Morgan Fairley

SO-AEA-646

☆ CHEER WORLD ☆

My Life as an Illinois All-Star Cheerleader

outskirtspress
DENVER, COLORADO

Outskirts Press, Inc.
http://www.outskirtspress.com

ISBN: 978-1-4787-1767-6

Outskirts Press and the "OP" logo are trademarks belonging to Outskirts Press, Inc.

PRINTED IN THE UNITED STATES OF AMERICA

Table of Contents

Introduction

I'M NOT REALLY sure that I knew what I was getting myself into…If someone would have asked me five years ago what cheerleading was I probably would have laughed and said "an excuse for a sport". Little did I know that this "sport" would change my life forever. Through all of the ups and downs, I now find myself pondering what or who I even was before I had cheerleading in my life. It is my biggest weakness, my constant struggle and my never ending addiction. The world of all-star cheerleading stretches beyond the imagination of a "normal" human being. I say normal because no one in the cheer world is normal, including myself. We have our own planet that resides on earth, it's a place so cut throat that even I question myself at times why am I so in love with this sport. The answer to that question is simple…It's the rush you get when you are on the floor in front of thousands of screaming people, the lights shining and the music blaring, the base pumping and all eyes on you…the moment when you hear nothing but your heart beat… and then your music comes on and instincts kick in.

I often get asked the question "what do I do as a cheerleader?" as I am sure that most all-star cheerleaders do. I'm almost positive that a thousand answers go through their minds as they get asked this question….but we know that no one will ever be able to understand what exactly it is that we do and what we go through…so instead we just say "I do flips and I toss people around". I'm writing this memoir because I'm tired of this question going unanswered.

More and more media attention is being drawn to this sport. It seems as if America knows that there is something there but they are only scanning the surface of what really goes on in inside this world. We find ourselves continuously trying to prove that cheerleading is a sport. Instead of focusing on why we should be a sport I've written this book to take you on my journey and my experience and in my opinion, why cheerleading isn't a sport and why we aren't being taken seriously.

PART I
The Illinois Cheer Company

1

THEY WERE LIKE goddesses walking by, the type of people that you can't take your eyes off. Every step they took seemed to be in slow motion, every smile seemed to brighten the whole room. Everyone in the gym wanted to be them… they were our inspiration; they made us work our asses off in hopes to be in their spot one day, or even better, compete next to them.

I believe there were about eight teams in our gym, maybe more ranging from levels one through five. There were three level five teams, one junior team, one senior small coed team and one senior large coed team. Everyone wanted to be on the large coed team, they were so talented and bound to place top ten at world's this year. I had been working so hard the past few months in hopes to be on this team. It was tryout day and I couldn't have been more nervous and excited. I didn't know one person in the gym. It was filled with hundreds of amazing athletes, but I knew it was somewhere I wanted to be. I wanted to get to know these people. Being a former power tumbler I knew I would be put on a level five team but I was unsure if it would be the one that I wanted.

They had us sit in rows on the floor by the number we were assigned. I was number 421. There were tryouts for the younger children earlier in the day so I was actually one of the first few groups to tryout that afternoon. They let us warm up on our own in the gym for a few minutes before the tryout began. I nervously threw my standing back handsprings to full, a newly learned skill that I had just started doing on my own without my private instructor's help. With all the adrenaline rushing through my body the height of my full was nothing to be worried about, it gave me all the confidence that I so desperately needed while being surrounded by all of these talented athletes that were throwing skills that I've only seen Olympian gymnast do.

When they called my group I timidly stood in front of a panel of judges next to five other girls. One by one they had us ripple off our tumbling passes, and with a smile on my face, I successfully landed my skills. Almost everyone from Inspire (the large coed team) retried out for the new season, so I knew that there were only going to be a limited amount of spots to fill. After they evaluated everyone's tumbling skills they wanted to test our stunting skills as well. There were so many guys on the team so if I were to be chosen I would obviously have to fly. I was a very inexperienced flyer. My nerves started to get the best of me. It came down to me and this also new super tiny, and cute blonde girl (who now cheers at the University of Kentucky). Not only was she intimidating because she had way more experience with flying, but she was also about twenty pounds lighter than I was. The judges had me fly on some of the guys from the team last year and when I was put into the air they had me pull body positions (heel stretches, scales, scorpions). Luckily I was flexible, so I actually looked very pretty in the air, but when it came to the level five stunts, like flying on your left leg and switching to your right leg, I completely bombed. I looked over my shoulder and the new girl was hitting all of the level five stunts. I instantly knew that she got the spot over me. I walked out of tryouts with a tiny bit of hope, but in the back of my mind I knew that I didn't make Inspire.

I went home that night and waited by the computer for hours for the results to be posted. My anxiety made time feel like it was moving by tremendously slow. As soon as all of the assigned numbers popped up on the screen, my eyes began to scan the page for number 421, praying that it would be under the team Inspire. It wasn't. It was under the team Destiny, the small coed team, or you could just call us the leftovers. We were the kids who weren't quite good enough to be on Inspire, but who were too talented to be on a level four team.

Tears immediately fell down my face. My mom hugged me and told me that I should be proud. I didn't want to hear her words of support, all I could focus on was that I didn't make the team I wanted to, but as you will continuously hear me say throughout this memoir, everything happens for a reason…She brought me back to reality and made me realize that I had ultimately accomplished my dream of being on a level five team and that I should be proud of myself, and honestly I was.

2

I REMEMBER MEETING everyone at our first practice during the summer, half the kids were new and half the kids were veterans from last year, it was definitely one of the most awkward practices. I also met our coaches, Randy and Synelle. Randy was a short, stocky guy with a funny sense of humor, he was our head coach. I would come to love his coaching style. Our assistant coach, Synelle, was a tall lean tumbling coach. He was someone who always knew how to put us in a good mood and bring a smile to our face. They made a great coaching team and it fit well with the personality of our team.

Until we finally warmed up to each other, the first few practices of that summer were quiet. Eventually we were able to start cracking jokes and having fun. I was always the more shy one in high school. I was very cautious of who I would get close to. I was bullied by my ex-best friend's new clique, so it put up some strong walls for me. I got close to my teammates but I would never hang out with them outside of practices. I was too afraid to be good friends with people.

All-star cheerleading is a year round sport unless you count the few weeks we have off between World's and tryouts. Summers are spent working on skills and then at the beginning of fall you get your routine. Competitions usually start in October and would go through April. After World's is over tryouts for the next season began immediately. You then have about a two or three week break until the new practices begins. During the summer most gyms have skill instructors come in from all around the nation to help their teams learn new skills and perfect the ones they do have. The skills camp I had with Destiny was definitely one to remember.

It was about 95 degrees that day with no air conditioning in our gym. The only air flow we had was from the big open warehouse door that was attached to the building. The skill instructor introduced himself as Tye, a well-known name in the cheerleading industry. Just the fact that he worked for Cirque Du Solei was pretty phenomenal. I'll never forget, while we were all stretching out one of my teammates was putting on her wrist braces because they supported her while she tumbled. Tye yelled from across the gym as loud and as sassy as he could…"Hey tiger claws do you need those for stretching…?" her jaw dropped to the floor from embarrassment, our teammates giggled around her but she just quietly replied "No" I felt so bad for her.

Tye went on to teach our team some new stunts; he was such a perfectionist. He would not let us move on to something new unless we had perfected what he had taught us first. I've always been respectful to any kind of instructor unless of course they disrespected me. I'll be the first one to call you out no matter who you are. He complimented me on my listening skills and asked me what my name was. He told me that I was beautiful and that he was going to make the gym owner put me on Inspire just to stand in front and look pretty. He boosted my confidence that day. I will never forget it.

Skills camp is when our team really started to get comfortable with each other. The heat seemed to help us not edit anything that came out of our mouths. We were sassy, we gave attitude, we cracked jokes and we had a great time working with each other regardless of the temperature. I am not sure that our coaches and instructors would have said the same thing though. There were two boys on our team, total opposite of each other; they would constantly bicker. I grew close to one of them at skills camp. I remember Tye had me try flying on that 95 degree day, but sweat kept dripping down my shins and calf muscles, so it made it impossible for my bases and back spot to hold onto me. I would just slowly slide out of their hands because of all the sweat. The boy I grew close to was the one that had to grab my legs. He was so grossed out and kept screeching every time he had to touch them. I kept paper towels next to me to try to keep the sweat off my legs, it was disgusting, but we were all so delirious from the heat that we thought it was hilarious.

At the end of skills camp Tye told our team a very motivational story about a horse and a farmer. I know that sounds strange, but up until this day I still think of that story whenever I am going through a hard time and it gives me that little extra strength and motivation I need to keep going.

3

CHEERLEADING STARTED TO become my life. I'd find myself coming home from school and rushing to get ready to go to the gym an hour before practice just to hang out and work on skills. Like I had previously mentioned, I was very shy and I never really talked to many people while I was at the gym before practices. Then one day... the day that ultimately changed my life and my love and passion for cheer, I met Zavell and Cassady.

This cute and lean darker skinned boy from Inspire came up to me and asked me if I wanted to stunt with him and his friend Cassady, who was also on Inspire. I got butterflies in my stomach. I knew that I was newer to flying but I couldn't deny the excitement I had that these guys from Inspire were not only talking to me but wanted to get to know me too. I remember the first time Zavell and I stunted. He put his cold hands on my waist then I grabbed onto his wrists, I couldn't help to think that they were so tiny and how was this guy going to be able to throw me over his head. I trusted him though and when I jumped and he threw me and caught my feet, I was surprised by the strength that he actually had. After a few minutes, a shorter super lean, dirty blonde boy walked in the gym with glossy eyes and a smirk on his face, he introduced himself as Cassady. I stunted with the boys awhile before practice started and Zavell made sure that I got his number before we parted ways.

Zavell and I began to text a lot. The more we got to know each other the closer we became. It wasn't long before Zavell and I started to date and once word got around about it in the gym, some girls on my team came up to me and said to me, "Oh my gosh, you're dating Zavell? You know he's like a cheerlebrity right?" That was when I learned what cheerlebrities were. In the cheer world, just like in the real world, we have celebrities but we call them cheerlebrities. How does someone get famous in the cheer world you might ask? Well some cheerlebrities have wealthy families who know how to market their son or daughter, some are strictly known for their raw talent, some for winning world's and some are known for the big named teams they've cheered on. These cheerlebrities have thousands of followers on social networks such as Facebook and Twitter. They even have fan pages and go on tours to visit different gyms all around the United States. They get paid a TON of money to do it. It's like being a famous player in the NFL, these athletes send out signed photos, shoes, pictures and T-shirts to thousands of fans.

After these girls told me about cheerlebrities I began to do some research. I suddenly began to realize how big the cheer world really is but at the same time how small it is. Social media sites keep the cheer world connected through tweets, through Facebook and most importantly through Fierceboards. Fierceboards is a social media site created just for the cheer world that has all the latest news, gossip, team placements, newest uniform trend and almost anything you want to know about a gym or cheerleader, it is on this forum. There are billions of all-star cheerleaders around the world and through media, gossip spreads within a matter of hours.

Finding out that Zavell was a cheerlebrity didn't affect my feelings towards him, he deserved the attention. He worked his ass off in the gym everyday working on new skills. He was throwing skills that level six gymnast throw at the Olympics, it was incredible.

4

THAT FALL ZAVELL and I hung out at his house a lot after practice. He lived in a nice town conveniently located a mile away from the gym. This also meant he had a lot of boys from Inspire over all the time. This is when I got introduced to the drug world within cheerleading. Being a senior in high school I had obviously been around weed; almost everyone in my school had at least tried it or smoked it on a daily basis. I wasn't too fond of smoking, I had never tried it nor wanted to, but it didn't bother me to be around it. The boys smoked weed almost every day after practice it was routine for them. I remember having to buy Swisher Sweets for them all the time at the gas station because I was the only one old enough to do so. Since they couldn't buy their own blunts to roll I am sure you are wondering how the boys even got their weed in the first place.....

Other than the coaches and the gym owner, there were other employees at the gym that taught classes and private lessons. One of the most popular private instructors in the gym was Matteo. This instructor was known for his ability to not only teach tumbling but to fix athletes who have mental blocks as well. As a cheerleader traumatic injuries happen all the time and when they do happen athletes become very scared to attempt the skill they got injured from after they recover. Mental blocks can last only a few days and more serious ones can last up to years. Having had one for a while I know how hard they are to get over. Every time you're about to throw a skill an image of doom slides through your mind and you picture the worst possible outcome. Then your palms start sweating and you start breathing heavier and your emotions sky rocket. I took a few privates with Matteo and my tumbling improved faster than I ever thought it would. He had such a calm and reassuring way of explaining things to his students.

Matteo was close to all of the boys on Inspire. He taught some of them almost everything they knew about cheerleading. Because they had such a close relationship they hung out together outside of the gym. Not only would they hang out with each other they would smoke blunts with each other. Sounds like a great role model for a young athlete, right? but that's exactly how they looked up to Matteo, like he was a God. I remember the first time walking in to his tiny apartment that he shared with his girlfriend, Brittney. I thought to myself this can't possibly be allowed and obviously it wasn't. As soon as I walked through their door they immediately tensed up and whispered to Zavell. They wanted to know why he brought me to their apartment but Zavell had told them that I was "cool" and that I wouldn't tell anyone, which I didn't. As I sat on their couch with their two little dogs fighting for my attention, I watched Matteo and Zavell roll a blunt and in the back of my mind felt panicked, but the feeling was soon broken when Matteo jokingly said "You know... anyone that comes into this apartment has to do a standing tuck at the front door". A standing tuck is a back flip with no hands, something level five athletes should be able to throw in their sleep. I went by his front door and threw the flip and when I landed it with a loud thunk, Matteo started laughing and said that he didn't think I would actually do it. It broke the tension and I felt a little more comfortable but in the back of my mind something still didn't feel right. After they were done rolling their blunt on the kitchen counter Matteo asked me if I smoked, as if to ask if I wanted a hit or not, I politely told him "no" and instead continued to sit on the couch and play with their dogs until they were done smoking.

Although what they were doing was highly inappropriate, I couldn't help but like Matteo's personality, he truly was a good hearted person and had a way with getting along with everyone. His girlfriend on the other hand didn't give me a good vibe but it was too early to tell who or what kind of person she was. The only judgments I could make of her was by the clothes she was wearing. Unlike most girls, I'm not really into fashion, I never dressed up. My daily outfits consisted of sweatpants and sweatshirts and my hair style was always in a messy bun. Brittney on the other hand, was dressed in brand named clothes with her make up done nice and her hair styled. I know you can't technically judge someone on their clothing style, but it was hard not to think that she may have been high-maintenance and high-maintenance, in my opinion, usually means bitchiness. I only went to their apartment once while I was dating Zavell, but I had a feeling that I would see them around because Cassady looked up to Matteo more than any of the other guys. I had that assumption because he introduced Cassady to cheerleading but also because of his mellow personality.

Cassady was one of Zavell's best friends, they always hung out together and since I was Zavell's girlfriend at the time I hung out with Cassady a lot as well. Cassady Facebook messaged me one day a bit flirtatious, asking for my number so that if I ever wanted to come into the gym early before practices to stunt then we could text each other. However, the texting "to come into the gym early" turned into a little more than just a way to contact each other. Cassady and I would text for hours on end every day about everything. He quickly became a close friend of mine and I couldn't deny that there was a little spark between us but I knew that Zavell and he were best friends so I stayed away from him.

Zavell was quite the popular guy. I recall going to a house party that one of his friends was having all weekend because his parents were out of town. Cassady was of course at this party. I've never been the one to drink, in fact I was one of the few kids in high school that didn't. The only time I had actually ever drank was at a family party in Mississippi for the New Orleans Saints super bowl game. (I'm from Mississippi, so the Saints' winning the super bowl was a huge deal for us). Being around these boys for some reason made me feel, well… kind of bad ass. So I made the decision to drink a little with them.

As the booze settled into my body I became more relaxed and

comfortable, I was able to laugh a little and an extra layer of confidence began to shine through which eventually lead to all of us getting in the hot tub. The house we were at had a really nice jacuzzi and I'm not sure who got the idea to go for a dip in it but I do remember that none of us had swimsuits accept for the one piece I carried with me in my back pack because I was a lifeguard. I sure as hell was not about to wear that thing but Cassady on the other hand thought it would be funny if he wore it. I have to admit it was pretty hilarious watching him walk around in it with his butt cheeks hanging out. Because none of us had suits some of us jumped in with our undergarments on and just chilled out for a while and talked. While we were in the hot tub Zavell was nowhere to be found and I asked Cassady where Zavell was. He told me that he had taken my car to go steal some weed plants from someone's backyard. The feeling of shock and disappointment ran through me all at once. I couldn't tell if I was more upset at the fact that he took my car without asking or that he was going to be do something highly illegal with it.

The booze allowed me to stay calm though and when I texted him to ask where he was he responded that he was almost to the house. Cassady wasn't kidding, when Zavell pulled up into the driveway he had about five plants that were about six feet high in the back of my car. When he pulled them out of the car there were leaves everywhere and my car reeked of pot smell. I was infuriated. I told him that he better clean out every single bit of the mess that he had made. He did clean it out but there was no way that anyone could have gotten rid of that smell. Being an older sister that my brother looked up to, the first thought that popped into my mind was "How am I ever going to get rid of that odor so that Sam doesn't smell it". How could I possibly explain to him what had happened? I decided to go back in the hot tub and worry about everything in the morning.

While I was in the hot tub, Zavell and some of the boys picked at the plants trying to get all of the bud off of them. The longer I sat in the hot tub the more the heat started making me feel dizzy. I was positive that the water was making the alcohol intensify. I got out with a big smile on my face feeling really relaxed. I wanted to go into the house to cool down for a little while. I entered through the sliding glass doors from the backyard and stepped into the kitchen, the only other person there was Cassady. I smiled at him and he smiled back and I could tell he was checking me out with that stupid grin on his face. You could feel the tension in the room but it was broken when a few people from outside walked through the door. Soon after I began to feel extremely drowsy so I laid down on the kitchen floor and snuggled with a little dog that belonged to the kid who was throwing the party. I remember I was about to fall asleep when Cassady came and picked me up and took me into the kid's parent's room. He laid me in their bed so that I would be more comfortable. We looked at each other and I knew right then that Cassady and I would turn into more than just friends. I never believed in drinking under age and I couldn't help but feel a little guilt in the morning when I woke up.

As much as I liked Zavell there was just something about him that wasn't relationship material. He was such a sweet guy but at the same time he was just a little too immature for me. It wasn't necessarily his personality that was immature it was more the way that he didn't know how to be in a relationship. I just couldn't see myself taking the next step with him so I relayed that to Cassady. Whether or not Cassady had good or bad intentions in helping me out, I guess I'll never know, but he convinced me to break things off with Zavell. Zavell was very upset and a little confused at first, but I knew that he would have no problem moving on, after all, he was a cheerlebrity and all the girls wanted to be with him.

Just like most breakups are things were a little awkward with Zavell at first. but as Cassady and I got even closer Zavell eventually left my mind. Cassady and I kept things on the down low since he and Zavell were best friends. We didn't want to hurt their relationship. Cassady and I would still come into the gym before practices and stunt with each other but people believed that that was the extent of our relationship, little did they know we were actually dating.

5

I REMEMBER THE light blue minivan pulling up into my driveway, obviously borrowed from his parents. Most teenagers don't drive minivans. He pulled up with the window down with a big smile on his face, his diamond earring shining in the sun. My mom was impressed at first sight. Someone picking me up to take me on a date was something she hadn't seen a guy do for me. As he walked up the driveway to shake my mother's hand and introduce himself, I couldn't help but feel butterflies in my stomach. He seemed like a real gentlemen, plus my mother had been telling me for a while that I needed to date a cheerleader so that they could understand my love for the sport.

We went out to eat at one of my favorite restaurants, Mongolian Grill. It was the first date we had been on and the first time we actually hung out with each other alone out side of the gym. After dinner we went on a nice stroll down the river walk and I knew immediately that this guy was going to have a huge impact in my life, I just wasn't sure yet in what way.

Cassady and I kept our relationship on the down low for a very long time. The only people that knew we were dating was my family and his, and of course Matteo because Cassady and Matteo were best friends. We didn't hang around each other in the gym a lot and he didn't show any signs of affection, and we definitely did not make it Facebook official. It wasn't what I pictured for a relationship but Cassady told me that he didn't want everyone in the gym to be in his business and it seemed like a great explanation to me at the time, so I went along with it.

Our first competition was in a few days and my team was ready to compete, Inspire, however got their choreography later than all the other teams in the gym and had to drop out of the competition but the entire Inspire team would all came to support us. Although we took pictures together at his grandmother's house before the competition, Cassady made it clear to me that he did not want to be seen walking around with me or holding hands with me or even talking to me at the convention center. I continued to play along with it but I couldn't help but feel a little sad, after all, it was my first competition and I had butterflies in my stomach.

Warm-ups are the most chaotic part of a competition. Just imagine a huge room filled with hundreds of cheerleaders, tension so thick in the air you could cut it with a knife, buzzers going off and people yelling and counting at the top of their lungs trying to be heard over each other. Warm-ups are set up in a rotation with three floors. You get five minutes on each floor. The first floor is usually a hard floor where you throw all of your stunts, baskets and pyramid. The second floor is a spring floor where everyone can throw their standing and running tumbling. The final floor is a cheer floor where teams usually mark out their routine and if they need to throw any last minute skills they can. In warm-ups I would feel such terrible anxiety that after running through everything I had the most terrible cotton mouth. Luckily they have water jugs set up at the end of warm ups to help this.

After warm-ups there is usually a staff member that will lead you to the competition floor where you will wait in line behind two or three teams for your turn to compete. This is the most stressful part of competing, waiting behind that curtain, hearing the music of the other teams performing, listening to the crowd screaming and everyone feeding off of each other's nervous energy. This was a small competition but I still couldn't help but feel anxious it was my first time competing on a level five team.

As our team got closer and closer to our turn, we huddled together and our coach, Randy, gave us a pep talk, he was always so good at those. It was what we needed right before we went onto the stage to compete, it wasn't just motivating but it kept our minds off of all the distractions around us for two seconds and brought us back down to earth. Then the announcer called our team's name and my stomach instantly dropped to the ground, this is it......

I skipped onto the stage waving and smiling at the crowd scanning for my mom and brother in the sea of people. ICC was a huge gym, and anytime one of their teams competed the whole gym came to watch, this made it difficult to spot people. That did not stop me from finding my family they were smiling and waving at me, probably the most comforting part of the competition for me so far.

I took my starting position and waited for our music to come on to start our routine. There's a moment an athlete has right before the music starts. You take a deep breath and listen to your heart beat and suddenly the whole world gets silent and then your music starts and you completely lose all train of thought and just do what you've been taught to do. I can honestly say the only thought I had throughout the whole routine was after I landed my running full, something I had never thrown in a competition before, and thinking "holy shit, I just landed that, hell yes!" It's the best feeling when you land a new skill for the first time in a competition. It pumps you up and motivates you to keep doing well throughout the rest of the routine. When the music stops and the routine ends it is the most relieving feeling in the world you instantly exhale. OR if you hit a perfect routine you tackle the teammate nearest to you. That day we didn't have a perfect routine. It's hard to hit a flawless routine in cheerleading. Just because you personally hit a perfect routine doesn't mean the person next to you did but that's what makes this sport so addicting, the team effort that it takes to reach your goals. There is no way to have a perfect routine unless you ALL have a perfect routine.

6

IT WAS MID-NOVEMBER and competition season was in full swing. We had our second competition coming up and practices were beginning to get a lot more intense. As a level five team your goal throughout the season is to make it to The Cheerleading World's, or in other words, the Olympics of cheerleading. At some competitions there are bids that you can receive if you score high enough. You must receive a bid to go to worlds. There are at-large bids (ones that do not pay your way to worlds but it invites you to compete), partial-paid bids, and full-paid bids. Obviously every team would love to get a paid bid considering worlds is the most expensive competition to compete at. Once you add up airfare, hotel rates, food and of course souvenirs, the costs easily becomes around $650 per athlete. To receive a paid bid your team must be VERY talented. I'm not saying our team was bad, but we were in a very competitive division and some of the teams we competed against were just absolutely amazing. Making it to worlds is a huge accomplishment for any cheerleader, considering only 5% of teams within all-star cheerleading make it.

Although Jamlive wasn't a bid competition it was one that prepared us for our first bid competition that was soon approaching. It is a competition that most gyms from around the area come to. It is a showdown to see who has the best in our state.

I remember hearing stories about this competition. It's one of the few that are held on a raised stage. I was told that if you landed your tumbling long then you would fall off the stage. You had to be extremely aware of your surroundings and very careful. What also made it so different was the fact that as soon as you are done competing you would walk to the side of the stage with an announcer and they would give you your scores immediately. If you are the highest scoring team in your division then you got to move to the other side of the stage where the "leader lounge" is. The leader lounge consisted of nice couches and a seat right next to the DJ, and it came with a few minutes of glory. If the next team had a higher score than yours, they would knock you off the leader lounge and they would assume that position.

When Destiny competed, we didn't have nearly as big a crowd as Inspire, another reason why we always called ourselves "the leftovers". We felt like no one in the gym paid much attention to us because we got overshadowed and outshined by Inspire. We were all really down to earth people though and we didn't let it bother us. We had a great performance at Jamlive and held our spot in the leader lounge which won us some T-shirts. I know it sounds kind of goofy but cheerleaders love T-shirts and sweatshirts. Anything new we can wear to show off at school the next day after a competition, we wanted it. I felt pretty awesome walking into school Monday morning with my new Jamlive T-shirt, even though no one had any idea what it meant, but it meant victory to me.

After the Jamlive competition, word around the gym was that we were moving to a bigger new gym in the winter. Our gym wasn't small by any means but for the amount of teams we had practicing at once, we were always crammed and sharing tight spaces. I personally didn't mind it, it brought a feeling of unity to me. I'm not going to lie though the new gym looked pretty sweet. It was rumored that there was going to be a weight room and all kinds of new amenities.

Cassady and I continued to keep our relationship under wraps. No one had caught on to it yet. It had been about three months that we've been dating and things seemed to be going really well. I would drive out to his work and wait for him to be done with his shift then we would hang out at his mom's house or go get pizza with his dad. I have to admit though I was starting to get a little anxious with the whole "let's keep our relationship a secret" thing. He introduced me to his parents, he told me I was beautiful and that I was such an amazing person. I couldn't understand why he didn't want to show anyone that we were dating…then one day it all fell into place.

We were riding in my car on the way to the gym and his phone kept blowing up with texts. When I asked him what was going on he told me that a girl, also named Morgan, wouldn't stop texting him. When I asked him why he just replied that he didn't know. This struck me kind of odd and he seemed to be acting a little suspicious, so I asked more questions. I asked him who she was and what she was texting him about. He told me he had an ex, also named Morgan. He said that he dated her for quite a long time. It turned out to be his first "real" love. He told me that she was sending him Brittney Spears lyrics through the phone, the newly released hit, *All Eyes On Me*. I found that kind of odd…I asked him why he still talked to his ex and he told me that he didn't want to talk to her but that she was psycho and that if he had stopped talking to her that she would go crazy and cause drama.

I asked him nicely if he would stop texting her and he said he would and as far as I knew he did. Being the stalker that I am I jumped on Facebook immediately to find out who she was. She was on a small senior all-girl level five team at a local gym; it had looked to me as if they had met through cheerleading. There were pictures on her Facebook of them cheering together at a former gym that had shut down about a year ago. I had a bad gut feeling about this girl and for some reason my instincts just told me to keep an eye on her.

The Thanksgiving holiday was upon us. My family is very small, but very close. We always did the same thing for the holidays. My parents are divorced and I chose to spend the holidays with my mother. Unlike a lot of divorced families, my parents live in two different states, Mississippi and Illinois so I didn't have the option to spend time with both sides during the holidays. I never minded though, my family in the south is a tad crazy and I enjoyed the peacefulness of my small family up north. This thanksgiving was a little different though, Cassady's parents were also divorced which meant I had two parties to attend. His dad's side of the family actually lived pretty close to my house and we had Thanksgiving lunch over at his grandmother's house in the morning. I liked his dad's side of the family a lot more than his mother's, they were a lot more laid back, the kind of people who you could tell were just genuine and so kind. His mother's side was the complete opposite, they came off fake to me and no one seemed to want to be there they acted more like they were obligated to be there. To me, that's not how family should be but I was raised in a very tight knit family and I knew the values and the importance of family. My mom and brother are the only ones that I've ever been able to 100% trust. I know that they would go to the edges of the world to help me and I would do the same and I would do the same for them..

I'm not sure what it was that day, but as Cassady and I were on our way to his mother's after Thanksgiving lunch with his dad's side, he asked me again if I wanted to smoke a blunt he had. For some reason I said yes, it seemed harmless after all. I tried smoking it, and whether it was just because I wasn't doing it right or because I've been told that the first few times you try smoking you don't feel anything, it really didn't have any effect on me.

We arrived at his mother's house for dinner and as soon as I walked in you could feel the awkward tension in the air. It wasn't the kind of family parties that I grew up around. At my family parties everyone would be laughing and having a good time, all the cousins would play with each other while the adults got drunk. This party was more like a wanna-be-high-class-even-though-were-a-middle-class-family party where no one really talked besides Cassady's little sister who could talk faster than anyone I knew. She would talk about everything and anything. She absolutely adored me and asked me to bring my cheer makeup over every time I visited so that I could do her makeup. She was the sweetest thing ever.

After his mother's party, we ended our evening with what I looked forward to the most all day, Thanksgiving at my mother's house. It was just her, my brother and I and she always made the best home cooked southern meals. It was always a place where I could just kick back, throw on a pair of comfy sweatpants and relax. There was something so soothing about the aroma of mom's cooking, all three of her little dogs snuggled beside your legs, and the faint noise of the bears game playing in the background…

Cassady told me that In order to actually feel the effects of smoking weed that I would have to keep trying it and I believed him, so I did. I tried once more with his friends in the back seat of his friend's mustang, and although the weed made me cough uncontrollably, I still didn't feel any side effects whatsoever, but Cassady was determined to make me feel what it was like to be high. I went home that night after hanging out with his friends for a little while and my ex-boyfriend texted me to see how I was doing. He was very irresponsible, didn't have a job, smoked a lot of weed and drank a lot of alcohol, thus the reason we split. He was a nice guy though, just surrounded by some bad influences. He knew me before I had got involved in cheerleading, before I had been open to trying weed and before I decided that I could be at a party and be the only one that wasn't drinking. When I told him that I had tried smoking weed but hadn't actually felt what it was like to be high, he jumped at the opportunity to ask me to meet up with him and smoke a blunt. Being the naïve kid that I was, I agreed to meet up with him.

I picked him up from one of his friend's houses and we rode around the neighborhood while he rolled a blunt in my car. When he was finished and offered me a hit I took it and almost immediately felt the drug start to work. I wasn't sure if it was because it was my third time trying to get high, and Cassady's theory proved right, or if my ex's weed was just maybe more powerful, but whichever it was this weed got me so high and I could not stand the feeling. I dropped my ex-boyfriend off back at his friend's house and my first instinct was to go to the gym and try to sweat it out. I was too dumb to realize though that the only thing to get rid of the feeling was time. That didn't stop me from going to the gym though, I was lucky that it was open 24/7.

Have you ever been so tired that everything around you seems to be a blur? Well that's how being high felt to me. As I ran on the treadmill everything around me seemed to be moving in slow motion and all the TV's that surrounded me seemed to be talking in slow motion. I suddenly realized that running on a treadmill wasn't the best idea, my body didn't feel like it wanted to be moving.

I texted Cassady and told him everything, I was hoping he would know how to get rid of the feeling but he was so angry at me. He told me that I needed to go home and just go to bed, so I listened to him and that's what I did. That was the last time I ever smoked weed.

7

DECEMBER CAME AROUND, and with that, came a new gym and new drama. I remember helping everyone move the cheer floors. Anyone that knows anything about cheer floors knows how big of a pain they are to put together. You can rip them a part in about ten minutes but it takes about three hours to lay one down and put it together. This new gym was huge, so big that the owner of the gym would ride a scooter to get from one end to the other just because walking took too long. Underneath the carpet that lies on top of a cheer floor, are wooden panels and under those wooden panels are springs. When we laid down our last wooden panel everyone that had helped assemble it, signed it by writing things such as "cheers to new beginnings" And "congratulations" to the gym owner. I couldn't help but have a huge smile on my face as I was signing the panel, after all our gym was becoming one of the top gyms, not just in our state, but around the world.

Practices in the new gym weren't the same as the ones in the old gym, mainly because everything was so spread out. It seemed to lack the unity that the old gym had before the new gym doors opened. This didn't distract Destiny for preparing for our first bid competition in Indianapolis in two weeks. We focused on ourselves and pushed through intense and stressful practices.

Cassady still continued to show no affiliation and affection to-wards me in the gym and now that it had been more than three months

I had really started to get fed up with it. I decided to do something about it. I talked to him and told him that I really liked him and that I wanted to know if he felt the same way back because it sure as hell didn't feel like it to me. He was really taken aback. It was the first time that I had actually stood my ground in our relationship and I wanted answers. I wanted to know if he really wanted to be with me and that if he did then he was going to have to prove it to me by showing and letting people know that we were official. I could tell that he was caught in a weird situation and it finally hit me that this guy wasn't keeping the fact that we were dating from people because he didn't want them in his business, it was because he didn't want girls to know he was off the market. I treated Cassady like a God and he didn't do the same back to me. I had more self-respect for myself than that and I stood my ground and told him that if he wanted to be with me than he would have to step it up. I gave him a few days to make his decision and made it clear that we were not broken up. I just needed to know whether or not he really wanted to be in a relationship with me. I gave him some time to think about it instead of having him make a rash decision. I told him that I wouldn't be hurt by his decision and that I just wanted him to be honest. That's all I ever wanted and asked from people. I would rather someone be honest with me than lie to me and lead me on.

A few days went by and Cassady told me that he was ready to be in a real relationship. I knew that when he made it Facebook "official" he was serious. It was a huge relief to not have to hide our relationship anymore, but of course as soon as it was made public, drama followed.

I got a text from a friend who was on Morgan's team. She told me that she was happy for me and Cassady but she wanted to let me know something that I probably would like to know. I picked her up and we drove to the gym to tumble around. As soon as she got in the car I was eager to hear what she had to say. I asked her what was going on and she asked me the question "When did you and Cassady officially start dating?" I told her that it was about five days ago and she seemed kind of relieved and said good. When I asked her why she told me that about a week ago, which is when I was giving

Cassady some time to think about whether or not he wanted to be in a relationship with me or not, that he was hanging out with Morgan at her house. My heart dropped to my stomach and a fiery hot sensation spread in my body within a matter of seconds. My mind started assuming the worst possible situations. Lauren continued to talk but I didn't listen all I could picture in my mind was Morgan and Cassady hanging out and I wanted answers.

I confronted Cassady about what Lauren had told me and he immediately looked guilty. I told him to be honest with me, like I had always asked of him because honesty is the best policy. He told me that he had gone over to her house and that they had watched a movie. I asked him if he had sat next to her and he told me that he sat on the opposite side of the couch as her. I found that really hard to believe but he swore to me that nothing had happened between the two of them, so I believed him. When I asked him why he was over there in the first place after I had asked him to stop talking to her a while ago, he told me that he wanted to see if he would be "missing" anything if we were to start dating. A disgusted look came over my face, I could feel it but I couldn't stop it. When I asked him what that was supposed to mean, he told me that he was unsure if he still wanted to be with her or with me but once he hung out with her and her family, it brought back old memories and reminded him why he wasn't with her in the first place and that was what made him realize that I was such a good girlfriend and why he wanted to be with me. I decided to believe him, he seemed to be telling the truth, but I still had my doubts, after all, they were each other's first loves.

8

WSF (WORLD SPIRIT Federation) was our first bid competition. It was being held at the convention center in Indianapolis, one of my favorite places to compete. The convention center was conveniently connected not only to a mall, but to the hotel that we were staying at. This meant we never once had to step outside into the cold Indy winter, unless of course you brought your dogs with you. This was another reason Indy was my favorite, the hotel we stayed at was pet friendly. My mom never wanted to leave her dogs at home

WSF has always been a popular competition which means all the big teams from around the US came, as well as all the local teams. Our team was actually predicted to do pretty well if we hit a perfect routine but we had to be flawless. Inspire was also competing in a smaller division, therefore they didn't have to necessarily hit perfect to place well. The only downfall for Inspire this weekend was the fact that they weren't getting their music until the night before the competition.

In cheerleading, your music is made to fit your routine. Every sound effect should be aligned to every skill and the timing of the music can be crucial if it doesn't match up with your routine. Usually the first time a team gets their music, the DJ will have to go back in and edit a few things so that the routine matches perfect to the counts. If they don't, it could throw your brain in a spin and cause you to miss skills.

I remember arriving at the Westin Hotel, a tall, beautiful building that when you walked in you were greeted by two grand stair cases winding up to the second floor. When I looked down, a projector had our logo on the floor with words that read, "Welcome Illinois Cheer Company." My eyes widened like a kid in a candy shop, I was at the top competing against some of the best teams, and I felt like royalty.

My family and I made our way to our hotel room and did a quick scan of the place. We excitedly went to the mall to get some food, we were starving and it had one of our favorite fast food restaurants, Chick-Fil-A. As I ate dinner with my family I texted Cassady and asked him where he was, he told me that he was out in the parking garage smoking with the boys from Inspire. I asked if he would meet up with me and he said that he was going to hang out with his guy friends instead of me and that he would be out late. I did not want to be tired for the competition so I decided to go back to the room and spend some quality time with my mom and brother and go to bed early.

Waking up a cheerleader the day of a competition is like waking up to Christmas day when you're a little kid. The excitement that you have running through your veins is one of the happiest feelings in the world. There is a certain pride you get when you put your uniform on and do your make up. I kissed my mother on the cheek as I left the room and she gave me a big hug, the kind that calms your nerves as you walk towards the convention center. When I entered the giant room filled with thousands of cheerleaders my stomach sank and my nerves hit me really hard.

In warm-ups, the stunt that I was basing was not hitting. We were having trouble with our full-up. A full-up is where the flyer starts in the bases hands and does a 360 degree turn to the top and lands over our heads. I began to panic and then my coach told us just to go straight up instead of performing the 360. This helped calm my nerves, going straight up was something we could do in our sleep. Other than our stunt, everything else was hitting good in warm-ups. This gave our team the boost of confidence that we needed right before we went onto the floor.

Standing behind the curtains before our performance I didn't know what to think about, that's the worst part of waiting, your mind starts to think about a thousand things until you get on that floor and everything goes silent and your mind clears.

During our performance our point flyer fell not only once, but twice. I couldn't help but feel anger. I wasn't necessarily blaming anyone, it was just really hard not to feel disappointment when I knew the potential we could have had if we hit. At WSF there was no margin for error. That's another aspect of cheer that makes it so addicting. We don't get 2 hours to prove how good we are like most sports, we only get 2 ½ minutes.

Results came in later that night and we were in 8th place out of eleven teams. Obviously we were all really disappointed but it gave us the fire in our ass to perform perfect the next day and at least move up a spot or two. Inspire had an almost flawless routine that made the crowd go wild, I couldn't help but feel jealous.

I didn't get to see Cassady much at WSF, although we were Facebook official, he still seemed to not want to show me off like I wish he would. He would avoid being seen with me and when we did see each other we were alone.

The next day was a little different. We had nothing to lose like we did on the first day. There was no way we could get first place now so we weren't as nervous as the day before. We had more anger and determination in us though. I'll never forget the feeling I had during our performance that day. It was the first time I experienced hitting a perfect routine, the MOST addicting part of cheerleading. When your performance is over, you know when you hit a perfect routine not just because the crowd is screaming, but because your coaches are having a seizure and your teammates are jumping all over each other. All the hard work you've done over the past seven months, all the blood, sweat and tears, and you know you only have two and a half minutes to prove yourself, that's when you know nothing in the world can make you feel more invincible.

We stayed in 8th place, we were sad to hear that, but we all felt amazing after hitting our perfect routine the second day. Inspire had received a partial-paid bid to worlds, but they weren't happy about it, they wanted a paid bid. I remember sitting there thinking to myself, "How greedy and un-grateful can you be?" We're over here working our asses off to receive a bid and you're pissed off that you didn't get a paid one. That's when my opinion of Inspire changed. It was at that moment I stopped looking up to them.

At the end of the competition news broke that a huge snowstorm was coming. Families were suggested to stay another night if at all possible. My family jumped at the opportunity to spend some extra time with each other, Cassady's family on the other hand, was adamant on going home that evening. I told Cassady that he was more than welcome to stay in our room for the night since he wasn't too happy that his family was going to drive home in the storm. He was stubborn and declined my offer and they left moments later.

It only took a half hour for him to text me and tell me how bad the weather was. He explained how the visibility was no more than 5 to 10 feet in front of the van. He had said that they hadn't even gotten out of Indianapolis yet. I could tell through his text that he was aggravated about something. When I had asked what was upsetting him he told me that his mom was getting on his nerves. A few minutes passed and I started to get worried because he wasn't responding to my texts. When he finally replied he told me that he had gotten into a huge fight with his mother and had ended up getting out of the car and walking away for a minute in the storm. Supposedly they were arguing about how he thought they should have stayed the night because they were never going to get home. I didn't say "I told you so", but in the back of my mind I was thinking it. I couldn't help but not feel sympathy for him, after all I had offered him to stay with us in our room, and his mother said he could, but he still refused to stay the extra night.

My family and I woke up early the next morning to the local news showing cars and trucks on the side of the highway for miles. I texted Cassady to make sure they had made it home. He texted back and told me that he was still about 45 minutes away from his house. We ended up getting home only three hours after his family made it home. What was supposed to be a four hour trip home for them turned into a fifteen hour trip. It was an eventful weekend, but I was glad to be back at my home in my comfy bed.

9

CHRISTMAS WAS RIGHT around the corner and joy was in the air. Just like Thanksgiving, my family and I would always celebrate by cooking a nice meal and snuggling up under a blanket and watching the movie A Christmas Story. Christmas with Cassady's family was just the same as Thanksgiving minus the weed smoking for me. I told myself that I would NEVER smoke weed again. Cassady on the other hand continued to smoke every day, if not twice a day.

Cassady, like Matteo, got along with everyone. He was really close to his coaches, closer than he was allowed to be as an athlete with a coach. Just like Zavell smoked with Matteo, Cassady did as well. Cassady also smoked with his assistant coach.. For some reason Cassady has this unique charisma about him, all people, not just coaches, seemed to have this huge trust in him, as did I.

His assistant coach was alone on Christmas day, all of his family lived back in Texas, and all of his roommates were out of town visiting their families. When Cassady heard that his coach was alone for the holidays he told him that he had a blunt and that if he wanted to, Cassady would come visit him for a little while and they could smoke. I felt horrible that his coach was spending Christmas alone, so I tagged along with Cassady and brought some of my mother's delicious homemade sugar cookies.

When we pulled up to his coach's neighborhood, Cassady told me that it was a very unsafe place to be and that the crime rate in this area was very high. On the outside, the house looked tiny and kind of tacky, but when we walked in I was taken aback by how nice it was. There was a very open living space with a gigantic mirror. His coach said he had it there so he could watch himself do standing fulls. From the front room we walked into an updated kitchen that was tiny but very cute. When I handed him my mother's cookies he was so grateful and happy.

I sat at the counter while the two guys rolled the blunt and began to smoke it, again the coach asked if I smoked as if to ask if I wanted a hit, but I told him that I tried it once and would never be doing it again. I'm not sure why I ever felt it was okay to put myself into these predicaments, not only was smoking weed illegal, but doing it with coaches made it so much worse. I guess it goes both ways, right? The coaches should never be socializing with athletes let alone doing these types of things with them. It never crossed my mind that I could get in trouble, I mean...I wasn't the one smoking, I was just around it. I suppose when you are young, or when you are blind to the true meaning of life you feel invincible.

Kids nowadays use the term YOLO (you only live once) for everything. They say it right before they do something dumb like getting messed up on drugs or drinking and driving. I've learned now, and I wish I had known it back then that YOLO does not mean we should party our asses off and enjoy tonight because we may not wake up tomorrow. Most likely you will wake up tomorrow and you will have to deal with the consequences from the night before. YOLO should mean that we should learn to appreciate the small things in life and learn how to live every day to our fullest by chasing our dreams, not alcohol.

Like I had mentioned earlier, I didn't have many friends in school. I didn't fit in with the crowd so instead I kept to myself. However, there were two people that kept me sane throughout my senior year, Keith and Caroline. These two always had my back. There was something about these two that made me feel so comfortable to be around. We had this unbelievable connection, the kind where they always knew when something was bothering me, and vice versa.

Keith, who lived with three other roommates in a nearby apartment complex, was throwing a New Year's Eve party. They weren't your typical "let's go out to the clubs and get wasted" type of people, they were more the type of people that would sit around at home and play their guitars and sing. One of Keith's roommates, Jimmy, had one of the most brilliant voices I'd ever heard in my life. I could listen to it all night. It had that deep bluesy soul to it and the kind of voice that made you want to dance and have a good time.

I was so excited for the party. It would be the first time that Cassady would be hanging out with my group of friends. I got all dolled up in a mini red sequenced dress, teased my hair super big and put on some high heels and red lipstick. I walked down the stairs where Cassady was waiting for me and as soon as he saw me his eyes lit up. I knew right then and there it was going to be a night to remember, I could just feel it.

I made sure to pack my pajamas, I knew that I would be drinking and there was no way I was getting into a car. When we arrived at Keith's apartment there were just a few people there, not too many, just enough. It was a good crowd, the type that would stay through-out the whole night. When I walked through the door I noticed a guy across the room, he immediately caught my attention, he looked so familiar…then it hit me, I screamed "CODY??" He looked at me puzzled for a moment then he shouted back "MORGAN FAIRLEY?" The last time I had saw Cody was at our 8th grade graduation dance. He was singing karaoke to *You Shook me all Night Long* by AC/DC; He had everyone in the crowd going wild. At that point I knew the night was only going to get better.

Cassady and Keith immediately left the apartment to go on a walk, tagging along with them was a fat blunt and a bottle of Jack that would later show up to the apartment empty. In the meantime Cody and I worked the beer pong table together owning everyone that dared challenged us. We went on a five game winning streak. Because I can't stand the taste of beer I was taking sips of my mixed drink instead, probably not the best idea. I got really drunk really fast but I didn't care, I was having such a good time surrounded by all my good friends, old and new.

Keith and Cassady returned to the apartment almost two hours later totally drunk. This is when the party started to pick up. Jimmy played the blues on his guitar with Keith, the beer pong games started to get intense, and people were stopping by left and right to say hi and wish us a happy new year. This party was probably the first time that Cassady ever really showed any affection towards me in public. He was taking pictures with me, holding my hand and wrapping his arms around my waste. It was the happiest I had felt with him during our relationship.

The countdown to the New Year came on and everyone started yelling at the top of their lungs throwing their first into the air "FIVE, FOUR, THREE, TWO, ONE…. HAPPY NEW YEAR!!! Confetti flew in the air, noise makers were being blown and Cassady looked me straight in the eyes and kissed me. That is when I knew that he really loved me.

The party slowly started to die down after the countdown. I was starting to feel tired and uncomfortable in my dress so I went into Keith's room and changed into my pajamas. I was super clumsy from the booze so Cassady had to help me change. After struggling to put on my PJ's I made my way to an empty bed while climbing over a pile of people that were lying on the ground passed out. I have never figured out why everyone was on the floor instead of in the bed but I fell asleep within a matter of seconds. I woke up around six in the morning feeling terribly sick. It was my first time really getting drunk and the first thing I did was leaned over to Cassady and said "Babe…I don't feel so good." Half asleep he got up with me and took me into the bathroom down the hall way. He told me to lean my head over the toilet and try to throw up. I tried and nothing came up. Cassady went and got some water for me and told me to drink it, but I couldn't. He then offered to go find me something to eat and I told him that I didn't want anything to eat either. I kept whining about how sick I felt. A little frustrated, but with some slight humor in his voice Cassady replied "I offered you water, I told you to throw up and I offered you food, those are the only three things that you can do to make you feel better if you are hung over, I don't know what the fuck else you want me to do." I quit my bitching and made myself throw up and I felt a hundred times better. We tip toed back into the room over everyone and fell back asleep. When everyone woke up around ten, we were all super hungry so we decided to go get a table for twelve at the local Ihop.

We were THOSE people walking into the restaurant with our hair a mess and in our PJ's and probably smelled a little because we hadn't showered yet. But I'll tell you we were the happiest people walking in because we had just had the best night of our lives. We sat down at our table and when I opened the menu my eyes caught a picture of a huge loaded omelet. My mouth started watering and I knew instantly that was what I wanted for breakfast. I went to the bathroom after everyone had ordered food and looked in the mirror and chuckled to myself. I found the image in the mirror of me in my oversized t-shirt and polka dot sweatpants so funny. I splashed my face with cold water to wake myself up a little more and when I returned to the table the server was bringing out our food. As she placed my omelet in front of me my stomach got a little queasy, it didn't look near as good as I remembered seeing it on the menu. I looked to my right and one of the girls had a big pickle spear on her plate it looked so delicious. I politely asked her if she was going to eat it and she said no and she kindly let me have it. I scarfed it down and quickly realized that pickles were my choice for a hangover cure.

I took a picture in the car with Cassady that morning and a peacefulness came over me, for the first time in our relationship I felt like he truly did love me...I had a feeling that 2011 was going to be an amazing year.

10

BECAUSE DESTINY DID not get a bid at WSF our next chance was coming up in a few weeks at one of the biggest competitions of the season, Cheersport. Cheersport is held in Atlanta, Georgia, the furthest I've ever been to compete for cheerleading. Unlike most competitions that hand out eight bids, Cheersport hands out around 40! Also, for the first time ICC's history, our gym owner was taking us to NCA in Dallas, TX. This is also one of the biggest competitions of the season. Because of the fact that these competitions are back to back weekends, only the big gyms compete. Team practices returned to their normal schedule and things seemed to mellow out in the gym. Every team kept to themselves as they prepared for the upcoming competitions. Little did anyone know that soon our world as we knew it inside the gym was about to come to a complete halt.

It was a cold January night, I was sitting in my car in front of Cassady's house saying good bye to him. My car wasn't warmed up yet so I could see his breath from the cool air. He sat in my passenger's seat nervously fiddling with his fingers with his head looking down like he was pondering about something very hard. My heart sank a little…it looked like he was thinking about something very serious and I started to get worried. When I asked him what was wrong he told me that if he told me that I would have to swear to him that I would not tell anyone. Not expecting to hear what was about to come out of his mouth, I agreed.

He took a slow, deep breath and told me that his best girlfriend, Jordyn, who was a flyer on Inspire, had sent him a text. Not surprised, because they texted often, I asked about what...after a long pause he told me that she had told him that his coach, also the owner of the gym, was sleeping with one of the athletes on Inspire. Instantly goose bumps ran up my arm. I was in complete shock, mostly because the coach's partner and co-owner of the gym was thrown in jail a few years earlier for having a sexual relationship with a minor, so for him to do the same thing just seemed insane, I mean...he had to have learn from his partner's mistake, right? I was unsure of what to even say to Cassady. Surely this had to be a rumor, it just had to be.

He went on to explain to me that it wasn't a rumor that Jordyn had told him that Annie (the girl who supposedly was having a relationship with the coach) had shown Jordyn the texts between them, and that Annie confided in Jordyn, about the relationship. Annie told her parent's about what was going on and immediately they took her not only off of the team but moved the entire family to a completely different state. The only person that Annie made contact with was Jordyn, she blocked everyone else from every social media site.

Annie had left a few days ago, without saying a word to anyone on her team and everyone was told she moved to Georgia to be on a top gym there named Georgia Allstars. It didn't seem to make sense to everyone that she and her family would just pick up everything she had here and leave to go to a completely different state, especially since she was one of the most talented girls on the team and seemed to be passionate about Inspire. It made a little more sense in my head now why she would just pick up and move. I still didn't want to believe it though. But why would Annie tell Jordyn something like this? No 16 year old would admit they were having a relationship with someone twice their age unless they really needed someone to talk to, and Jordyn was her best friend.

The drive home from Cassady's house that night was the longest drive ever, every single emotion a human being could feel, I was feeling all at once. My mom is my best friend and when I got home I immediately told her everything. She was in just as much shock as I was. I told her that I didn't want to be a part of a program like this. I couldn't continue cheering knowing that the owner may have had a relationship with an underage girl.

I sent an email to my coach, Randy, that night. It was very short and to the point, something along the lines of:

Dear Randy,

I have decided no longer to cheer on Destiny. I apologize for any future obstacles for Destiny that may occur from my decision, but please know that my leaving is for a very good reason. You are the most phenomenal coach I have ever had, and I wish you and Destiny the best of luck with your season.

Thank you for all you have done for me, Morgan

I didn't expect such a quick response from Randy but he got back to me that night. He was very taken aback, which was understandable. He wanted to know why I decided to just up and quit the team and that it must be something pretty serious to make me stop cheering. He said that I was one of the hardest workers on Destiny and that he knew I loved being at the gym more than anything. He said it just didn't make sense to him. I felt he deserved to know why I quit, so I sent him back a painful email telling him what I had been told that night. His immediate response was: "Wow", that was the absolute LAST thing I thought I would hear you say." He told me to not make any rash decisions that it could be a rumor and to still come to practice the next day. He told me that he had known the owner for many years and he didn't believe he would do something like that, especially something that would put his company in jeopardy.

I agreed to Randy's suggestion and showed up at practice the next day, but word had quickly started spreading through the gym, and people wanted answers. The owner wasn't giving any. My mother decided to send an email to the owner that included everyone in the gym. She asked him to explain himself and that he had athletes and families relying on him to respond. He did respond in a short brief message that he would not do anything to jeopardize his business and that if people did not want him in the gym that he would step back and let the assistant coach of Inspire take over. He said that his main concern was keeping the teams together. He didn't deny or admit to the rumor. All the evidence seemed to be pointing towards him being guilty and the fact that Annie had blocked everyone from her life just proved, in my opinion, the situation to be true. If it wasn't true you would think that she would tell her old teammates that it wasn't and that she really did just move because she wanted to be a part of another gym, but she never did.

Some of the athletes from Inspire showed up at the next practice, others left because the owner wasn't coaching them anymore, and some left because of what he was accused of doing. Destiny, despite everything, was still together and with the left over kids from Inspire, we considered combining the teams and calling ourselves Desire.

After that awkward practice of being Desire for one day, news spread through the gym that the owner was stepping down and resigning from his business; ICC's doors were closing.

I felt like a part of me was dying, everything I had worked for all summer and fall was being ripped right from underneath me. An email was sent out soon after everyone got the news that ICC was no longer and it said that Darlene, a gym owner from Indiana, was buying out the gym and giving the teams the opportunity to stay together if they would like and they could cheer under her gym name, ICE (Indiana Cheer Extreme). Most athletes stayed but I decided not to. I didn't get a good vibe from her and I didn't feel like I could move on that easily from everything that had just happened. I needed time to collect my thoughts after all of these events that had just taken place and I would decide from there whether or not I was going to continue my cheer career or even where. That's when Famous Athletics was created.....

PART II
Famous Athletics

11

WORD ON THE street was a new gym was opening. I received a text from Matteo telling me to come to a meeting that was being held at a local restaurant and that there would be all the information I needed there on a new gym. My mother and I hopped in the family van and drove over to the meeting. Despite the fact that Cassady decided to stay at ICE, he still attended the meeting to keep his options open and also to support his friend Matteo. Inspire was trying to stay together as a team but a lot of the boys left to go to another gym that was about an hour north. This caused Darlene to pull up some of the "leftover" boys and girls from Destiny to Inspire. This put Destiny in an even shittier position not only were they the leftovers but now Darlene was taking the athletes with the best skills from Destiny and putting them on Inspire, leaving Destiny in the dust. This gave me the reassurance I needed to know that I had made the right decision to leave the gym.

At the meeting, Brittney, Matteo, and Jeff an all private instructor from ICC explained that they were working for a new and upcoming gym named Famous Athletics. They told us that they were opening in a few weeks at a badminton club. Yes…you read that correctly, they were renting out space from a badminton club. They were going to do this until their building was being finished (it was still in construction). They told us that they were having an 8 week team and that they were going to try to take the team to worlds. I felt kind of skeptical when I heard this… teams practice year round to make it to worlds so how in the world would a team be prepared in 8 weeks? And not only that they told us we would only be competing at ONE competition. That gave us one shot to get a bid, that's two and a half minutes to make it or break it. At that time this was unheard of. It took one week just to learn the choreography of a routine let alone be ready and be perfect in seven weeks! When the meeting was over Matteo texted me. He reassured me that this team would be successful and to trust him. He hadn't yet lied to me and he had helped me gain my confidence back in tumbling so I had no reason not to trust him. I told him that I would be at tryouts, after all, I wasn't cheering so it couldn't hurt to give it a shot.

I walked into the badminton facility and all the way in the back of the room was a seven and a half panel cheer floor...cheer floors are nine panels wide but since there wasn't space in the warehouse for nine we had to make do with what we had. I walked through the badminton courts, birdies flying everywhere, to get to the floor, I couldn't help but chuckle to myself, this was by far the most ridiculous place I've ever cheered at; I trusted Matteo though and I knew that he wouldn't let me down.

After taking off my sweatpants and jacket I joined a group of girls in the middle of the cheer floor for tryouts. Jeff, Brittney, and Matteo introduced themselves as our coaches and thanked us all for coming out. I was surprised, there was actually a good amount of athletes that showed up, most of them were high school kids which scared me; all-star cheerleading and high school cheerleading are two completely different types of cheer, or at least at that time they were.

Although the girls were in high school they had outstanding skills and I came to learn that a lot of them had actually been a part of an all-star cheer gym at one point or another in their lives. Tryouts went really well and I was ready to get back on the floor and start cheering again. Calls were made to those who did and didn't make the team. I believe there were only about three girls that didn't make it. We would end up being a small all girl level 5 team, a division that was very cut throat and difficult to compete in which means you would have to be an very elite team to make it to worlds.

Our first practice was spent getting to know each other's strengths and weaknesses. We figured out who our flyers, bases, and back spots would be and also who would be center for jumps and last pass for tumbling. Last pass was usually the best tumbler on the team and center jumper was usually the best jumper. At the end of the evening our coaches explained to us that practices were going to be almost every single day and that if we wanted to make worlds we would have to put aside all other commitments and dedicate all of our time to this team. They explained to us when our first competition would be and when Worlds would be if we obtained a bid. They wanted everyone to be 100% committed and if they weren't going to be then they should not be on the team. With that being said, a lot of girls found out that Worlds would be on the same day as their prom so they had a decision to make. Half of them stayed and half of them left making our team a little bit smaller but still strong in skills.

It only took about three practices until the gym owner, Heather, flew in a choreographer for us. The nice thing about this team was that there was no monthly fees, no choreography fees and if we made it to worlds, our gym owner found a sponsorship to pay our way, so we were essentially cheering for free. We had a couple of fundraisers throughout those few weeks to help pay for uniform costs. Unlike most teams who spend about 14 hours to learn choreography we learned ours in six. We had no option though, most teams learn their routine in the summer when they are out of school and have time during the day to learn it. We had to use our practices that were three hours a day and we only had the choreographer for two days.

Learning our routine went fairly smooth. Our choreographer was very peppy but strict when he needed to be. I really enjoyed performing the routine he gave us. It was sassy, fierce but most importantly clean. Our coaches would continue to preach cleanliness to us. They told us that it was what was going to make us stand apart from other teams. They told us that if you actually break down our entire competitor's routines that we all have the same skills and that it would come down to who could best execute and that would be who would win the bid to Worlds.

After we got our routine practices started to get intense, and the fact that I was coming from track practice every day too made it even harder. I could feel my body getting into tip top shape. Our coaches would warm us up with insanity work outs and condition us at the end until someone would throw up. They expected me to be the leader and they made me set the pace for the other athletes to keep up. Our team became closer through this conditioning. It exposed us in a weak state of mind which in return made us lean on each other to get through tough practices. We motivated each other and cheered each other on and we were all in this together. We had one goal in mind and that was to get a World's bid.

Brittney made us a bulletin board with all of our names on it. Under our names were three skills that she wanted us to achieve. At the end of every practice if we got our new skill we would get to mark it off and if we got all three of our skills by our competition then we would get rewarded. I know it sounds childish but it really did give us something to work for and strive towards. There wasn't a better feeling than landing a new skill on your own for the first time, it boosted your confidence and gave you a sense of pride within yourself.

As a token for all of our hard work the gym owner allowed the team to see the new building that was under construction. It was due to be finished in a few weeks. As we walked into the unfinished warehouse all of the girls scurried fast into the gym while I stayed behind. Everyone was screaming with excitement, the place was gigantic. While they saw something amazing I saw the exact opposite. I may have not known a lot about how to run a gym or a business but I did know that it was always better to start your business off small and grow rather than starting too big and this place was too big. The cheer business in Illinois is tough and competitive. Athletes hop from gym to gym, as well as the coaches. One year you could have eleven teams in your gym, and the next you could have a fall out and only have four. In order to be successful you have to start off small, even the floor we were practicing on in the badminton court would have been a more ideal way to start up a business. Where they got the money for this gigantic warehouse still confuses me till this day. Supposedly they got a huge chunk of money from Nike but I found that really hard to believe. If they did have the money where were all the athletes going to come from? In order to support a facility this big you would need at least a minimum of 150 athletes. I've never seen a new gym have more than 60 athletes.

12

BECAUSE IT WAS my senior year I was constantly trying to figure out what I wanted to do after high school. All my life I had wanted to be a teacher. I just couldn't figure out which college to attend to do so. I considered going to Purdue, the cheerleading coach was really nice and he would have loved to have me on the team but I just couldn't see myself fitting in there. I looked at Florida State, I was from the south and would love to go back and they had a pretty laid back cheerleading team that I knew I could make as well, but once again there was something keeping me back.

My mom is my best friend, I know that you hear kids say this sometimes, but she really is the only person, besides my brother, that I could 100% trust. People always joke around about how it's just a phase and I won't be able to stand her one day, but I'm almost 21 years old now and she is still the first person I go to about ANY problem that I have. I know that she will never judge me, never look down on me and will ALWAYS support me as long as I tell her the truth. This was one of the few rules that I had growing up. Along with always telling the truth I had to always let her know where I was going and not to lose my cell phone. If I lost my phone then she couldn't get a hold of me and she would panic. It taught me responsibility. I can honestly say that I never go a day without saying "good morning, good night, and I love you", to her. The bond between my family is ultimately what kept me from going away to college. I couldn't bear the thought of being more than ten miles away from them, call me a baby I just call it good parenting. I came to the conclusion that I wouldn't fit in at a four year college so instead I decided to save a bunch of money and go to the local community college.

Cassady hadn't planned on going anywhere for college either, I don't think he ever really had a plan. Just from the talks we had he didn't know what he wanted to do with his life. To me this wasn't a huge deal he was still so young. He ultimately decided that he wanted to take his first year off after high school and cheer all-stars for one last year. In cheerleading if you are 18 by August 30th you can still cheer, which means some seniors stick around a year to cheer, they are called "super seniors". That's if he could even pass his senior year. If he failed he wouldn't be able to graduate and he was right on the border of failure. I talked to him about renting out an apartment with me while he cheered one last year and he was ecstatic. My mother found a perfect unit for us on the first floor of a building. The area was beautiful, it was an escape from everyday suburbia life. We were surrounded by wooded areas, there were lakes within the complex where we could fish and paddle boat, a convenient store and a huge hill that in the summer had volleyball courts and in the winter was a ski hill, it was like living in your own little resort year round.

We signed the lease late in February for $950 a month, with taking possession being the first of May. We determined that I would be bringing in most of the rent money since I had just missed the deadline to cheer an extra year. I would be working all summer long at the local pool, lifeguarding. Our relationship was starting to get serious. We joked around that he was stuck with me for a year now due to both of us signing the lease. I knew that I must have meant something to him.

Because Cassady was still on Inspire, he was still competing in Atlanta and Dallas. I was excited for him but I was sad that I wouldn't be there to support him, not only could I not afford it but I would be missing practices for our 8 week team at Famous, and every practice for our team was crucial.

I gave him a note before he had left on the long 12 hour drive to Georgia. I had written the note in study hall the day before. I told him not to open it until the day he competed. It read that I was so proud of him and how I wish I could be there in the crowd cheering him on but I was there in spirit. He loved his note and we texted all weekend. He explained to me that he was always with his boys just smoking. He also told me that his family was getting on his nerves and that their performances did not go as well as expected. They did not get the paid bid that they had wanted. He told me that he was just ready to come home, I told him to just be patient and that he would be home soon and everything would be better. But once he got home things never did get better like I had told him they would…

Like I had mentioned, ICE was going to Georgia and Dallas, two of the biggest competitions of the season, which were also held on back to back weekends. After Cassady's experience in Georgia he told me that he was having second thoughts about being a part of ICE. He mentioned that he couldn't stand Darlene, their coach. I told him that Famous Athletics was still an option and that it would be nice to be a coed team and that he would be a tremendous asset to us. He took it into consideration and decided that he wanted to. After all, his best friend, and the person he looked up to the most would be his coach, Matteo. The only thing holding him back was a release form from ICE.

In all-star cheerleading if you are a level five athlete and you compete with a level five team you have to get released by the gym owner to go to another level five team. Cassady knew that the gym owner of ICE, also his coach, Darlene, would never release him to compete with our team, so he did the un-thinkable. He went to Dallas the next weekend, put on his uniform, and on day two and right before his team went on the floor he pulled his coach aside and whipped out the release form and told her that if she didn't sign the paper then he wasn't going on the floor to compete. Startled, and not wanting to ruin her gym's name, she signed the paper. Cassady was officially allowed to join Famous.

Although I was ecstatic, the rest of the athletes on Inspire were not. Not only was the team hit with the reality that Cassady would no longer be on their team but they once again did not get the paid bid they were hoping to receive. Supposedly a huge fight broke out in the hotel lobby later that night, between the athletes and Darlene, emotions were running high and people's feelings were deeply hurt. Inspire was becoming a hot mess. Cassady, as I'm sure the rest of the team, couldn't be more relieved to be home from the stressful weekend.

13

ONCE THE GIRLS on our team found out that Cassady was joining they were even more excited about our upcoming competition which was only about two weeks away. We spent the last few practices adding Cassady into the routine and perfecting all of our skills. He seemed to be the missing puzzle piece that we needed. Once he came the routine began to fall into place perfectly. The goal board that Brittney had made us a week ago was almost completely scratched off, everyone was getting new skills left and right. I had never been a part of a team with such hard work ethic and dedication, I was never more proud in my life as I was then to be a part of that group of athletes.

It started to get warmer out which meant Indian runs. An Indian run is where the team jogs in a straight line, one person behind another and the last person in line has to sprint all the way to the front and so on and so forth. I was a natural runner. I had been in track for seven years and Indian runs were something that I did on a daily basis. Most of the girls on the other hand had a hard time with these. With the sun beating down and already having gone through conditioning beforehand they would jog at a very slow pace, it was my job to push them to their limits, and I did. I remember one practice our coaches were upset at us and Brittney told us that we were conditioning until someone threw up. One of the athletes jokingly said to me, "Quick, someone make themselves throw up so we don't die." I couldn't help but laugh at her comment. Brittney didn't think it was funny though and we ended up being worked to the point where our legs wouldn't want to move any longer. The thing I liked about Brittney and Matteo though was that at our weakest point, when our legs could barely walk any longer, they told us to throw a skill. They told us that in the middle of a full out routine you would feel like your body is going to give out and that's when you need to be able to throw your skills. They were right, a moment comes over you right before you throw a skill when you're at your weakest point that you take a deep breath and tell yourself " I got this.", then you push through the pain with your team cheering you on in the background. When you land the skill, the biggest most uncontrollable smile comes over your face with your teammates clapping for you, you can't help but feel proud. It was the best way to boost everyone's confidence.

It was our last practice before our first and possibly last competition. We received our sports bras and spandex that we would be competing in. Because we were such a short season team we didn't have time to order our uniforms. The outfits were simple, a nicely fitted black sports bra with a mesh back that read Famous on the front in the brightest rhinestones you'd ever set your eyes on. Our spandex shorts were V-cut, a higher rise around the waist, and lengthier towards the mid-thigh so that our butts weren't hanging out. It was very classy and I am not going to lie, I felt bad ass wearing the outfit. It showed off our muscles that we had gained over the past few weeks training so vigorously. We were going to look like an army walking into the competition. Brittney, knowing the fashion world as she does, bought the prettiest makeup for us, a very simple yellow and black smoky eye shadow that shimmered in the light and vibrant red lipstick to make our faces pop even more. She also told us to do our hair half up-half down with huge curls and for those who had short hair, to get extensions. This is called hairography. When you have long hair that flips around in the routine, it draws the judges and crowds eyes to you, it makes everything look bigger and better.

The last practice was very emotional for me, I loved this team, and I didn't want it to be our last practice. I was going to put my heart and soul into this routine and give it everything I had. We broke for the last time on our 7 ½ panel floor and parted ways, the next time we'd see each other was the night before the competition for a quick run through of the routine at the location of the competition.

CSG (Champion Spirit Group) offered teams to come the night before so they could run through the routines in the warm-up area behind the stage. Teams were to arrive at 7PM and be prepared to get only about fifteen minutes of practice time. We got there a half hour early to secure our spot but when we got there we were the only team. Really confused, we went to the warm-up area to ask the attendant if they were still holding practice, the lady told us yes. We continued to stretch while we waited until 7PM. To our surprise only one other team from Kansas showed up. This worked out to our advantage because we needed as little distraction as possible. Although we could have practiced for an hour our coaches decided to prepare us by acting like we were in warm ups and gave us five minutes on each floor to perform our skills. Everyone hit everything perfectly, it was exactly what we needed the day before our big competition. We had pep in our step and fire in our ass; we were ready to bring it the next day at competition.

The next morning, my best friend, Caroline, came over to curl my hair. It was nice having her there. I needed to be around the ones I loved to calm my nerves. My momma cooked me a nice light breakfast of scrambled eggs and toast but I didn't eat much of it, my nerves didn't allow it. After Caroline was done with my hair I put on my makeup and put on a black and yellow Nike jacket that I had got while I was out shopping with Brittney the weekend before. Cassady spiked his hair into a fo-hawk and put on his black compression shirt and black shorts. Due to the fact he joined the team late, we didn't have a uniform for him, but he blended in well with the rest of the team.

I hugged Caroline and making sure not to leave without that big motherly hug, I kissed my mother goodbye and said goodbye to my brother and walked out the front door. It was a beautiful day out, about 55 degrees and clear blue skies, I took a deep breath and smiled, I had a good feeling about today.

I took a picture with Cassady in our bad ass outfits before I jumped in the car with him. On the way to the convention center we were jamming out to *Lose Yourself* by Eminem with the beginning lyrics running through my head on repeat.

"Look, if you had...one shot...one opportunity...to seize every-thing you ever wanted...in one moment...would you capture it? Or just let it slip. "

I had never wanted something so bad in my entire life.

When we arrived at the convention center, filled with thousands of athletes, my heart began to pound. It was finally here, the day we had all been waiting for, everything we had worked so hard for. It seemed to have flown by so fast; it seemed like just yesterday that I was at tryouts and surrounded by complete strangers.

Negative rumors were going around in the convention center about us. There were whispers that there was no way an 8-week team could get a bid to worlds. After all, this was something that other teams had been trying to get all year long. They wanted to see us fail and they wanted to believe that it was not possible. We were there to prove all of them wrong.

We waited in an upstairs lobby before warm-ups, finishing any last touch ups to our makeup and hair. When the time came to get ready to walk to the warm-up room, our coaches gathered us around and told us that we were to walk in two lines side by side, chest up, chin up, big smiles on our faces; they told us to look intimidating. They told us to focus on what our goal was and not anything that was going on around us. As we started off in our two lines, arms linked with the person next to us, a crowd of parents formed around us to send us on our way with claps and cheers. I lead the line with the other team leader, Lauren, we were like the moms of our team, she was the loving and compassionate one and I was the motivator. We linked arms, smiled at each other and began our walk down to the warm up area.

As we walked through the crowd of people with pride in our step, they couldn't help but stare, they were intimidated there was no doubt about that. When we got to the warm-up area our nerves started to sky rocket and the pressure started to become reality. We got onto our first warm-up floor, where we threw our stunts, everything hit perfect besides my basket. My flyer was having issues finishing her skills. She was letting her nerves get the best of her. I did my best to stay calm as her base and looked her in the eyes and told her that she had this. All of our tumbling hit flawless on the second floor, leaving us some extra time to just chill out before we moved on to our last and final floor. When we got to the last floor we just marked our routine to our music, making sure to do any last minute skills that we felt we needed to do. After the third floor a staff member directed us to the line behind the stage where two teams were ahead of us to compete.

Our coaches brought us together and said "This is it, all that you have worked for, all the blood, sweat, and tears that you have experienced, this is your moment to prove to everyone that hard work will always pay off, go out there and hit a clean, fun routine and you got this!" With that said we broke from our huddle and lined up behind the stage. Everyone gave last hugs to each other, reassuring each other that they had this. As I finished my round of hugs to everyone I stood in line and wiggled my toes, a sudden sense of horror shot through my mind. The pendent that I always wear in my shoe was not there.

This may sound strange, but right before I go out onto the floor to compete a thought of my grandfather's pops into my mind. They are both passed away and I know that both of them are looking down on me and are with me when I compete. I always put a pendant of an angel in my shoe that my mother had given to me on my 18th birthday. It was a reminder that I always knew that they were with me. My panic diminished when I had realized that over the winter break that past year I had gotten the angel pendant tattooed on my back. They were always there with me. They were the angels on my back that day.

When the announcer called our teams name, Revolution, to the floor, we entered through a banner to the biggest crowd I had ever performed in front of, everyone was really interested to see how we did. This was it. The crowd calmed and the room got silent, all I could hear was my heart beat, with my head down, I waited for our music to come on.

When I heard the ding that played at the beginning of the music, my face lifted up with a big smile and instincts kicked in. I did the beginning motions and moved to my standing tumbling spot, as everyone stepped back together and did our tumbling at the same time you could tell by the thud of the cheer floor that we had all landed in perfect unison. We all fell to the ground as two of our most elite tumblers threw standing back handsprings to doubles; we could tell from the cheer of the crowd that they had landed. After that came the jumps, something we were surprisingly good at, it was the tuck that a few athletes had trouble connecting. As the crowd yelled HIT after every jump and PULL for when we tucked, I knew that everyone had landed. We moved from jumps to our stunts, timing was everything, everyone needed to be in perfect synchronization in order for us to get that bid to Worlds. We clapped and set for our stunt, when we went up and moved to our new spots and double downed, I looked at our coaches and saw them going crazy. I knew everyone had hit perfect. Running tumbling was also flawless, all that conditioning made our skills look like we could throw them in our sleep. From there we moved to baskets, something my group was having trouble with in warm-ups. As we set for the basket I screamed at Haley "You got this girl!" When we threw her she kicked beautifully and as she began her double twist down, her first one was perfect but her second one she opened up too early and her legs came flying apart, our jobs as bases was to catch her and not let her or her feet hit the floor so that we didn't receive any deductions. But we couldn't...her feet brushed the ground slightly, but from all the adrenaline rushing through my body I didn't even notice, we tried to play it off like we were just setting her out. After baskets we moved to pyramid, something we had struggled with the most during practices. I took a deep breath and caught my flyers foot as we put her up in a prep. Because my group was the outside prep and not the main tricking stunt, I could see if our pyramid hit or not. As our flyers were thrown through the air, flipping and turning, I knew that we had just hit a perfect routine. I dipped to throw my flyer and catch her, when I set her out and moved to my dance spot I saw our coaches throwing their fists into the air and the crowd was going wild, tears started to poor down my face, all of our hard work had paid off. The only thing left to do was dance my ass off and that I did. After our routine ended I threw my fist up in the air and screamed, it was the happiest moment of my life.

That evening our team met back up in a ballroom in the convention center to hear our team placement after day one. Our coaches gathered us around with our score sheets in their hand as we waited nervously to hear what they had to say. They had a blank expression on their face and after a long pause they threw their hands up in the air and announced that we were in first place! We only had one small deduction, the judges had caught that we had let our flyers feet touch the ground, frustrated at myself, I put it aside and focused on the positive; we were in first place! Although this was wonderful news, getting first was just one of the few hurdles we needed to get over throughout our World's bid journey. To obtain a bid at CSG you didn't have to place well just in your division you also had to outscore every other level five team at the competition. CSG were handing out 6 at-large bids and 3 paid bids. Our coaches told us that we were in the running to get a bid but because the scores were so close we had to hit perfect during day two.

After they told us our standings they broke down our scores for each part of our routine. The judges complimented us on our cleanliness, jumps, tumbling and pyramid. Our dance, however, needed to be cleaned up and that our formations were off. The dance was our lowest score. It should have been our highest considering there are no skills in dance but it was an easy fix. Brittney had us go through count by count to make sure that everyone was on time with each other and every formation was symmetrical; that should easily boost our dance score an extra point. After we were done making the changes to our routine our gym owner surprised us with a new sports bra to wear for day two. They were a lot different than the ones we had worn the first day. They were one shouldered, all black, outlined in yellow, with our logo on the front. They were sassy and fierce. I absolutely loved them. I couldn't wait to walk in the convention center tomorrow and show them off.

I went home after our brief practice and relaxed the rest of the evening. I had a big day tomorrow and I didn't want anything getting in the way of that. I relaxed on the couch with my family and our dogs, munching on the homemade spaghetti my mom had made us. It was exactly what I had needed after such a long but exciting day. My mother asked me how Cassady was acting towards me at the competition since I had told her in the past how he really doesn't like to be seen with me around crowds of people. Because we were on the same team though, she knew it would be a little harder for him to avoid that situation.

But the situation wasn't different. I didn't mind it because I was focused on doing well during our competition. Cassady wasn't anywhere near our team almost the entire time before warm-ups. Inspire was also at the competition still trying to get their paid bid, so I had assumed that he was probably off hanging out with his old friends, it didn't even cross my mind that he'd ever be doing anything else. I didn't make a big deal out of it. My mother on the other hand had a real bad feeling. She knew that Morgan's team was there competing and she didn't like that. I told her that she was just worrying too much and looking too hard into things. Feeling kind of strange after she had brought that up I decided to go to bed and not worry about it. I had more important things to worry about and I couldn't let anything distract me.

I woke up the next morning a bit more tired than the morning before but still just as excited. Caroline was there bright and early before church to curl my hair again. I am so thankful to have such a wonderful friend like her. I sat in the bathroom eating the same breakfast as I had the day before, picking at my scrambled eggs and toast and talking to Caroline as she curled my hair. After she was done I put on my new sports bra and makeup, said my goodbye's to my family and my friend and then went out to Cassady waiting for me in the car. The car ride was a little different that day. Cassady was acting a little more quiet than usual. I asked him if he was even excited about today's competition and he said that he was but I got the feeling that he was either nervous or thinking about something else, whichever it was I continued to focus on myself and my emotions. I put our cheer music on and started to picture our routine over and over again in my mind and I could feel the adrenaline starting to rush through my body.

People acted a little bit different when we walked into the convention center that day. They weren't looking down at us they were looking up to us. We got so many compliments on our outfits and how pretty we looked. No matter how cut throat the competition was on the floor most everyone off the floor was genuinely nice.

Once the time came we lined up just as the day before and headed down to warm ups, heads up, chest up, chin up, a smile on and ready to work. Warm-ups were a little less stressful that day. They flew by smoothly and everything hit on the first try. This left some extra time to gather ourselves and have a sip of water. As we headed to the stage our coaches told us to do the exact same thing as we did on day one, but even cleaner. They reminded us of the changes we had made in the dance and with that they left us to go take their seat in front of the floor.

As everyone gave their last round of hugs, knowing in the back of their minds that this could possibly be our last time with each other, a peaceful feeling came over me. I felt like the pressure and nerves had been lifted from my shoulders. I told my team that no matter what happened on that floor that I was still the happiest and most blessed person to have met and worked with such an amazing group of people.

We were ready, this was it. It was now or never. The announcer called our team's name and we took our starting positions and before I put my head down I saw my family and smiled at them. Our music began and everyone lifted their heads and began to do work. Our standing tumbling landed and as we nervously waited for our elite tumblers to throw their doubles, they did and landed them both. We transitioned to jumps and listened to the crowd yell "Hit, Hit, Hit, Pull!" And I knew from the energy in the room that we had just landed all of our tucks. As we moved to stunts I took a deep breath and grabbed my flyers foot and yelled at her that she had this. Because we were in the center of the floor and all the other stunt groups were behind us or to the side, we could not see if everyone hit their stunts or not… but when I looked to the front of the floor where our coaches were sitting I could see them jumping around throwing their fist into the air and at that moment I knew that we had all hit perfectly. Next was running tumbling, which flowed as smoothly as day one. As I made my way to baskets the thought of yesterday popped into my head, I could NOT let my flyers feet hit the ground. I cheered Haley on as she stepped in my hands, as our group threw her she flew in the air and kicked her leg high and began her double twist on the way down. The first spin was beautiful and my heart stopped as she began her second spin…it was perfect. All that was left was the pyramid and dance. Our pyramid was flawless as I threw my flyer for the last time during the routine and set her on the ground. I walked to my dance spot and knew in my head that there was no way we didn't get a bid to World's, we had just hit two nearly perfect routines both days. We were unstoppable!

As soon as I walked off the stage I was tackled by my family and friends that had come to support me. They were so proud of us. When everyone was done getting hugs from their families, our coaches had us gather around in a circle in the lobby of the convention center. They had the biggest smiles on their face, they couldn't have been more proud of their team. They congratulated us and told us how amazing we did. After all the brutal practices, all the worrying, all the struggles… we had achieved our dream. I couldn't help but cry tears of joy and all that was left to do now was wait for the award ceremony.

I have never been a fan of award ceremonies. They stall by playing music for us to dance to, they throw beads out to the crowd and sometimes even beach balls to toss around. After about twenty minutes of this craziness they finally started to announce the winners. They take as long as they possibly can just to announce who got first place. We knew we had won our division and for that we received sweatshirts but I was more concerned about the World's bid. When the announcer began to read off the recipients of bids, listed in order from lowest scoring all the way up to the highest scoring bid (the last three being paid), we stood in a circle and held hands with our heads down praying to hear our names. We figured that because our routine had high execution but was very simple and had little difficulty that our score wouldn't be as high as most teams that took the risk of adding in more difficult skills in hopes to not get more deductions. We assumed that if we were to receive a bid it would be one of the first three names called…but after they called three team names and one of them were not ours, we began to get very worried…then the fourth name was called…and the fifth name was called…our hearts began to sank…then the announcers said "the highest scoring at-large bid… goes to…FAMOUS ATHLETICS REVOLUTION!!!" Not only did we get a bid, we were a tenth of a point away from getting a paid bid! Later on I couldn't help but think that if we had prevented our flyers feet from hitting the ground on day one then we could have had a paid bid, but it was okay because we had a sponsor for worlds anyways.

We took our spots up on the stage next to the other bid recipients; confetti was dropped from the ceiling as pictures were taken of everyone. I couldn't help but notice while I was on the stage, Inspire's sour looks on their faces, they once again did not receive their paid bid for the fourth time in a row. Once the crowd died down I gathered my belongings and headed home. I was exhausted from this weekend and a big comfy bed sounded like the best remedy ever.

As I laid in bed that night, I couldn't help but have a huge smile on my face, I was going to World's for the first time ever and with the greatest group of athletes a girl could ask for. I couldn't wait for the adventure that lay ahead of me during the next few weeks.

14

TWO DAYS AFTER CSG was Cassady's 18th birthday. When I had asked him awhile back what he wanted as a gift, he told me a tattoo of his last name spreading across his shoulders. My mom bought him exactly what he wanted. It was a big tattoo and we had practice in two days, I knew that he was going to be in pain, but he didn't seem to care, he loved it.

Everything in my life seemed to be picture perfect, I was going to World's, Cassady and I's relationship was at its highest point and we were finally starting to become really comfortable around each other, the end of the school year was right around the corner and to top it all off I was moving into my own apartment in about two months. It all seemed too good to be true. I just knew that something bad was going to happen, and that's when I received a text from a family friend.

Alyssa, a girl I had known in the cheer world for a few years, texted me saying that she had something she needed to tell me. A text that starts with "I need to talk to you about something" is never going to end well. I took a deep breath to prepare myself for what she was about to say. I don't think I could have been prepared for what was to follow. Her and her family was also in Georgia for the same competition that Cassady was at a few weeks ago. Her little sister competed on the same team as Morgan and they had let Morgan stay in their hotel room for the weekend because her parents weren't going. Alyssa told me that while they were there, that she had walked in on Morgan and Cassady in their hotel room, snuggling on top of the covers. That same horrible feeling that I had gotten a few months earlier when I had been told about her and Cassady hanging out while we were "on break" came over me again like a firecracker, I was absolutely furious!

I called Cassady immediately and asked him if what Alyssa said was true, and of course he acted surprised and said no. He explained that he was hanging out with his boys all that weekend and that he didn't get anywhere near Morgan. When I asked him if he was telling the truth he said that he swore the only two times he had even seen Morgan during that weekend was when he and his buddy were going down an escalator and Morgan was on one too on the opposite side. He said that she tried waving to him but they turned and walked the other way as if to act like they hadn't seen her and then in the warm-up rooms because their teams were competing around the same time.

When I told Alyssa what he had said, she respectfully told me that she wouldn't make something like this up and that she had no reason to in the first place. She just thought I needed to know. She said that she wasn't sure if they had done anything more than just cuddle, but that was more than enough for me because not only did I ask him not to talk to her but he told me that weekend he was just hanging out with his boys and no one else.

When my mom got word of this she was furious because the first thing on her mind was that I had just signed a yearlong lease with this guy and that he could possibly be cheating on me. She called Mike, Alyssa's dad, who she was friends with, he told her that he too had seen them in their hotel room laying on the bed next to each other, and an adult for sure had no reason to lie.

Cassady stuck with his story and claimed that Alyssa and her family were just crazy cheer people trying to start drama. Although I chose to believe him, that was the day when I lost trust in Cassady, and I've learned throughout my life now that without trust, a relationship will never work.

Because I could no longer trust Cassady I found myself snooping through his Facebook messages. I came upon one between him and Morgan during the weekend of CSG, my heart dropped. I tried reading the messages but most of them were deleted so I couldn't make out what the entire conversation was about. I NEEDED to see those messages, he'd been claiming for months now that he hadn't talked to Morgan. I thought really hard trying to figure out a way to find those messages and then it hit me, when you have a Facebook account, it's linked to your email address and when you get messages on Facebook they are sent to your email address as well. Although I wouldn't be able to see what he was saying I would be able to see what she was saying. I had to pray that his email account had the same password as his Facebook account.

I went to AOL.com and typed in his email address, then typed in his password from Facebook hoping that it would work, and it did. I scrolled through his Facebook notifications, looking for messages from Morgan, and there they were, all 50 something of them. I had hit the jackpot. I clicked on the first message and it read:

"If you cared about me you'd be here writing."

Okay that's not so bad…He's not talking to her right? I opened the next one…

"We need to talk."

"If you love me like you say you do and eventually want to be with me I will see you at 2:30 tomorrow to talk."

Sent March 13th, the day that we received our world's bid. All I could think was "are you freaking kidding me?" My mother was right, she had a feeling he was doing something wrong that weekend, and oh boy was he! I thought he was hanging out with his boys at the competition, little did I know that he had actually seen her while he was there. I couldn't believe what I was reading. The messages went on to say things like *"I miss you and want you, I better be seeing you on your birthday."* She even sent him one on his birthday that said *"Well I'm going to bed, no one is on Facebook to keep me awake. Goodnight, happy birthday! Hope you have a great day tomorrow! You're finally 18 now, quite a turn on actually because were illegal now."* with a winky faced attached. For his birthday I'm assuming they were supposed to meet up because messages were also sent saying *"Call me when you're done getting your tattoo, thanks for ignoring me, I'm sitting in my bed half naked for you and you aren't even answering me, I haven't seen you in three weeks, sorry that I miss you."* Needless to say, my blood was boiling, but I continued to read, and this was the message that really set me off:

"This is going to happen eventually, so why not now...If you want to be with her then be with her...I'll back off and we can just be friends. I know I treated you bad, and I'm not proud of it and I want to make it better, and I'm trying my best to prove it. We have had three good years together and I personally don't want to give it up but if you do then that's your choice...I love you and I know that deep down you still love me and I hope we can work things out between us because we had something special."

Cassady and I had been dating for over six months now, we were Facebook official, we had pictures together on our pages, we had signed a lease to an apartment for a year and my mom had just bought him a $500 tattoo for his birthday. Words cannot even describe the anger I was feeling at this point. I told my mother everything. You think I was mad, you should have seen her. We stood in the living room pondering what to do. I decided that before even going to Cassady that I wanted to talk to Morgan, one on one, and see what she had to say. I got her number from Alyssa and texted her very kindly and respectfully saying "look, I saw these messages that you sent to Cassady on Facebook, I promise I will not be mad at you, in fact, I will be so thankful if you are honest with me and tell me if there is something going on because I'm about to move in with this guy and it will really save me time and heartbreak if you are just honest with me. She told me that in Georgia they hooked up, not to what extent, but that they had. Whether or not she was trying to stir up drama or if she was telling the truth, I decided to call Cassady.

When I had told him that I had talk to Morgan and saw all of the messages, his excuse was that she had always messaged him and texted him and that if he ignored her texts and messages that she would go crazy and start drama. Sounds kind of familiar doesn't it? It's exactly what he told me when I first found out about them texting each other at the beginning of our relationship. He went on to use the fact that I didn't have his side of the conversation in the messages. He told me that his responses were always short to try to get her to stop talking to him. I obviously couldn't tell him that he was lying because I didn't have his side of the conversation, but it just didn't add up. I needed to see the entire conversation...so I texted Morgan again asking if she still had the conversation on her Facebook messages. She told me that she did and when I asked her if I could see them she replied "No." I figured it was because she didn't want anyone to know what she was saying in those messages. She had a good-girl image and didn't want that tainted. I asked her over and over again to please let me see them and she refused. She told her mother that I was aggravating her. When her mother found this out she wanted to speak to me on the phone and I was more than willing.

When Morgan's mother called me five minutes later, I answered the phone very politely and respectfully and explained the situation to her. I explained to her that I was about to move in with this guy and I needed to know the truth. When I told her everything I knew, she stubbornly told me that her daughter would never do or say such things and to leave her alone. I got into a huge argument with her yelling at the top of my lungs that her daughter was a sneaky little bitch and I have the emails to prove it. I explained how she stayed home from school to see him and was laying half naked in her bed waiting for him. She refused to look at the emails, which was not a big surprise to me, she didn't want to believe her little girl wasn't an angel. She hung up the phone on me saying something along the lines of "Don't ever talk to my daughter again, and we will make sure she will never have contact with you or Cassady." This was not what I wanted to hear. I wanted to see what he said in those messages and without them I really couldn't prove that he was lying. He begged me to believe him and for some reason I did. To this day I can honestly say that I didn't believe him, I more so decided to just put it in the back of my mind. I really thought I loved him. Maybe it was because he was the first person to take me on a date, or because of the way we could always laugh around each other, but whatever it was something made me stay with him. In life, I've learned that God has a plan for you and that sometimes you don't know what that plan is. Everything happens for a reason and maybe at that moment you may not know what that reason is, but with a little patience, you will find eventually find out.

15

BECAUSE CASSADY AND Matteo were so close, I found myself getting a little closer to Brittney, after all I was around her all the time and I had nothing else to do but talk to her while they smoked. She was a very smart woman. Her mind was constantly on high gear and coming up with new ideas. She and Matteo made a great couple. He was extremely laid back and always the people pleaser. Brittney was the business side of the relationship, she was always on the go and making things happen, together they were unstoppable.

As I got closer to Brittney she exposed me to her second life outside of the gym. She loved the excitement of the big city lights. She was the type of person that wanted to be famous. She was a model and a dancer and has a website highlighting her talents. This is the total opposite personality of mine. One day she showed me her wardrobe closet stacked miles high with designer brand shoes. I had asked her what was the most she had ever spent on a pair of shoes and she told me $900. My jaw dropped, that was almost a whole months' worth of rent for me. One night she introduced me to this website that she worked on explaining to me that guys pay her and buy her expensive gifts to chat with them. She suggested that I should do it with her sometime because I could make a lot of money. I was very skeptical, why would guys pay money just to talk to you through the internet? I just felt like there was more to this website than just conversation with these gentlemen. I told her about my concerns and she told me that they would ask her to take off her clothes and the more she removed the more they would pay her. She told me that the most she's ever done on the website was to get in the shower with a white t-shirt on. It still didn't seem right to me. I told her that I didn't want to be doing something like that. I would find out later down the road that she did way more than just talk and have wet t-shirt parties on the website. My mom obtained photos of the webcam sessions from some of her "clients" and they weren't as innocent as Brittney led me to believe.

I turned her down on that proposition but she insisted that I come to a photo shoot with her in the city. When I asked what it was for she told me that it was just for fun and that I could wear bathing suits and cute dresses. I accepted this offer and she let me go through her closet and pick out a couple of her outfits to wear for the shoot.

I remember it was freezing that night in the windy city, we ran over train tracks in our heels, barely being able to feel our toes. When we got inside the building we got into an elevator and she pushed the button to the penthouse, we were going all the way to the top. I knew the minute we walked in that this photographer must have been successful there was no way someone could afford to live in a place like this in Chicago if they weren't. I was amazed at how luxurious it was.

When I walked through the door and looked to my left I was immediately greeted by bottles and bottles of alcohol; someone offered me a drink but I sure as hell wasn't about to take a drink from a stranger, so I politely declined. As I made my way into the studio with my bag of clothes, I was amazed at how big the place really was and it had a spectacular view of the city. I followed Brittney upstairs where a photo shoot was already going on, one of the girls from Americas Next Top Model was there, and she complimented me on how beautiful I was. I momentarily felt like a celebrity for a second, it was strange seeing someone from TV in person. I smiled and told her thank you. Brittney introduced me to the photographer and then led me to get my makeup done by a professional artist; it was the first time I had gotten my makeup done by someone other than myself. It was strange having my face air brushed. When he was finished and I looked in the mirror, I was surprised; he had made my face look so natural, as if I wasn't wearing any makeup at all.

Once the time came to get in front of the camera I went into the bathroom and changed into pink bathing suit that Brittney had let me borrow. I walked out and everyone kind of stopped what they were doing and starred. I was very shy and felt uncomfortable but Brittney coached me in front of the camera and told me to relax. Everyone in the room was amazed by my body. They told me that it was the most amazing thing they had ever seen. This made me blush and feel a little more awkward but at the same time it also boosted my confidence. While I was standing there the photographer got in front of me and I became nervous. I felt so awkward. He gave me a chair to sit on and gave me directions as to what to do with my hands and feet. Brittney told me to relax so that I didn't look so tense and after I took a deep breath in I started to get more comfortable. I went on to take a few more photos in three different outfits and then watched Brittney as she posed for her shoot. She was not afraid of the camera, not one bit, she loved being in front of it. She was a natural, you could tell she was born to do this.

It had started to get late and I texted my mom that I really didn't want to stay the night at Brittney and Matteo's, I was such a homebody. I made up an excuse and drove home that night. I was exhausted, I wasn't really into the city life like Brittney was. I am more of a country girl. I would rather be home playing with my dogs and hanging out with my family. I got a bad feeling, a feeling of almost guilt. I didn't need to be showing off my body like that. I wanted to be a teacher one day and although I wasn't nude, I still wouldn't want images like that anywhere for my kids to see. I wanted to be a good role model and I didn't feel as if those pictures were appropriate. That was the last time I ever did a photo shoot and it was as close to the model life as I would ever get. I was happy in my peaceful home that night. There was no other place I would have rather been.

The next morning my mother woke up really early to let her dogs out and while they were outside she hopped on the computer and went to Facebook and noticed that the photographer had tagged me in photos from the night before. She woke me up immediately and told me that I needed to un-tag myself so that no one would see them. It is Facebook though, and anything that you put on Facebook will be seen by someone. I went to school that day and a rumor was going around that I had some really sexy pictures up on my profile. I ignored what they were saying. I didn't want to draw any more attention to the pictures than there needed to be. People forgot by the next day and I was so thankful that my mom had caught the pictures before someone else had. She had and always will protect my reputation.

Spring was in the air and Worlds was right around the corner. I have to admit that once our team got our bid we became a lot lazier at practices. We didn't take things as serious as before and goofed around a lot, probably because we knew that we wouldn't do well at World's. Being able to go seemed to be enough of an accomplishment for us. Our coaches on the other hand had bigger plans for us, they believed that we could make day two in our division. They constantly got angry at us for not trying as hard as we had trying to obtain the bid. Instead of just adding difficulty into our routine though, they changed it around a lot, which did not make us happy. We obviously had had a successful competition with the routine we did perform and we didn't see the need to change it around right before World's. The owner also had told us that they were adding in a competition the weekend before we left to go to Orlando. They told us that they wanted us to perform our routine one last time before World's which I could totally understand. But in my opinion it would have made more sense to keep practicing the newly changed routine and perform it for the parents at a pep rally before World's.

We went to the competition. It was held at Navy Pier in Chicago and unlike CSG, it was a very small one-day competition. Hardly any level five teams were there. I remember sitting on the couches outside the performance area when my phone suddenly started blowing up. I looked to see what all the chaos was and I got tears in my eyes and had to leave my team for a second to gather myself, I didn't want them to see me crying. A girl in my grade had been posting mean things about me on Facebook and a bunch of peers had jumped in with her and made fun of me too. I was so hurt. Throughout my senior year I was bullied by a group of girls who had nothing better to do with their lives than taunt me. They would say mean things about me, put election signs all over my yard, steal other people's Christmas decorations and put them in my lawn and egg my house and car. It all started at the beginning of senior year when I stopped hanging out with my long time best friend because she decided to start hanging out with the mean girl clique in our grade. I for one did not want to be around them. She wasn't who I used to know and I wanted nothing to do with her or any of them. They saw this as an insult and instead of just letting me be they decided that harassing me would be more fun, and apparently my peers thought it would be fun too. Cassady was somewhere in the building so I texted him and asked him to come find me and that I really needed someone to talk to. When I had shown him what they were saying he held me and told me to not let them dictate my emotions and that I was a wonderful girl. He wiped the tears from my eyes and told me to go wash up in the bathroom because we had to go to warm-ups.

This warm-up room was the least chaotic one I had been in probably because it was spaced out and there weren't many teams. Warm ups went pretty well. My friends were all there to support me. I had told them not to expect anything fancy because we just changed our routine and that we were probably going to look like a hot mess, and we did. I couldn't tell you what did hit during our routine. I was absolutely humiliated and I let everyone know. I walked around after the performance with a sour look on my face and arms crossed. I knew that we shouldn't have gone to this competition in the first place. I just knew it was going to be a disaster..

Our coaches yelled at us for having bad attitudes and looking back at it I don't blame them. We deserved to be yelled at because we goofed around during practices and didn't take them as serious as we previously did. We needed to keep in mind that they were changing things so that we would do well at Worlds. It was time for us to step it up and realize that we weren't just representing ourselves at Worlds, we were representing a new and upcoming gym and it was up to us to represent them the best we could.

After that competition I decided to invite all my friends over later that night to have a bonfire at my house. Cassady was staying out by my house a lot more, it was nice because we were about to move in with each other and we needed to know what it would be like to live together. Most everyone at the bonfire was drinking besides Caroline and I. After New Year's I didn't think I would be drinking for a while, it wasn't the best feeling in the world and I knew that I could have just as much fun without it.

My mother never trusted Cassady again after what had gone down with those messages between him and Morgan, but she supported me and just wanted me to be happy. That didn't stop her from checking on him though. While he was out in the back drinking she checked his phone and saw that he had been texting a girl named Kaleigh, a girl from Inspire, she was asking him if he could get booze for her. The fact that he was texting any girl was enough for my mom to get upset, she didn't want anything to do with him and she made it clear. She went up to bed and I chose to ignore the text and headed back out with my friends. Cassady and Keith were drunk already, Caroline told me that they had thrown back around eleven shots, I knew right then that someone was going to get sick later on just not sure who though.

The bonfire continued late into the evening and everyone was having a great time talking and eating s'mores. I loved being around these people, they were genuine and laid back, the kind of people I knew would never hurt me. Later that evening, Cassady and I were sitting with Keith and his girlfriend inside my screened in porch. Keith and his girlfriend were sitting up against the wall and Cassady and I were sitting on a glass table, all the chairs had been taken and put outside around the bonfire. We sat there for a while talking about life and anything else that popped into our thoughts. As were sitting there I heard the glass table start to crack from the weight of Cassady and I sitting on it. Because I was sober and my reflexes weren't delayed, I sprung off the table before it collapsed, Cassady on the other hand continued to sit on it while it broke, crashed and shattered to the ground. He was lying in a pile of glass surrounded by 3 inch glass daggers nearly an inch away from his body. Probably because he couldn't feel a thing from the effects of the alcohol, he thought this was humorous. I was in shock though, yelling at him not to move. I told him to grab my hand and I pulled him up. Once he stood up we checked everywhere on him for cuts or shards of glass, somehow he managed to not get a single piece of glass in him. After that he told me that he didn't feel well and that he needed to throw up. I went with him to the bathroom and watched as he filled two toilet bowls up with puke, I was so glad I didn't drink. Cassady still felt sick even after throwing up so I went and laid down with him in my bed. I told everyone we were going to go to sleep and the few people that were still there could sleep on the living room couches if they would like. They ended up sleeping on the trampoline outside.

With only a few practices left World's was just around the corner. Our team had gotten over our bad attitudes and practices started to get back to how they used to be. When we all showed up to the badminton court on Monday our owner was there and our seven and a half panel floor was not. She told us that she had a surprise for us, a little confused we asked what it was. She told us to jump in our cars and drive across the street, that the new gym was finally done being built and that our last few practices were going to be held there. Everyone jumped in their cars and drove the quarter mile to the new gym. When we got there we all ran in to this huge beautiful gym, it looked like something from a dream. Not only was there one floor, they had three! They had a tumble deck with a rod floor, a tumble track and a trampoline! Not only that, the lobby was gorgeous with tables, chairs, vending machines and flat screen TV's. We helped the owner put together some chairs from Ikea and then began to practice in our new gym and on our new nine panel floor.

I loved our new big gym but I had that same feeling when ICC moved into their new building. Because it was so spacious, it made the team feel further apart from each other. Maybe it was just me but I actually enjoyed the seven and a half panel cheer floor that was in the middle of a badminton court. Just thinking about it brings a smile back to my face.

The second to last practice our gym owner had another surprise for us...new uniforms for World's. Not just sports bras and spandex but REAL uniforms. They were absolutely gorgeous, the most beautiful uniform I had ever set my eyes on. They were cropped top, all black with a gun metal metallic grey stripe going down the side of the sleeve. On the front of the top was the same bright rhinestone logo that was on our sports bras that we wore from day one at CSG. The skirt fit nicely with the same stripe going down the side of the hip that was on the sleeve. The spandex underneath the skirt was yellow. When I put it on for the first time I had a teammate take a picture of me so I could send it to my mom. It fit me absolutely perfectly. I couldn't wait to wear it at World's.

It was the day of our last practice and I had mixed emotions of happiness and sadness. For the first time ever I was going to World's but it was also our team's last practice ever together, I couldn't help but feel a little blue. Practice ran as it always had, our coaches were a little easier than usual on us though, they knew that we were all emotional and wanted to take in every moment before it ended. To finish off our final practice the coaches had all of our parents come into the gym and sit in front of the floor to watch us as we went full out for the last time before World's. Halfway through the routine my flyer karate chopped me in my throat so hard that I couldn't breathe. As any cheerleader knows, it takes a lot to quit in the middle of a performance. I continued the routine gasping for air, once the music ended I ran over to the water fountain to try and clear my throat. It felt like a softball was lodged in my esophagus, I could barely swallow. I ended up losing my voice until I landed in Orlando. Our team broke for the last time; the next time we'd see each other would be in the Sunshine State making our way to the All-Star Resort at Disney Land.

16

MOST EVERYONE TOOK the same flight down to Orlando. It was a 7pm flight scheduled to land in Florida around 9pm. Cassady and I were on an earlier flight though, which was scheduled to land around 5pm. I have always been a procrastinator when it came to packing but I had made sure that I had everything I needed for the weekend. I made sure to stuff everything into a carry on, not only did I not like waiting for luggage but I didn't want to take the risk of losing it either. World's is a two day competition but you could only go on to compete day two if you had placed top ten in your division on day one. Our division only had 14 teams, this is why our coaches believed that we could make it to day two and possibly place top ten.

I gathered my belongings that Friday morning and jumped into my mom's minivan, she was so excited for me and made me promise her that I would take a lot of pictures. She is a picture person and loves capturing memories on film so that in future years we can look back at them. I'm so glad she taught me this because pictures really do capture time and time is a precious thing. When she dropped Cassady and I off at the airport she gave me a huge hug and told me good luck but most importantly to just enjoy the opportunity and have a good time.

Cassady and I made our way into Midway Airport, we had already checked in online so we went straight to security, the line was surprisingly short. I am a flying professional, I know all the rules when it comes to what you can and can't take on the plane, mostly because for a while as a kid I would travel back and forth between Mississippi and Illinois to see my father. We went through security pretty quickly and made our way to our gate. As I sat down next to Cassady waiting to board the plane I asked him how he was going to smoke in Florida considering he couldn't take it on the plane. He told me that his boys from Inspire were driving to Orlando, carrying with them bundles of weed, not just for themselves but to sell to people while they were down there. World's wasn't just the biggest competition of the year it was also the biggest party of the year. Sunday night at World's was always known for their block party. After everyone was done competing they blocked off MGM Studios for us and brought in a DJ and giving us free access to unlimited rides.

As Cassady and I boarded the plane we couldn't have planned for what was about to happen next. We took our seats shoving our carry-ons into the overhead compartments. After we buckled up we texted our parents one last time before the plane took off. Once we were up in the air things seemed to be going smooth until the pilot came over the intercom and told us that we would be landing in Nashville. Nashville? That didn't sound anything like Orlando, what the heck was going on? The pilot explained that there were some weather issues and the flight could not continue until they got the okay. When I got off the plane in Nashville I called my mother immediately, she told me that a severe tornado had just hit the Birmingham area and that the airport had also been hit, she told us to get comfortable because we were going to be there for a while.

I don't think comfortable was the best word to describe our situation, we were getting really antsy waiting, it was already five and we were supposed to be in Florida and we weren't anywhere near Florida. I began to get slap happy looking for ways to entertain myself in the airport, there wasn't a whole lot to do. I had received a text that the rest of the team was boarding their flight in Chicago and that they were probably going to get there before us and we had left six hours earlier than them. While I was waiting there I couldn't help but think of the teams going to World's from Birmingham. I prayed that they were all okay and we'd see them at the competition the next day. A few more minutes went by and then a lady told everyone that they were finally ready to board the plane and continue our flight. We were so ready to be at the hotel. We boarded the plane and I took a deep breath and tried to relax my brain. I figured that sleeping would make the time go by a little faster and to my disbelief I actually dozed off pretty quickly. The next thing I remember was waking up to Cassady poking me on my shoulder telling me to wake up that we had arrived in Florida. I texted my mother immediately to let her know that we had landed safe and she was happy that we had finally made it.

Cassady texted Matteo to ask if they had landed yet and Matteo told him that they were actually getting off the plane right then and to have us meet them by the buses. When we made our way to the buses, my jaw dropped. We were not greeted by our team but instead we were greeted by a group of the most orange oompa loompas I had ever seen. A few of the girls on the team decided to get a spray tan before World's, but a tan was the furthest thing from what they got. Some of them even looked green it was so bad. I couldn't help but die laughing when I saw them. They were the type of people that were always laughing at themselves so they played along and everyone made a huge joke out of it. Luckily it faded to a nice bronze color after swimming in the chlorine pool for a little before we had to compete.

When you compete at World's and you stay at the All-Star Resort, your package deal also comes with hopper passes. These passes allow you to hop from park to park. I had never been to Disney World except when I was three and I can't remember anything from that visit. I was extremely excited to get a picture in front of the castle, but I was even more excited to try mickey mouse pancakes AKA the breakfast of champions.

When we pulled up to the All-Star Resort I couldn't help but feel giddy, it made me feel like a kid. We checked in really late so there really weren't that many people around. Once our gym owner gave us the keys to our rooms I made a quick detour to check out the place. It had a gigantic pool with a tikki bar by its side to serve alcoholic beverages and everywhere you looked there was a Disney themed character added in to the atmosphere in some way. There were big dalmations attached to the hotel's walls and paw prints lined the pathways in between. There were gigantic hockey nets set up with the Mighty Ducks beside them. The benches were in shapes of dog bones; this place was awesome. I decided to make my way up the stair case that was enclosed in a huge fire hydrant and followed the paw prints to my hotel room. While everyone stayed out a little later I had decided to get some rest, we had a big day tomorrow and I wanted to be well rested. Cassady told me that he was going to meet up with his boys from Inspire, my guess was to smoke weed.

The next morning I woke up feeling great. I got up a little earlier than everyone so that I could do my hair and makeup before the room got crowded with girls running everywhere trying to get ready. I went to the cafeteria after I was done and decided that maybe I shouldn't get Mickey Mouse pancakes today. I never ate heavy before a competition so instead I just got a bagel and some orange juice. As I made my way back to the room I could see that the girls had woke up and were scrambling around to get ready. I decided to stay outside while they were doing their make-up, there was no reason for me to be in the way so instead I sat on a picnic bench underneath a shade tree. It was really hot that weekend nowhere near the cold temperatures of Chicago.

As I was waiting on the bench I actually received a group text from our coaches that we were to meet everyone where I was sitting in fifteen minutes. I went to get a bottle of water before everyone came down, it was starting to get more and more humid out as the sun rose higher and higher.

When we were all gathered around the bench, the owner handed out our hopper passes and told us that if we make day two after today's performance that we had to be in bed tonight by 11pm. Our coaches told us the game plan for the day. They explained that in ten minutes everyone needs to have their uniform and shoes on and ready to get on the bus. I was already ready so I just sat there and waited until it was time to go. I called my mother and told her that I wouldn't be able to talk to her now until after I was done competing, she wished me good luck and told me that she loved me and that she'd be watching me live on the computer from home. World's was huge, not only would it be broadcast on ESPN in the future but it was also airing live on the internet for everyone to see.

On the bus ride over images of what I imagined the ESPN Wide World of Sports building would look like raced through my head. I had been told stories of how amazing it is. I was told you would be surrounded by the best of the best athletes and the Milk House, which is where the competitions are held, is huge. Supposedly when you step on stage you wouldn't even be able to see the end of the crowd because it was so large.

When we got there it was everything I imagined. There were palm trees, millions of cheerleaders and cameras everywhere covering the event. I couldn't help but be in awe when I passed some of the teams from Chile and China...their uniforms were so different than ours, it was amazing to see the differences in culture. That's another thing that made World's so awesome, the people that you get to meet, although it was hard to communicate to most foreign teams they were always so friendly and we loved getting photos with each other. We even tried on each other's uniforms.

Before we walked into the warm-ups I took a peek over the edge of a balcony to see the stage we would be competing on, although it was a very nice stage, I have to admit that the stories of the place being "So big that you couldn't see the end of the crowd" was a bunch of crap, it was actually a rather small area just crammed with a bunch of people.

When we got into warm-ups I was so taken aback by how small the area was. I had to keep in mind though that Worlds was a big DEAL and not a big competition; Atlanta and Dallas are actually twice the size of World's, that's because those competitions host all the lower leveled teams as well as the senior teams. Only 5% of the entire cheer world would actually be competing here, but 100% of the cheer world was watching, either in the crowds, on their TV screens or on their computer screens at home.

Warm-ups went really well, I couldn't remember being more nervous in my entire life. As we waited behind the stage for our turn, the thought of my family and grandfathers popped into my mind as they always had, reassuring me that everything was going to be okay. I hugged all my teammates and told them how proud of them I was. I gave Cassady a hug and then resumed my spot in line. When they announced our name, I'll never forget that moment. Taking that first step on the World's floor, it was a moment of glory. I had always dreamed about this day, never sure if it would actually come true but here I was, waving into a crowd of thousands upon thousands of people.

I took my spot and put my head down waiting for our music to come on. Once I heard that familiar ding we began our routine. Everything that I had seen was hitting, but when I looked over to our coaches I didn't see them jumping around like they had done at CSG, instead they had a look of shock on their face. I knew that something must have gone wrong but I just wasn't sure what. When our music ended and our routine was over I didn't have the invincible feeling like I had had a month earlier...It was more a feeling of confusion this time. I immediately began to ask my teammates did your stunt hit? Did you do your tumbling? What went wrong? When I watched the replay with the team after our performance, water in my hand, I noticed our first error. A group had dropped a straight up stunt, a level three skill, I was furious, but I continued to watch the tape and everything else flew by smoothly until pyramid. The group on the opposite side of me dropped a prep, which is a level one skill. That was it, I had lost it, I threw my cup of water on the floor and yelled "Who the hell drops a level one stunt at World's?" and proceeded to stampede out of the room to the outdoors, I needed some fresh air. My team joined me, tears falling down everyone's cheeks. These were not tears of joy. Our choreographer came out of nowhere. He must have been watching us from the crowd or something because he was the last person I expected to see. He gathered us and told us that we shouldn't be crying. He told us to look him in the eye and lift our heads up and he said that when he had first heard that an eight week team needed choreography because they were going to try and make it to World's, he thought we were insane and that there was no way a team could accomplish that, but we proved him wrong. He told us that we should be proud of how far we had come in such a very short time and to not be so down on ourselves; it was exactly what we needed to hear at the time and even though we were upset, he did have a point. We did ultimately reach our goal, and we should be happy about that. I wiped the tears off my face and tried to look at the bright side, at least now we had all day Sunday just to relax and enjoy Florida.

17

ALTHOUGH I WAS ashamed of our performance, I have to admit that it was nice to be able to relax the next day and take in the full Worlds experience. I woke up and had my Mickey Mouse pancakes drizzled in syrup and relaxed by the pool the rest the morning with the other athletes that didn't make day two. Our coaches ended up telling us the night before that we had gotten last place, but looking on the positive side we were still 14th best in the world, not too bad for an 8 week team.

We would pass our time sitting by the pool by playing the game "Have you ever" I learned a lot about my teammates that day, stuff I would have never expected. It was interesting to really get to know them now that the season was over and we had nothing else to do but talk about our lives. It was really hot in the Florida sun so we would take turns taking each other's water bottles and filling them up in the cafeteria. When it was my turn I made my way over to the water fountains and on the way in stopped to say hi to Matteo, Brittney, and the rest of the adults that were there drinking at the tikki bar. Cassady was also there hanging out with them. When I had asked Cassady what he was drinking in his water bottle he told me to taste it and when I did I made a sour face, it was an alcoholic beverage. I whispered t and asked where he had gotten it from and he pointed with his eyes at Matteo. So not only did he smoke with his coach, his coach also bought him alcohol. He asked me if I wanted one too but

I told him no that I was just getting water for myself and the girls by the pool. I made my way back to where we were sitting with the water bottles strung over my arms. When I got back we all jumped in the pool and started to stunt and throw each other around. I was having a great time with everyone and it was nice not to have to worry about competing.

When you are a cheerleader, cheerleading is your life; you don't just cheer inside the gym you'll find yourself cheering outside of the gym as well, throwing stunts and showing off your skills in front of a crowd or just trying to get a cool picture in front of a restaurant, a building, a monument and almost anything that has a cool background. This is why I feel terribly sorry for anyone that is NOT a cheerleader that vacations at Disney World while World's is going on. Not only are they bombarded by thousands of screaming and obnoxious athletes, they have to deal with us stunting almost everywhere we go; we take over the resort like we're the only ones there.

To pass some time before I went to the Magical Kingdom with Cassady, a group of cheerleaders was gathering in a nearby grassy area to stunt and tumble around with each other to show off their skills. Although I wasn't a flyer on my team, I was a pretty talented coed flyer and I wasn't going to pass an opportunity to stunt around with some new people. I went to my hotel room and quickly changed into a sports bra and spandex and of course my white Nfinity cheer shoes.

When I ran to the area where everyone was stunting, Cassady was there waiting for me, we stunted together a lot in the gym and we couldn't wait to show off our skills. We soon found out though that our stunting was just average to some of the tricks that these people were doing, they were absolutely insane. Matteo was there too, he was a phenomenal stunter, he cheered on Kentucky for four years which is one of the most well renowned schools for cheerleading. He and Brittney could do some of the most elite stunts ever.

While I stunted with Cassady, a tall Cuban boy approached me and politely introduced himself as Jorge. He then asked me if I wanted to stunt with him, I of course accepted his offer and we stunted for a while in the hot Florida sun. It was around 95 degrees that day with the humidity at its highest. Regardless of all the sweat dripping from our bodies and making it hard for him to hold onto me, Jorge and I actually worked very well together. Matteo was nearby giving us tips on how to do a rewind, a skill that required Jorge to throw me into the air, let me back flip and then catch my feet when they came around; it was a very elite skill but with Matteo's help we were able to perfect it. I couldn't help but chuckle at Matteo, he was standing nearby spotting us with a towel over his head. His head had gotten sunburned on top along with his shoulders the day before and he was feeling the side effects. While Jorge and I were taking a break I asked him where he cheered and when he told me Top Gun, my jaw dropped. Top Gun was one of the most prestigious gyms in our country, having won multiple World's titles. When I asked him what he was doing here and why he wasn't competing he told me that he had gotten kicked off his team at the beginning of the season and that he was there supporting some of his ex-teammates. I still thought it was amazing though, I was in the presence of a World champion and to my disbelief he seemed very humble. I guess I assumed that because he was a World champion that he would have been a little cockier, but I was wrong. Cassady and I got along very well with Jorge so we invited him to come along with us to the block party later. He told us that he wouldn't be able to get in because he didn't have a wrist band but we told him that we'd find a way to get him in, so he agreed to tag along.

Even though I was in Florida that didn't stop me from being an adamant runner, I couldn't go two days without running so I put on my tennis shoes and went for a jog before Cassady took me to see the Magical Kingdom. As I was running I took in the view, it was so awesome to be surrounded by so many people that had the same passion as me it was like being in my own little cheer world.

When I finished jogging I went back up to the hotel room to take a shower and get dressed. I wanted to look nice for my picture in front of the castle. I put on a cute floral print skirt and a plain black tank top to go with it, straightened my hair and put my bangs in a braid and bobby pinned them to the side. When Cassady picked me up he told me that I looked gorgeous. I was never the one to do my hair or get dressed up so it was nice for him to see me all dolled up.

He thought it was silly that I wanted to go to only one park just so I could take a picture, but to me, it meant so much more. Everyone had a picture in front of the castle, it wasn't just an American symbol, for cheerleaders it was a victory photo. When we got off the bus butterflies fluttered in my stomach, I showed my hopper pass to the staff member and after he scanned it I made my way through the gates towards the castle. It was dark out and the castle was lit in wonderful interchanging colors. I stared at it like I was a kid that had just met Santa Claus. It was so big and grand. I ran towards it through the sea of people with Cassady by my side. When I got close enough I had him take a few pictures, it was trickier than I thought it would be with all the people looking up at the castle and walking by. They kept walking in the view of the camera. I wasn't angry though because I did the same thing myself a few times. After I got my photo in front of the castle we headed back to the hotel to meet Jorge, we had figured out a way to get him into the block party.

When we got back I ran to my room really quickly to throw on a more comfortable dress while Cassady went to meet up with Jorge. After I was finished I texted Cassady asking where they were and when he told me that they were in the room down from me I made my way over there, I was excited for what the night had in store for us.

When I got to the room Jorge and Cassady complimented me on my dress and I told them thank you and then asked what they were doing. They pulled out a bottle of Jack Daniels and between them and another girl took shots, they asked me if I wanted any but I told them that I didn't want to drink, once again I was scared from New Years and probably wouldn't be consuming alcohol for a while. After they were done we made our way towards the crowd of cheerleaders that were waiting at the bus stop. It was weird seeing everyone in dress clothes, I was used to seeing their hair done with crazy makeup and either in a uniform or sports bra and spandex. While we were waiting in line a kid who was obviously drunk started hitting on me, he asked me what I was doing after the block party and I just responded to him that I had a boyfriend and he backed off. Once the bus pulled up we all piled in and took our seats. On the way there we got to know Jorge a little more. We found out that he was a really cool guy and that he was actually looking for a job in the cheerleading industry. We told him that our coaches Brittney and Matteo actually owned their own choreography company and that if he was interested in moving up to Chicago that we could probably get him a job. When we told him this his eyes lit up and he asked us if we really could do that for him, we chuckled and told him that of course we could.

Once the bus pulled up to MGM studios we stepped out and made our way to the huge line to get in. We had decided that in order to get Jorge in I would wear my wrist band loosely so that after I walked in Cassady could walk back out with my bracelet and then Jorge could slip it on and walk back in. The planned work and once we were all in we made our way to the block party. It was still early and people were still on their way over so to kill time we went on a Toy Story ride. Because the park was shut down just for cheerleaders there were virtually no lines to go on rides. It wasn't so much of a ride as it was a virtual game. We rode in a little buggy together that dragged us through rooms filled with 3D objects that would pop out at you and you had to try your best to shoot at them and get as many points as you possibly could. The person with the most points won.

After we were done going on that ride a couple of times we went back to see if the block party had picked up a little more and boy did it! Thousands of crazy cheerleaders were everywhere grinding on each other to the music that the DJ was playing; you could tell most of them were wasted by the way that they stumbled everywhere and slurred their words, but no one did anything about it. I felt a bit uncomfortable. The party started to get crazy, Cassady and I tried dancing together and it wasn't hard for Jorge to find a girl to dance with either, but as time passed everyone started to get a little bit more out of control. Some kids were trying to climb up on the stage that was being blocked by police. These athletes had gone buck wild. The police got overwhelmed by the amount of force and they were clearly outnumbered. Their only solution was to shut off the music and turn on the lights. This didn't stop the athletes from partying though. The crowd broke out in song singing "Shots" by LMFAO, yelling back at the staff members and police that nothing was going to stop them from dancing but the police did shut the party down. They called in more police and forced everyone out of the area. It was like something out of a movie. I'll never forget that night.

Buses upon buses were waiting outside of the park to take everyone back to their hotels, once we found our bus we hopped on and listened to everyone complain as they made their way in to take their seats. Rumor was that the party was going to continue back at the resort but I was exhausted from the day and decided to go back to the room and go to bed for the night. I was told the next morning that the party did continue by the pool but was shortly shut down by the staff. Cassady would later tell me that he spoke to Matteo and Brittney and that they would be more than happy to have Jorge come work for them and that he could even stay in the loft that they had at their house.

It had been a long, exciting and memorable weekend but it was almost over. All that was left to do now was go to bed and wake up early the next morning and enjoy one last breakfast at the All-Star Resort. No surprise that Cassady stayed out a little later with the coaches. I texted my mom goodnight and told her that I loved her and then rested my head on the pillow and dozed off.

The next morning I awoke to the ringing of my phone alarm, I stumbled out of bed and threw all my clothes and belongings into my carry on and made my way downstairs to the cafeteria. I had breakfast there one last time and then made my way to the bus station.

The plane ride home went a lot smoother than the one getting here and although I was sad that our journey was finally over I had a lot to look forward to when I got home. Our move in date for the new apartment was right around the corner and so was Cassady and I's senior prom. I couldn't help but think that might have been my last performance as an all-star cheerleader. I had missed the birthday deadline to cheer again by two weeks. I was unable to cheer as a super senior so the only way that I could cheer would be to be on an international team, where there is no age cap. These teams mostly consist of college students and college students had other priorities which made these teams rare to come by. I had a gut feeling that this was not my last performance though and I had hoped in the back of my mind that it wasn't.

18

EVEN THOUGH WE were still in school, Cassady and I's lease started in May and we decided to move in early. Cassady wasn't at the apartment much the first few weeks, his school was nearly an hour away and he didn't want to wake up really early to go to class so I spent the weeknights by myself. Even though I only lived about three miles from my mother's house, I still had a very hard time transitioning to living on my own. It was strange not being around my family all the time and not having moms home cooked meals, or having breakfast made for me every morning; it was definitely a lot harder than I thought it would be.

Cassady and I's proms were on the same date so we had to choose which one to go to. That decision wasn't too hard for me though, I didn't like most people in my school so going to his senior prom was no problem for me. His friends were all very friendly. Cassady lived in a town further south out in the corn fields where everyone knew everything about each other. Since I wasn't going to my high school's prom, I made sure to text Caroline and tell her to stop by for a little while so we could get pictures together. She looked beautiful that day, in a classy navy blue dress with her hair pinned up with a few strands flowing down the side of her face. My dress was the most gorgeous thing I had ever owned in my life, it was white with gold sequins lining the dress in a soft flower pattern. The side of the dress had a slit going down my left leg and a nice open back to show off my angel tattoo.

Cassady wore a white tux to compliment my dress and we looked very good next to each other. My mom and brother came over and took a few pictures of us at our new apartment and then we jumped in my car to head to his hometown. We took pictures at Cassady's best friend's girlfriend's house with one other couple, I really enjoyed that we had only six people in our group. It wasn't chaotic and the other two couples were very laid back just like Cassady and I were. In fact we were so laid back that for dinner before prom we actually went to Culvers, one of my favorite fast food restaurants. We grabbed a quick bite and then headed over to the ballroom that was only about fifteen minutes down the road. When I walked in I was greeted by groovy butterflies and wacky designs, their prom theme was Alice In Wonderland, something I had never seen before, but it was unique, I liked it. Once we checked in and gave a group of volunteer teachers our tickets we made our way to the grand room. When we walked in we were greeted by at least 60 huge round tables, this was by far the biggest dance I had ever been to. My school barely had a thousand kids in it whereas Cassady's grade had nearly a thousand kids by itself.

Everyone that was there was assigned a number that lead you to a table where we would first eat a three course meal. Cassady and his friends had warned me that the food was bad, that's why we went to Culver's beforehand. I tried their food and they were right, it tasted awful. That didn't stop us from having a great night though; we danced our butts off on the dance floor, rocking out to our favorite songs. About three hours in people started getting curious as to where the after party was going to be; because Cassady and I had our own place we had told people that we were going to have an after prom party, but being the homebody that I was I told him that I was exhausted and just wanted to go home and sleep in our bed tonight and watch a movie. He said that he was actually pretty tired too so we decided to leave early and go home. I know to most I would be considered boring but there was just nothing more that I loved than snuggling up in a blanket at my home. When we told people that we were no longer having a party no one was really upset, it was a far drive for them anyway and there were plenty of other parties that they could attend.

After prom ended graduation was right around the corner. It was now June and the pool was open and I was working there every day to pay bills. I didn't mind though, I loved working as a lifeguard, not only was it a great job, the management made it fun to work there. As I was filling out my availability one day for the upcoming week I came upon our graduation date. The pool was being rented out that night for a birthday party and they needed people to work it, I pondered for a second if I should work it or not but then I decided I would. I went to my mother and asked her if she would be mad at me if I didn't walk at graduation, she told me of course not, I was getting my diploma no matter what. I explained to her that I would rather be at work making money and having fun rather than sitting in a three hour assembly to announce who had graduated. Not only did it sound like a bore fest to me, I didn't want to walk with my class anyway.

Ironically the pool was located right across the street from my high school so as I sat there on graduation night and I couldn't help but smile to myself; I was so relieved to be out of that hell hole. I had to drag myself out of bed every day to make myself go to class and at one point I even considered dropping out and getting my GED because I couldn't stand the thought of being around a place like that any longer. It was all over now, I had made it. My experience there had made me a stronger person and I knew that I was going to be successful. Community college started in a few months and I had all my classes picked out. I couldn't wait to get started on my teaching career. It was something I had dreamed of my entire life.

Cassady just barely graduated high school, it boiled down to him passing his finals that would determine if he would walk at graudation or not, and thankfully he passed. He was the type of student that never did homework or projects, but when it came to tests he was naturally book smart and passed them with flying colors. I was the total opposite. No matter how many hours I studied as soon as a teacher plopped a test down in front of me I second guessed myself and bombed almost every time.

Unlike me, Cassady did love his school and classmates. He went to his graduation ceremony high as a kite and walked with his grade.

I was unable to attend the ceremony because I spent most of my days at the pool working since it was our main source of income.

Because Cassady and I didn't have a prom party we decided that we were going to have an ABC (Anything But Clothing) graduation party instead. He invited a bunch of his friends, and I invited a bunch of mine and to my better judgment I invited some old friends as well, assuming that maybe they had grown up a little. Caroline came over early to help me make my hot pink duct tape outfit while she fashioned a sheet tied around her acting as a toga. When I walked into our kitchen I died laughing, Cassady was wearing nothing but a beer box around his waist, it was quite the sight.

Once everyone started piling into our tiny apartment I started to get a lot more tense, of course I had told people that they could bring a friend if they wanted but most of the people didn't have the decency to tell me how many they were actually bringing. People I had never met in my life were rolling in our back door like they had known us for years. The party started to get a little crazy, girls were starting to take off their clothes and the noise level was getting way too high. The only drink I had had all night was one shot of Jack Daniels, enough to barely even get me buzzed. I spent most my night running around making sure that people weren't destorying my new home. Caroline isn't a drinker and being the good friend that she is she helped me get a lot of people out of my apartment. I didn't want to get a noise complaint the first month I was living there. The party started to die down after we had herded most of the problem makers out the door. I let the remaining few people know that they could sleep at my house if they wanted but most of them chose to walk home. As the last group of people were heading out the door one of the boys started to sway back and forth and he turned really pale and threw up all over my carpet. I was so angry, I told him just to leave and not worry about it. Thankfully he hadn't obviously eaten anything beforehand because the puke was just pure alcohol. He apparently had too many shots. I was stressed out from the long night and told Cassady to clean up the apartment. I just wanted to get in my bed and go to sleep. It was the last time I had a party in our apartment. The next morning we spent hours cleaning up the place from head to toe. I told my mom that it was not a fun night and that I was never going to have another party again. She laughed and told me that life is all about learning lessons and from now on if I wanted to go to a party I should go to someone else's house so that I wouldn't have to be responsible for cleaning up the mess the next morning. I soon started to realize that I really wasn't the party type at all.

While I was working 40 hours a week at the pool Cassady continued to cheer at Famous Athletics. Because our team had done so well they had a good turnout for tryouts and had around 60 people show up. Although this was fantastic for a first year gym, I still couldn't figure out how they were supporting a building that big with only 60 athletes, but Cassady was having fun so I just put the question in the back of my mind.

Jorge was now living with Brittney and Matteo in their town home. Jorge and Cassady worked for Brittney's and Matteo's choreography business over the summer as well as instructing a few classes at Famous. This brought in the little extra money that we needed to pay bills. We lived pay check to pay check but I didn't mind, I enjoyed my simple life and as long as I had my family and a roof over my head, I didn't see the need for anything fancy.

Jorge and Cassady traveled a lot together that summer to different high schools around Illinois teaching cheerleading squads new skills and choreography for their new upcoming season. I quickly found out that Jorge was not the person I thought him to be when I met him at World's. We invited Jorge to come over to our place a lot that summer for dinners or just to hang out with Cassady so they could smoke. When I had asked them how their days went when they worked with these high schools, Jorge told me a story of how he snuck away to a class room to have sex with one of the coaches while Cassady stayed with the girls and taught choreography and skills. I was in shock. I had no idea that Jorge was that type of person. When I told him that I thought this was wrong, his response was "Morgan, are you crazy? I'm Cuban, It's in my blood!" Although his comment made me laugh I couldn't help but think about how wrong it was and how unprofessional it was. It made my blood boil to think that these high school coaches were around kids all day and they partook in activities like this. I couldn't wrap my mind around them being good role models to their students when they acted like this. And not only did Jorge sleep with a coach while he was on the job, he also texted some of the athletes that he had met at these camps! These girls were minors. Not only was this highly unprofessional to be texting clients they were also underage and he could get in huge trouble for something like that. I shook my head at him and told him that he should really be careful with what he said and did because he could easily ruin his entire future if he got caught in a sticky situation with an underage girl.

During the month of July bills got harder to pay. The unfortunate thing about working at the pool was that if it stormed then it would close down which meant no money for me. That summer happened to be one of the rainiest summers on record. Because bills got harder to pay, Cassady's checks from Famous and Brittney and Matteo's company became much more vital. From a business stand point I feel that it is your legal duty to pay your employees when you say they are supposed to get paid. Most families rely on paydays; they schedule their bill payments and grocery outings around them. If employees aren't going to get paid on the scheduled payday it could possibly throw them into a bad situation, this was the exact situation that Cassady and I were dealing with. Brittney and Matteo were a few days late in giving Cassady his pay check and I started to get very nervous. We had bills to pay and we needed that money. I asked Cassady if he could please ask them for his check because they were already late in giving it to him. He obviously didn't pressure them because there was still no check a few days later. I got impatient and decided to take the situation into my own hands. I texted Brittney and told her that she was running her business very unprofessional and that there was no reason that they should be giving Cassady his check so late. I told her that we had bills to pay and we needed that money now. She got very defensive when she saw this text. She didn't respond to me but she texted Cassady immediately and said that if I were to ever speak to her like that again that he would be fired and that she had his check ready for him at her house. Cassady blew up at me, he was furious that I had gone behind his back and texted Brittney about his check. I argued back at him that me texting her obviously worked because she said she had the check and it was ready for him to be picked up at her house. I told him that we couldn't afford to wait around any longer for the money. I couldn't understand why he would be angry at me? He hadn't had one ounce of anger towards Brittney and Matteo for not paying him and it didn't make any sense to me. We had gotten in such a big argument about it though that he ended up staying the night at their house, it was the first time we had gotten into a big fight.

After my text to Brittney he never had a late check again, although it tainted my friendship with Brittney and we no longer spoke. I was just glad to see the checks coming in steady again. This wasn't the only thing that made me stop talking to Brittney and Matteo though, not only could I not stand how unprofessional they were, I'll never forget one weekend how they handled a very scary situation with Cassady.

19

CASSADY WAS STAYING at their place for the weekend because they all had to wake up early in the morning to go to a skills camp together. As Cassady explained it to me, he woke up early that morning and made his way down their hallway to go to the bathroom, right before he opened the door he blacked out and the next thing he remembered he was waking up on the floor in a puddle of urine with a huge hole in the bathroom door. He went on to tell me that Brittney and Matteo said they heard a loud bang so they ran out of their bedroom to see what had happened and when they got to Cassady he was having a seizure. Although it hadn't lasted for long, it was still a seizure, a very serious medical condition that you should never take lightly and on top of that he had fallen into the door so hard with his head that he put a hole in it. Panicking after he had told me this I asked him if they had taken him to the emergency room and he told me that they didn't. He had told them that he was fine and didn't need to go. I don't care who you are, in my opinion if you have a seizure that knocks you out on the ground, makes you pee yourself and you hit your head so hard on a door that you put a hole through it, you should be going to hospital, if not for the seizure then at least to see if there was a concussion or not. This made me have even more resentment towards Brittany and Matteo. Not only did they not take him to the hospital they allowed him to proceed to a cheer camp. I couldn't understand why Cassady would ever want to surround himself with people that just didn't seem to truly care for his best interest. But as always, he remained friends with them, they were his idols and his heroes and he looked up to them more than anyone in this world. I had my own opinions about them though and he knew that I didn't want anything to do with them.

August was a lot better month for the pool, there was less rain, which meant more hours for me and fewer struggles to pay bills. It was almost the end of summer though which meant I needed to find another job. Cassady's job with the choreography company was also seasonal so he needed to find a new job as well. I tried to figure out a place where I could make a lot of money with fewer hours since I would be in school during the fall. The idea of serving crossed my mind, I lived close to a Buffalo Wild Wings and I thought it was the perfect opportunity for me. I immediately went and applied, making sure to get there 30 minutes before the restaurant opened. When I walked in I asked the hostess if I could speak to a manager, I knew that was the quickest way to a job. When a shorter man walked up to me and asked me what I needed, I introduced myself by shaking his hand and told him that I was looking for a job. He was very impressed that I hadn't just filled out an application and dropped it in their wooden box like most applicants. He told me that they were actually hiring and he would love for me to come for an interview the next day. He had me fill out an application and we scheduled a time to meet. Getting the job was fairly easy but they told me that for the first few months that I would have to start out cashiering because they wanted me to get used to the computer system. I told them that that was completely understandable and that I would be more than willing to. Cassady also found a job at a different Buffalo Wild Wings. He worked at a location that was further away from the one I was located at. It was a relief to know that we had both found jobs before our seasonal jobs were over. I knew that we would be okay financially for the rest of the year.

Once summer ended it was a bittersweet feeling. I was sad to stop working at the pool but at the same time I was more than excited to start my first year of college. I had gotten all my books and supplies that I needed. My main focus was to get straight A's. I was there strictly to learn and socializing was the last thing on my mind.

On my first day of school I woke up giddy and ready to take on the day. I packed all of my books, ate a quick breakfast and ran out the door to my car. Traffic wasn't too bad on the way there it was only about a fifteen minute drive from the apartment, however this college was known for its minimal parking and I should have known better than to get there only five minutes before class. It took me nearly twenty minutes just to find a parking spot. I walked into my first class late that morning but I wasn't the only one and that was reassuring. The instructors in college are a lot different than the teachers at a high school, they don't care if you don't show up to class or if you have your IPod out listening to music or if you are on your cell phone texting to your friends and they most certainly didn't care if you failed. They are getting paid regardless and in a weird sort of way, colleges don't mind if you fail or drop out because if you do then they know that most likely you will need to re-enroll into the class to try and pass it again which meant more money in their pockets.

I fell in love with the college atmosphere, it was a lot different than high school, no cliques, no drama and I didn't have to socialize if I didn't want to. I found myself in the library most of my time studying and getting ahead on all my projects. This was another thing I liked about college, teachers gave you syllabuses during the first class which meant I could get ahead of all my work if I wanted to and I took advantage of that.

The only grade I was interested in teaching was elementary. I loved working with little kids and I wanted to make a huge impact in their lives, just as some of my teachers did when I was younger. One of the classes I was taking, Education 101, had us go into a classroom immediately to observe what it was like to teach in an elementary atmosphere. We had to do this on our own time outside of school and we got to choose which school we wanted to make our observations in. I chose a fourth grade class at the elementary school that my brother had attended.

When I stepped into the classroom I was greeted by 20 young children all with huge smiles on their faces. The teacher introduced me and told them that I would be here for the week to observe and help and they all got excited. I had actually known a few of them because I had gone to school with their older siblings.

I learned a lot that week about teaching. It wasn't as easy as I had imagined it in my mind. I got to see the reality of what it was like to be a teacher. Obviously there were fun little moments but most of the time the teacher was spent trying to get her students to focus. I also noticed that her job didn't just end when the school day ended. She spent hours after school grading papers and talking to parents. As I sat in the teachers' lounge, where they all ate lunch, I listened to their conversations about how they had to figure out a way to re-teach a topic because their kids weren't understanding it and how some students were giving them a hard time. I didn't realize that being a teacher came with such a large amount of stress. I think the thing that got me the most though was the technology that was being used inside the classrooms. When I was growing up the only time we used a computer was to look up books in the library or when we were en-rolled in keyboarding classes. Now every classroom had computers in it and almost everything the students were taught was either on a computer or on a smart board which is a gigantic computer. It was a lot different than I had imagined.

After observing that class I found myself in the library one day pondering if teaching was something that I wanted to do for the rest of my life. It wasn't that I thought it was too much work or too stressful, I just wasn't sure if I could picture myself waking up every morning and being happy to go to work. My mother always told me that I should find a career that I loved doing every day and that if I could then I would never have to work a day in my life. I thought really hard and I still wanted to make an impact in children's lives...but in what way? What was the one thing that I could wake up every morning and love doing? The only thing that popped into my mind was cheer-leading. It was the one place that I never get tired of being at. I loved being in the gym, it was my second home.

I went to see my mom that day and told her my dilemma. She chuckled and told me that she knew I was going to do this. When I asked her why she wouldn't have told me not to go to college in the first place to save me some time, she laughed and told me that I wouldn't have listened to her and that I needed to figure it out on my own and she had a point. I talked to her about how I loved cheerleading and I knew it was the one thing I could be happy doing every day but that I didn't know how I could make that into a career. She told me that I could own my own gym eventually and it made sense and it sounded like a good idea to me. Being in the gym my senior year kept me from going insane and dropping out of school. It gave me a place to go where I could be surrounded by people that supported me and I wanted to give kids that same kind of place to go to. We talked about how to get into the cheerleading business and decided that it was best to start off by building up my resume. I would have to look for ways to get jobs as a coach, choreographer or even better all three. My mother and I began to do some research on the industry and we were shocked with what we discovered.

20

IN CHEERLEADING THERE are about 67 National Championships held within one year. I know this sounds crazy but most sports just have one National competition because there's only one nation within the United States, right? Well this is a huge part of why cheerleading isn't a sport. There is no universal scoring sheet. Every competition you go to can essentially have a different score sheet. This means that for each competition teams have to rearrange their routines to meet the expectations of that competition's score sheet, sounds like a bunch of crap doesn't it? That's like football players and coaches having to re-work their plays every week because the games that they will play in will have different scoring systems. For example touchdowns could be worth seven points at one game and worth three points at another game.

Cheerleading is "essentially' owned by Jeff Webb, CEO of Varsity Brands. When people hear the company name Varsity they usually think cheerleading uniforms but little do they know Varsity owns about 30 other branches of cheerleading. It gives you the illusion that you have a choice in what company you choose to do business with but in actuality it is owned and controlled by Varsity. Varsity's sale revenues exceed 300 million dollars a year. Yes, cheerleading is a 300 million dollar a year industry.

In other words, cheerleading is not becoming a sport because Varsity does not want to be included under title nine, Why? Because

Varsity's real revenue comes from their uniform sales and everything else they do is pointed towards those sales. To be a cheerleader a majority of families have to buy into Varsity's endless money pit. Teams will attend between eight and ten competitions a season and those competitions are ran by Varsity, although you may not realize that because their under names such as WSF. Each one of these competitions cost anywhere between $75 – $175 per athlete, per competition, which means competition fees for a year run at an average of $1,200 per athlete. That fee doesn't include the $300-$400 cost of a uniform and a $60 registration fee to the USASF (U.S. All Star Federation) who regulates the safety rules of cheerleading (also a subsidiary of Varsity Brands). Not to mention the monthly fees that you pay to the gym that average about $130 per month and the traveling fees such as airfare, gas, hotel rooms…etc. Cheerleading easily becomes a whopping three to five grand sport that families have to pay out of pocket. That is per child. I am sure you can imagine the amount of money families pay for two or three kids. You would think with all the money that these families are spending that they would at least get free admission into these competitions but they don't at most of them. Most competitions charge an entry fee of about seven to sometimes even twenty dollars per competition. Because the sport is not regulated these vendors are allowed to host "National" competitions. But there is only ONE Worlds competition and this is why teams strive to not just make it to World's but to place top ten in World's because it is a TRUE representation of your teams' skill.

Finding out all of this information I soon began to realize how big this business is and not only was it a career I could be happy with the rest of my life but it was also one of the few businesses that was on the rise during our nation's economic recession. I knew once and for all what I wanted to do with my life. I dropped out of school and picked up more hours at Buffalo Wild Wings and started on my new aspiration to become a gym owner.

Although I was not cheering any more I was still involved with the cheer world. Everyone I knew and hung out with was a cheerleader. I remember one night in the middle of August Cassady came home from practice and told me that Jorge had been fired from Famous.

A little taken aback I asked what happened. He told me that one night Brittney and Matteo had Madison over, a girl from Cassady's team, who had happened to be drinking a lot that night and ended up sleeping with Jorge. Word made it around to the gym owner and Jorge was fired for sleeping with an athlete. Even though they were only a few years a part it still broke conduct and I completely understood why they would fire him. But what didn't make sense to me was why wouldn't Brittney and Matteo get fired as well? They were also still coaching at Famous and they were the ones allowing it to happen in their home. I had later found out that Brittney and Matteo explained to the owners that Madison, who also worked for Brittney and Matteo's company, was a co-worker of Jorge's so it was not a conflict of interest in their mind. That still wasn't an excuse to have an underage athlete from the gym in your house drinking and sleeping with a staff member. The issue got swept under the rug as it always seems it does in "my" cheer world and Brittney and Matteo still got to keep their jobs.

Summer had officially ended and my brother was back in high school which meant football season. My mother and I would always make a date out of going to Sam's games. Our family has always been really supportive of each other and going to sporting events was one of our most favorite things to do together. While we were sitting in the bleachers during Sam's first game my mom received a text from Mike, Alyssa's dad, the one that always kept us updated on cheer news. When she read the text a look of disbelief came over her face and then she shook her head saying "I knew it, I just knew it, I had a bad feeling about this woman". When I asked her what Mike said she told me that he was reading the newspaper and that he had seen Heather, the owner of Famous, in it. She had been arrested for an outstanding warrant. I was in absolute shock. I asked my mother if he had said what the warrant was for and she said that he didn't know. My mother is an amateur private investigator and I knew she was going to get to the bottom of this.

She went home later that night and confronted Heather on Facebook. Heather's story was that the newspaper had made a mistake and that they were in the process of correcting it. She claimed that she was out with staff members the night of the "arrest" and that her child had been in the hospital all week long, but my mother knew better. The police don't make mistakes like that and she felt that there was something more going on and she wasn't going to quit until she found out what it was.

My mom contacted the police department and not only did they send over the mug shot and a copy of the arrest warrant from her arrest they also told her that the Girl Scouts had a law suit against her and that Heather had made an settlement agreement with them but she had quit making her payments. She missed her court appearance to settle this issue, thus the reason she had a warrant out for her arrest.

We immediately told Cassady, who told Brittney and Matteo. They didn't seem to believe it was a big deal but my mom and I thought otherwise. Their boss, the one who was paying them, was a criminal. Not too long after this incident Heather stopped paying her coaches. Their eyes finally started to open to the situation that there may be more truth to the story than they wanted to believe. I had called it from the beginning, I knew that this facility was way too big to be a first year gym and it now made sense to me that six months in they would stop paying their coaches. They weren't making enough money to support their business.

Cassady was the first to leave Famous. He wasn't making much money from Famous in the first place but for the sake of his cheer-leading career, he needed to get out of the gym before the team's first competition, otherwise Heather may not release him to cheer at another gym. He did not want to be put in that situation again. By the looks of it Famous wasn't going to make it through the whole year and he didn't want to be a part of another gym that shut down in the middle of the season. After much consideration he decided to go back to ICE where Darlene shockingly accepted him back onto the team but she told him that there were to be no monkey business going on like last year. He respectfully told her that he understood and apologized for what he had done.

Matteo and Brittney were the next to leave; they weren't getting paid so they sure as heck had no reason to stick around. Some of the other coaches did choose to stick it out for the sake of the kids.

Heather was finding money from somewhere to keep paying them a little of what they earned. We found out later that checks and money had been taken from the Booster Club. Heather was never charged, arrested or convicted of this but the gym did eventually close down at the end of season.

Even though Cassady was no longer affiliated with Famous my mom and I still wanted to help the athletes that were over there. We wanted to make sure that they knew what was going on in their gym. We knew we weren't allowed in the facility, so my mother got the brilliant idea to put together a packet with Heather's mug shot, police reports and an explanation of the "release rule". We put it on everyone's cars while they were having their last practice before their first competition. It was crucial to get it to the parents before they had competed. Our intention was never to bad mouth Heather or break teams apart but instead it was to help those families be aware of what was going on behind the scenes and also for the level five athletes to be aware about the release form that they would need if they had competed for Famous. We did not want to let these athletes go through what Cassady had gone through with ICE without giving them something to think about. We felt it was our obligation to let people know what we knew. They could make up their own minds.

After we were done putting the flyers across the windshields of everyone's cars we found out later that night that the front desk lady had saw us doing it and took them down as fast as she could. Most families did not get to see the flyer and those that did, chose to ignore it. We did what we could so we let them be and focused on Cassady and his new team ICE Lightening.

21

WITH A NEW team came new friends for Cassady and not just a lot of friends, but one in particular, his name was Trevor and Cassady and him became inseparable. Every day after practice they would sit on our back patio and smoke weed. Trevor was a very nice guy and very funny too, I didn't mind having him around all the time in the beginning but as time went on that would slowly change for me.

Although Cassady and Trevor were best friends they were on different teams at the gym. Trevor was new to cheerleading and had less experience than Cassady but he was a quick learner. Trevor attended a local collage on a football scholarship. I found it strange that he did two completely different sports. I asked him how he had gotten into cheerleading since he was playing football and he told me that his friend had gotten him into it about 6 months ago and that it had actually saved his life. When I asked him what he meant by that he told me that he was a heroin addict and once it started to get bad he locked himself in his room for a week straight so that he could get over his addiction. He told me that one of his close girlfriends suggest that he come to one of her cheerleading practices at ICE, she promised it would be good for him. As soon as he stepped in the gym and began to learn new skills he told me that he had fell in love with cheerleading immediately and that if it wasn't for her or the sport that he might still be in a bad place. I found this really hard to believe, just getting to know him and speaking to him he didn't seem like the type of person to be addicted to heroin, plus he was so young. I didn't see how anyone that age could even find a drug like that but I was naïve.

Cassady and Trevor's first competition was right around the corner and I had mixed emotions. I was so happy to see them perform but at the same time I knew that being there was going to kill me. I hadn't been cheering for four months now and I craved it more than anything. Once competition day arrived I met up with my mom and we drove over to the convention center for Jamlive. It was the first time walking into a cheerleading competition for me that I was not competing. I remembered this competition from the year before and it brought chills to me when I thought of ICC and how much I missed that gym. But everything happens for a reason and from its closing I had the opportunity to cheer with some of the most amazing girls on Famous.

It felt so awkward paying for admission to get into the competition and it felt even weirder sitting in the crowd with my mother and watching teams compete. It was like putting an alcoholic in a liquor store, I was craving to cheer again. I was choking up just sitting there watching teams perform. When Cassady's team took the stage I waited nervously as they began their routine hoping for them to hit a flawless one, but it was far from that. They had many deductions throughout their performance and their pyramid didn't even go up. Once the music cut off they all had disgusted looks on their face. I found Cassady and hugged him, and told him that they would do a lot better at their next competition in Indianapolis. He nodded his head and walked outside to get some fresh air and I could tell that he was frustrated so I just took my seat next to my mother and watched the competition for a little longer.

As I was watching, the announcer had said that up next was an international team from Bensenville. My mother and I whipped our heads around and looked at each other with huge smiles on our faces; an international team and it was located not far from my apartment! I sat there anxiously as I watched them take their spots on the floor. Once their music came on and they began their routine they had a lot of deductions but I saw what they were trying to do and more than that I saw the potential in them. I knew right then and there that I wanted to be on that team. As soon as they walked off the floor I ran up to one of the athletes and introduced myself as Morgan and that I was looking to cheer on an international team. The man introduced himself as Jeff, and told me that he was one of the owners of Cheer Illinois Athletics and although he was out of breathe he was so polite. He told me that he would love for me to come check out the team and we exchanged numbers. After the competition I texted him as soon as I got into the car.

He was very friendly and apologizing for how sweaty he was. He joked around about how a lot of the team was old and just cheered for fun but they ended up making it to World's the previous year. When I told Cassady and Trevor about how I had seen them at the competition and that I was going to their practice next weekend, Trevor told me that one of his best friends cheered on the team. I was so excited to hear this so I asked him for her name and looked her up on Facebook. I messaged her hoping that she didn't think that I was some creeper, but when she saw that I mentioned Trevor she knew that I must be pretty nice. They were obviously very close and I was surprised that he had never mentioned her to me before. We chatted briefly about the team and she explained to me that everyone was really laid back and the coaches were awesome. She said that the practices were pretty stress free. She seemed like a pretty nice girl and I was more than excited to meet her and the team. She had also mentioned that they were going to another competition in two weeks in Indianapolis, the same one that Trevor and Cassady's teams were going to. If I was lucky maybe I'd be competing there as well…

PART III
Cheer Illinois Athletics

22

I WAS VERY shy walking into my first day of practice, I wasn't sure what to expect. As soon as I walked into the gym, the coaches, Jacquelyn and Donielle, asked me right away if I was a flyer. I told them that I wasn't able to fly well on all-girl but if there were some guys underneath me then I'd be fine. They introduced me to two guys, Cisco, who had the body of a lineman and Ray, who was very cut and lean, they both seemed super excited to meet me and Jacquelyn told them that I would be their new flyer and to teach me the stunt sequence.

I felt very bad for the flyer that had been in that spot all season but I did as I was told and gave the stunt sequence a shot. The boys were very kind in explaining to me the counts and what to do. We hit the stunt sequence on the first try. My double downs were a little shaky but they told me that it was something they could fix after a couple of minutes working with me on them. We worked so well together, the three of us, I knew instantly that we were going to have a close bond.

After the coach saw that we could hit the stunt she told me to split center with Katie, the other flyer. She was actually Trevor's friend, the one who I had actually been talking to the night before. We smiled at each other as we took our positions splitting center, I had a feeling that we would become close friends too. Once our coach started putting me in the routine I asked her if this meant I would be competing at WSF in Indy, she told me she hoped so. I felt so much excitement and I could feel the energy shoot through my body; I was finally going to be on the floor again and for the first time ever in a competition I would be flying!

We only had two weeks until WSF so I had to learn the routine quickly, that wasn't too hard for me though, learning routines was second nature to me at this point. I know two weeks is a really short time but that's all it took for me to fall in love with this team. It was completely different than the team I was on at Famous Athletics. Practices were a lot more laid back like Katie has said they would be and everyone was older, which was also very nice. Cheer Illinois Athletics soon became my second home and my teammates soon became my family members.

On the team there were three girls that I became close to, Courtney, who was a lot like me, very mature, had motherly instincts and was also in a steady relationship. Katie, the one who I had met online before I joined the team, she was the party girl; she was the one that brought all the fun to our group. Then there was Steph, the Jewish baby of the group, the big goofball that always kept us laughing. They told me that it was rare that they ever got close to any other girls. They liked their trio and they called themselves the "bad bitches". I was an exception though they said and for some reason we all got along so well they even added me to their Group Me text that was titled Bad Bitches, a place where we could chat with each other all at one time. Our team also had a Group Me that was titled Power, our team's name. It came in handy when competitions came around, the coaches would send out long messages about where to meet up, what time and what to wear at competitions and practices.

It was our last practice before WSF and the routine had finally come together. Right before we went full out for our last time before competition I resumed my spot with my head down, I couldn't help but have a huge smile on my face, I was so thankful to be cheering again. It was my passion, my fuel, my happiness, and most importantly my drive to live. When our music came on I lifted my head and began the newly learned routine. I loved the feeling of adrenaline running through my veins, I lived for this feeling.

Our routine went fairly smoothly, a lot better than what they had performed at Jamlive, and with that we broke and went our separate ways, the next time we'd see each other was in Indianapolis! The girls and I had decided to have a sleepover that night at Steph's house, it was the first time I had hung out with them outside of practice. I was a little nervous for some reason, I guess because I hadn't had a sleepover with any girls besides Caroline in over two years. When I followed Steph home she pulled into this amazing driveway that wrapped its way around the front of beautiful house. I couldn't believe this was her house, it was gigantic. When I walked in her father introduced himself and offered to move my car into the garage for me. He was the type of person that wasn't going to let me say no, so I kindly handed him my keys and he pulled my car into their heated garage. Her dad was a very nice man and a lot friendlier than most dads. He told us to make ourselves at home and to not be too loud because he had work in the morning.

Our sleepover wasn't too exciting, we did what every girl does at a sleepover, we stuffed our faces with food and talked about our lives until we fell asleep. We made sure not to stay up too late we knew we had a drive ahead of us tomorrow. I was going with my family but they were driving on their own and needed the rest. I learned a lot more about the girls that night. I found out that Katie and Trevor weren't just close friends but they were best friends and they seemed to have an on and off relationship. I also learned that Steph was dating one of the guys on our team, they too had an up and down relationship. They butted heads a lot but you could tell they were madly in love with each other. Courtney was in a relationship similar to Cassady and mine, her and her boyfriend had been dating for a very long time and they were more than comfortable around each other. As I laid there on Steph's bottom bunk I thought to myself how nice it was to be hanging out around girls again. I was always around Cassady and his friends at the apartment so I never got to enjoy any girl time. It also didn't help that I had only had one girl friend. I was very cautious of what girls I hung around with. I knew that most could be manipulative and backstabbing but I could already tell that these girls were not like that.

The next morning I woke up a little earlier than the rest of the girls and gathered all of my things and drove back to my apartment to pack the items that I would need for the weekend. It was strange going back to WSF, the last time I had competed there was with ICC, it was our last competition before the gym had shut down. I started to get goose bumps thinking about it so I shook my head and continued to pack. Because I had only been on Power for two weeks, I wasn't able to have a uniform made for me that quickly, so instead they asked a girl from a level three team in the gym who was injured if I could borrow her uniform. She kindly let me take it for the weekend, instructing me not to wash it. I jokingly asked her if she was sure because after the weekend the uniform might smell a little bet, she laughed and told me that she was sure that her mother liked taking it to the dry cleaners because it was too fragile to wash at home.

Once I had all my things packed I drove over to my mother's house where her and my brother were finishing up some last minute chores before the trip. Our family minivan had seats in the back that would fold down allowing us to make a bed in the back. I usually slept the entire ride while my mom and brother jammed out to Kid Rock in the front. Indianapolis was only three hours away but to me it only felt like three minutes. I would fall asleep as soon as we drove out of our drive way and usually wake up at Lucas Oil Stadium downtown Indianapolis, the Colt's football stadium. I knew that we were only a few miles away from the Westin. When we pulled up we gathered our bags and the dogs and entered through the front doors, letting valet take our car to the parking garage, we wouldn't need it the rest of the trip. When I walked in I looked to the floor where last year's hologram of ICC's logo appeared, this year it wasn't there.

23

I HAD A feeling this year was going to be better at WSF, I had new friends, I was flying for the first time ever in a competition and Cassady had finally started to act like he was my boyfriend. After I unpacked my things I texted the girls to see if they had made it yet, they were still about 45 minutes away so I killed time by walking over to the convention center and checking out the stage, it had looked the same as last year. As I stood there in the empty room, which would be filled with thousands of people the next day I couldn't help but think to myself how much had happen within the past year. My thoughts were soon broke by a phone call, my family was going to the food court for dinner and they wanted to know if I would like to join. I told them that I would meet them at the Chick-Fil-A as we always had when we first got to Indy.

Something that I really enjoyed about cheering for CIA, was that all teams that competed were required to be at each other's performances. It created a great family atmosphere and it was a nice support system. CIA was not a very small gym though; they had roughly eight teams most of them in the younger divisions which meant they competed fairly early. So even though Power didn't compete until the evening we still had to be up around nine the next morning to support the other teams. With this in mind I didn't stay out too late. I met up briefly with the girls, Cassady and Trevor to say hello and then made my way back to my hotel room to get some rest.

The next morning I woke up early, the first team competing from our gym was our special needs team. This was also something that I loved about CIA, they were one of the few gyms that had a special needs team in the area. A few of the athletes from Power and other teams in the gym, volunteered their time to helping create and perform a routine with special needs children, it was a great opportunity for them and the kids loved being on stage!

Because it was early in the morning I didn't need to put on my uniform and do my makeup so instead I threw on some yoga pants and a sweatshirt and made my way down to the convention center. On the way I grabbed a light breakfast from Starbucks. When we were in Warm-ups with Starz, the special needs team, it was the first time I had actually seen them perform and they were an amazing team. I couldn't help but smile at how excited they were to go on the stage. As I watched them on stage, faces glowing from excitement, I found my eyes starting to tear up, I loved this sport so much and I knew right then and there that owning a gym was something I could see myself doing for the rest of my life. When their routine ended everyone in the crowd went wild. Although the cheer world could be really cut throat, it was also one of the most supportive places at the same time.

I watched the rest of the teams from the gym compete and then went back up to the hotel room to change into my uniform. As I was getting ready my nerves really started to rear it's ugly head. It was my first time ever flying in a competition and I wasn't sure what to expect. After I finished getting ready I gave my family hugs, and my mother told me to not be worried that my papa's were watching over me. This made me smile and feel a little more relaxed. I grabbed my shoes and headed towards the ballroom that our gym had rented out for the weekend. Courtney was going to do my hair.

When I arrived downstairs my team was scattered everywhere, stretching, doing their hair and makeup or simply just zoning out in their own little worlds listening to music from their Ipods. I walked over to where Courtney, Katie and Steph were sitting, they had already finished getting ready so they were just relaxing. As I sat next to them while Courtney curled my hair, I asked them If they had stayed out late the night before, they told me that they hadn't but later tonight they were all going to hang out with the boys on the team. They asked me to join them and I told them I would see how I felt after the competition.

Right before we went to warm-ups our coaches gathered us around and had us mark through the routine just to get our blood flowing. They explained to us that we had a chance to get a bid to World's at this competition and that we needed to hit a very clean, very flawless routine so that we wouldn't have to go to any other competitions the rest of the season. Due to the fact that 80% of our team consisted of college aged students, we all were paying out of our own pockets to cheer and we didn't have money to travel, like most teams. Our season was dedicated to chasing a Worlds bid, the sooner we got a bid the better, that meant less traveling, which meant less money spent.

When we got to warm-ups, my heart dropped a little, the team that Morgan competed on was right in front of us and she was the absolute last person I wanted to see. The girls saw that I was upset and when they asked what was wrong I pointed out Morgan. They told me to just have a kick ass warm-up and to make her stare at you. I loved them so much they were so supportive and what they said made me laugh. They were right I needed to focus on myself.

As we took our spots on the first floor we lined up in our stunt groups. I made my way to Ray and Cisco and gave them hugs and told them that we had this. As we set for our stunts and our coaches began to count I gave my foot to Cisco while ray grabbed my waist, as they both threw me in the air over their heads I did a 1 ¼ spin and stopped at the top, pulled a body position and did a double twist down. As they set me out of their arms I couldn't help but have the biggest grin on my face. The rest of warm-ups went well, everything hit perfectly which got us all pumped up to go on stage. We only had two other teams in our division and we knew we weren't going to win first place because one of the teams, that would later go on to win World's was there, they were phenomenal and we knew we stood no chance against them. They were going for a paid bid though which meant we still had a chance to get a regular bid but we had to beat the other team in our division.

As always, the thought of my grandfathers popped into my head before I took my spot on stage they always calmed me down right before I had to compete. Not only was the crowd huge at WSF, the lights were extremely bright when you are on stage which made it difficult to see anything but the floor. When I tried looking for my brother and mom I couldn't find them but I knew that they were there somewhere cheering for me. As I waited for our music to start the room went silent and the only thing I could hear was the sound of my own breath then the speakers blasted our music and our routine began. As I moved towards Ray and Cisco to perform our stunt my nerves started to take over my mind, being a flyer was a lot more stressful than a base, all eyes were on you so if you fell everyone would see. As we set for our stunt they both yelled at me "Come on girl, you got this!" It was so strange to be on the other side, just a few months ago it was me yelling at my flyer to encourage her before she had gone into the air. I took a deep breath and waited for them to throw me, as I spun around and landed in their hands just as I had in warm-ups, the most indescribable feeling came over me. I thought it was amazing when I was a base and our stunt hit perfect but as a flyer the feeling was ten times more exciting. All of the pressure you felt right before you set for your stunt was lifted off your shoulders immediately after you hit your stunt. The rest of the routine was flawless for everyone, we ended up hitting a perfect routine. Because of the short amount of time I was on the team, I wasn't worked into the pyramid yet so I just stood on the side and watched as my team performed. I was made fun of the rest of the season for standing there and jumping up and down like an idiot from all the excitement I had from hitting a perfect routine. I looked like I was a little kid being told they were going to Disney Land.

After our performance our coaches called us in to our ballroom for a quick meeting to go over our standings and score. When I walked in, the vibe in the room was not what I had expected. It was very gloomy and sad, as if a dark cloud was hanging over everyone's heads. I sat down with a questionable look on my face and our coaches explained to us that the judges gave us a legality deduction, one of the biggest deductions you can get in a routine. A legality deduction is when something illegal is being performed in your routine it can bring down your score dramatically. When we asked what it was for they explained to us that when we were coed stunting, one of our spotters wasn't close enough to the stunt. In all-star cheerleading when there is partner stunting going on (just a guy and a girl) there needs to be a spotter right next to the stunt to be able to catch the flyer if for any reason she were to fall. This deduction had put us in last place and the mood of our team had completely turned around. Just a few moments ago we felt like we were on top of the world from hitting a perfect routine but we were quickly brought back down to reality with this news. Our coaches told us to keep our heads up because you never know what could happen on day two and we need to go into the competition tomorrow trying even harder.

A lot of the guys from our team went out drinking that night and the girls hung out with them. Cassady and Trevor also went out with them. I decided to be the party pooper and went back to the hotel room with my family and our dogs. I was exhausted, so as soon as I walked into the room I laid down on the bed, makeup still on my face and fell asleep. When I woke up around 9 pm, I had a few texts from the girls and Cassady, asking what I was doing, when I told them that I had fallen asleep they laughed and called me a baby, I chuckled to myself because I knew they were right.

I woke up the second day and took a shower to wash off all the grimy makeup off my face. I finished drying my hair and put on my uniform. Before I left the room my mother told me that we had the room for an extra night but her and my brother weren't staying because they had work and school the next day but if I wanted to stay there with Cassady and some other teammates that I could. I thought this would be a fun opportunity to spend some time with Katie, Trevor and Cassady, so I told her that I would talk to them before we competed and let her know.

As I made my way down to the ballroom to get my hair curled by Courtney, I texted Cassady and asked him if he wanted to stay another night, he told me that that sounded awesome and he would get Trevor to stay as well, all I had to do was talk to Katie. When I got to the ballroom the girls were already done doing their hair, their curls had stayed in from the night before so I was the only one who had to get their hair done. I sat down in front of Courtney and while she curled my hair I talked to Katie about staying the extra night she told me that she would have to talk her parents but she thought they would let her stay. She called up her dad right away and begged him over the phone, for a second I thought that he was going to say no but then Katie started repeating "thank you" over and over again, so I knew that he had given in.

When our team was ready to head towards warm-ups our coaches pulled us all together once again and told us basically the same thing they had the day before, except that we had to perform even better. I knew that this was going to be hard for our team, we had a flawless routine the day before and there wasn't too much more we could improve on. We kept our heads high and did as we were told. Warm-ups flew by just as smoothly as day one and as we waited behind stage again I had a weird feeling in my gut, I wasn't sure why though so I just shook it off and walked onto the stage waving blindly into the crowd.

When our music started and the routine began I couldn't shake this weird feeling I had, I didn't let it show while I was performing, but the feeling wouldn't leave. As I set my foot into Cisco's hands and grabbed Ray's wrist we dipped together and then as they threw me and I spun my foot slipped from underneath me and I found myself nearly parallel to the ground... I was falling for the first time as a flyer in a competition and the only thought that popped into my mind, was "hell no, I will NOT be that flyer that falls and costs the team their performance, or even worse, our bid." I lifted my body up and squeezed every single muscle I had and just prayed, somehow Ray and Cisco managed to push me back to the top and we finished our stunt. I was so shaken up from the near fall that when I moved to jumps and performed my back flip, I didn't make it all the way around and I touched down. When the music stopped and our routine was over tears immediately began to pour down my face. I walked off stage and Cassady was there and took me right into his arms and held me close. When all of my teammates saw I was crying they asked me why the hell I was crying, I told them I messed up flying and I let the team down. The oldest one on our team, Roger, put his hand on my shoulder and said "Morgan, are you kidding? You haven't let us down at all, you did exactly what you were supposed to do as a flyer, you stayed tight and you fought for your stunt and it stayed in the air." Then he asked me: "What's the bigger deduction, a bobble, or a drop?" Sobbing with big red swollen eyes I responded… "A bobble." and then he told me "exactly." He had a point, I did all I could to stay in the air and that's all I really could have done, especially as a new flyer. Once our team had parted ways and I started walking out of the competition room, my mother was the first one to greet me, she wrapped her arms around me and gave me a big mamma bear hug and told me that she was proud of me and jokingly said that she had no idea how the hell I stayed in the air. I looked at her with tears in my eyes and told her it was cause I had angel wings on my back and that my papas were keeping me up…When I said this, she too got tears in her eyes and then told me "Yes sweetie, you are absolutely right."

While I walked around the convention center waiting for awards I had people that I had never met in my life come up to me and ask me if I was the flyer that saved the stunt earlier, and when I told them yes, they told me that it was the most amazing save that they had ever seen. A few months later it even was put on YouTube named "Most epic save ever" and got a couple of hundred hits, it made me feel a lot better about myself and gave me the confidence that I needed to continue to fly well.

Only thirty minutes after our performance was awards and to no surprise we had stayed in last place and didn't receive a bid. Cassady's team did fairly well, they received a bid but they were going for a paid one so they weren't too thrilled with their results either.

After the awards ceremony Cassady, Trevor, Katie and I said good bye to our teams and families and made our way to the hotel room. We hadn't had a great experience with our performances the past few days so we were determined to make the night one to remember. Being the party girl that Katie was, the first thing she asked when we walked through the door was if anyone had alcohol. Cassady told her that he had a shot or two of tequila left if she wanted it. She took the two shots, barely enough to get her buzzed, and we all threw on our swim suits and decided that it was time to go for a swim in the hotel pool.

As we ran down the hallway in our bath robes and towels, laughing and jumping on each other's backs, the feeling of happiness came over me; a night with some good friends was exactly what I had needed after today's performance. When we got to the pool there was an older couple in the hot tub which was enough of an audience for us. We flipped into the pool and began to stunt with each other, it got to the point where the older couple would applaud us and laugh at us if a stunt went wrong and the flyer belly flopped into the water. After a few minutes our fun was interrupted by a staff member, we didn't realize that the pool had closed at 11pm and it was now almost midnight. We wrapped ourselves in our towels and made our way back up to the hotel room. The boys ended up rolling a blunt and going outside to smoke it. Katie and I decided to stay inside and have a little girl time while they were gone. I asked her if Trevor and her were an item and she told me no, but I had a feeling there was something more there, when they were around each other they acted like they were dating, always flirting and kissing. I told her that they should date but she said that if they did that one of them would probably end up killing each other. I would come to learn that they had one of those relationships that they were always stuck trying to figure out which was better, being just friends, or more.

When the boys got back we sat there for a little while and watched TV, but soon boredom kicked in and they wanted to go do something wild. I asked them what there was to do at 3AM in Indianapolis. The boys came up with the idea to go look at the huge Christmas tree that was located a few blocks from the hotel. Being the homebody I was I wanted to stay in and go to sleep but they all convinced me that the tree was a must see, so I put on my yoga pants and jacket and we made our way down to the lobby.

As we exited the hotel, a gust of frosty Indy wind hit my face, it was freezing outside. I told them that we should make it quick because I wasn't dressed in very warm clothes and that I was most likely going to turn into an icicle. We hurried down a few streets, it took about fifteen minutes to get to the tree but when I turned the corner and saw how big and beautiful it was the cold walk had suddenly become worth it. We took stunting pictures in front of the tree and with all the enjoyment running through our bodies we came up with the brilliant idea to take pictures all around the city. We stayed within three miles of the hotel making sure not to stray too far. The city was like a ghost town, the only sign of human life was one of those street cleaning cars that brushed the sides of the road while everyone was sleeping. We took advantage of the fact that there were no cars in the streets and took the risk of stunting in the middle of the street in front of a huge sign that read *The City of Indianapolis*.

After our journey we headed back to the hotel and laid on the elevator floors for a little while. The ceilings were made of mirrors so we were able to take funny pictures of each other. While we were laying there laughing and having a good time I looked at my phone to see what time it was and it read that it was a 4:45 a.m. I couldn't believe how late...or I guess early it was. Time flies by fast when you're having fun. I told everyone that we needed to head back to the room and go to bed, we had to be out of our room in three hours for check out and we had a three hour drive that we needed to make.

I don't think you could have called it a good night's of sleep it was merely a nap when I woke up two hours later. I could barely keep my eyes open as we walked out the door. I was so glad that I wasn't driving, there was no way I could get us home safe. Cassady, however prided himself in his driving skills and let everyone know that he would get us home in one piece. I sat in the back of the car with Katie, who fell asleep as soon as she sat down. Apparently Cassady hadn't been as awake as he said he was because he kept the window wide open with the freezing air coming in the car to keep him awake. I can't stand being cold and since I was sitting behind the driver's seat I felt as much wind as he did, if not more. Half way into the drive Cassady leaned over his seat and told me that he could no longer drive, that he was falling asleep, I told him to not worry about it and that I would finish the rest of the drive.

It had been a long weekend. I experienced flying for the first time in a competition, almost falling for the first time in a competition, gotten closer to Katie and Trevor, stunted throughout the city of Indianapolis at three in the morning and most importantly I had found a new family.

24

AFTER WSF, TREVOR and Cassady became even closer. Trevor was well known in the drug world, he didn't just smoke it he dealt it too. I'm not sure what Cassady's infatuation was with Trevor, I believe it was his mellow personality. Cassady seemed to be drawn towards those type people. Whatever the reason, he started to become Trevor's wing man when it came to making drug deals. I found myself alone at the apartment more often than not. Cassady was never at home and if he was then Trevor was always with him. Cassady would let me know when he and Trevor were going to make drug deals, or when they were going to buy more weed from Trevor's supplier. It never dawned on me that they could have been thrown in jail for what they were doing. It had become such a normal everyday thing for them. They were so calm about it that it made me believe that what they were doing wasn't a huge deal. The bigger Trevor got as a drug dealer the more popular he became and the more weed they kept stashed at our apartment. Trevor lived in a dorm and with the amount of weed he was selling there was no way to hide it from his RA, so instead he used us. At one point they were hiding pounds of weed in zip locked bags behind our washer and dryer.

The reality of what they were doing hit me when Trevor told me that his supplier was thrown in jail and that the cops had been doing an undercover investigation for a while. Trevor wasn't concerned over the fact that this guy who supplied him weed was in jail now and that the police could possibly connect them and press charges against him, the only thing he was concerned about was how he was going to continue to get weed until his guy was out of jail.

I'm not sure what it was, but at that moment when those words came out of his mouth, I was done with him. This kid was a recovering heroin addict and walked around claiming that he is some great guy for getting over his addiction and that he is so strong and proud of himself for being "clean." I don't care what anyone says, weed is an addictive drug. There is a feeling that you get when you are high and it is a feeling that you can get addicted to. In reality, you can have an addiction to anything, a runners high, biting your nails; heck there are TV shows that are now showing people being addicted to drinking gasoline and eating couch cushion. So for Trevor to call himself "clean" is crazy. In my opinion, he was addicted to selling and smoking weed and I knew that he wasn't going to get any better and not only that, Cassady was smoking more than ever. It was coming down to the point where they could no longer eat without smoking first because they didn't have an appetite. I told Trevor that he needed to be careful and think about what he was doing but like most young men, he believed he was invincible and they continued to sell and smoke weed and in the meantime Cassady and I were drifting further and further apart.

Cassady and Trevor became really close to the guys on my team. When one of the owners of CIA, Jeff, invited me to his New Year's Eve party, so were they. I was excited about this party, the last time I had drank was last New Year's Eve and so I was ready to have a little fun. I picked out a classy half sequined off the shoulder champaign colored dress and wore some black high heels to go along with it. I wore my hair in a slicked back high ponytail with light neutral makeup, completely different than last year.

When Cassady, Trevor and I arrived at the party, jello shots in hand, we were greeted by Jeff, who had made it clear earlier on about the rules of the house. If we were drinking we were to hand over our car keys, we were planning on drinking so we handed Jeff our keys. I appreciated how cautious Jeff was but I could understand why he would be, he had a bunch of underage people at his house drinking.

A lot of members from Power were there and tagging along with them were their friends. It was a decent sized party, not too big, but not too small.

As soon as I walked into the kitchen the girls bombarded me with hugs and we made sure to get pictures before we started drinking. They all looked beautiful, and apparently sequins were in for New Year's because everyone was wearing it. After we got done posing for photos we began to take shots. I hadn't drank in over year and still considered myself inexperienced. I was trying a little bit of what everyone was drinking, everything from Patron, to Baileys, to alcoholic whipped cream. I couldn't stand the taste of anything, that's why shots became my best friend, it was like ripping a band aid off. Just a quick swig and then grab a can of pop and chase it down and it was like it never happened in the first place.

All the shots settled in quickly and after I had decided I had had enough I went to find Cassady. Not to my surprise, he was off somewhere smoking weed. I started to get a little nervous because the countdown was only a few minutes away but just in the nick of time he barged through the front door with some of the boys and joined everyone for the countdown. It wasn't as fun as the year before, maybe it was because I was with an entirely different group of people but it just didn't feel the same. As soon as the countdown was over and Cassady and I kissed everyone went down to Jeff's basement. He had an assortment of games ranging from darts to air hockey and of course a table set up for beer pong. Cassady decided to spend a little time with me and while we were down there we tried playing air hockey but we couldn't focus because we were laughing so hard, I'm not sure why, probably because I was so tipsy.

After a little while I started to feel incredibly sick, just as I had New Year's Day the year before and I knew that I needed to make myself throw up. I walked up the stairs to the bathroom and locked the door behind me. As I lifted the toilet seat up, I sat on my knees, pulled my hair back and stuck my finger down my throat. After a few tries everything finally came up and I had instantly felt better and 100 times more sober. I decided that drinking still wasn't for me and I didn't feel like the feeling it gave me, it was not worth the sickness.

I plopped myself down on the couch next to Cisco in Jeff's French room. I believe Cisco was stoned out of his mind. We sat there and talked for a long time about our lives. I learned so much about him that I never knew; it was honestly my favorite part of the party.

After a while we were interrupted by a few of our teammates looking to relax too. Soon after, everyone else filed in one by one buzzed from the long night. We were all starving and decided to cook some frozen pizzas and watch some TV for the rest of the night. There were still a few people down stairs playing beer pong, how they could drink for so long just amazed me. I was a lot more comfortable upstairs eating pizza and laying under a blanket the rest the night.

I thought that because I had made myself throw up the night before that I wouldn't be hung over the next day, but man was I wrong. As Cassady and I woke up and gathered our belongings I couldn't help but cringe from the raging migraine I had. Cassady dropped me off at my mom's while he went to work. I ate pickles, snoozed on the recliner with our dogs and just relaxed trying to make my headache go away.

25

THE DEEPER I got involved in the cheer world the sooner I wanted to start figuring things out about opening our own gym. I couldn't wait for the day where I could give kids a second home to come to, not only to cheer, but to learn the meaning of family, respect, and hard work.

After Matteo and Brittney left Famous, they apologized to us for not believing what we told them about the owner and the business and it gave us a reason to make amends. We told them about our dream of opening our own gym and they told us that they had always wanted to open their own gym but with their jobs as private instructors, coaches, and their choreography business they just didn't have the time. We told them that we were planning on opening our gym down on the gulf coast of Mississippi in hopes to get back to our roots and away from all the drama up north. We kept them in all of our plans, we knew that if we did open a gym one day that they would be great employees to start the business with, not only did they have a phenomenal resume, they also knew more about cheerleading and how to coach it better than anyone else I knew.

My mother and I went to work on naming the business, choosing colors and a mascot, etc. We knew that it would take a while to open our gym correctly, instead of doing it overnight like a lot of gyms did, we wanted to take our time over the next two years to plan, organize and start our connections in the south. As soon as my brother graduated, the plan was to jump in a U-Haul the same day and high tail it to the coast having a home and business established right before the move.

I came up with the name Mississippi Venom, our colors were going to be green, yellow, and black and our mascot was a venomous snake. We had a logo made up and everything, we even formed our LLC. My mother got the idea to make a Facebook page for our gym to help spread the word that we would be opening in two years. Word got around Mississippi like wild fire. Even though the south is well-known for cheerleading, Mississippi has very few all-star gyms so the rumor that a new gym was opening up was very exciting to them. Once the word was out in the south that we were opening a gym we received a phone all that would ultimately change my life forever.

Marcie was her name, a sweet southern bell momma who was always on the run doing things for her children; taking them to soccer practice, cheerleading practice and schooling events. She called me out of the blue one day and asked us when we were planning on opening our gym. We told her that it would be in two years. She told us that if we wanted to open in six months then she had a place and the clients to do so. My mother and I nearly fainted with this news. We asked her how in the world she would be able to do something like that and she told us that she had actually owned a cheerleading gym and that her and her partner opened the business a few years ago because she wanted to give her daughter a place to cheer. She told us that her gym grew insanely fast and that she didn't realize how big the need was for a gym in her area. When we asked why the business was no longer opened she told us that it had just grown way too big and too fast for her and that she didn't have time for it. Her partner left and opened his own gym and they just decided to close their doors. They explained that they still owned the building and that they could rent it out to us if we'd like. They knew for a fact that we could open with 150 athletes because there was such a high demand for more gyms.

My mother and I couldn't believe what we were hearing, this had to be a dream. We told Marcie that we were interested and that we would talk about it and let her know within the week what our decision was. My mom and I came to the conclusion that it was an opportunity too good to pass up and that it would be best if we go and check out the building. While we were down there we would check out some other buildings as well, just in case we didn't like Marcie's building. Marcie told us that even if we didn't rent out her building that she still knew that we would be able to get enough athletes.

The way that Marcie made it sound, with all of the athletes that we could have in our first year, we knew our gym was going to be bigger than planned and my mother and I knew that we couldn't run it by ourselves. We had originally wanted to open very small and just build from the ground up but with this opportunity being presented to us it almost seemed too good to pass up. We told Brittney and Matteo about the phone call and what Marcie told us. We asked them if they would be interested on moving down with us and opening a gym. Their expressions were exactly the same as my mother's and I when Marcie told us the news. They said that they were interested and that with such short notice only Brittney would be able to make the trip down to Mississippi to check out the building with us. It looked like we were just going to have a girl's weekend.

When I told my father about the news we had received and that we might be moving down in six months to open a business he sounded ecstatic and so proud for me. I told him that as soon as our plane landed that we should all meet up and have dinner at the Seafood Shack, it was a tradition that my dad and I had whenever I arrived into town. The first thing I wanted was seafood, it was always so delicious and fresh in the south and I wasn't about to break that tradition.

As soon as our flight landed Brittney, my mom, and I jumped in our rental car and headed towards the nearby hotel. Once we unpacked our luggage at the room we called Marcie and told her that we had made it safely and we arranged plans to meet at the gym the next day. We then made our way to the Seafood Shack a few blocks away from our hotel to meet up with my dad. As soon as I saw him I gave him the biggest hug ever and introduced him to Brittney. I explained to him that she would be one of our partners if we decided to open the gym. You would've never guessed that he and my mom were divorced, they still acted as if they were best friends. I was very fortunate, unlike a lot of children, the divorce that my parents went through was very easy. It basically boiled down to my mother not wanting to raise my brother and I around his family and that she wanted to take us up north for schooling, She told him that he could come with if he wanted but she was leaving whether or not he was coming. He chose to stay in Mississippi so he could continue to be by his family and work for the family business. The family business was an auto repair shop and air conditioning business named JD's One Stop. It was started by my dad's father, my grandfather, who had passed away about six years earlier. He was one of the grandfathers that I always thought about before I walked onto the competition floor.

At dinner we talked about our plan, and although he knew nothing about cheerleading, my dad did know a lot about owning a business. Although he struggled a lot with his business, he seemed to be proud for me, and excited that we would be closer than 12 hours away. After dinner we said our goodbyes. We had a long day ahead of us and we wanted to be well rested for what the day held in store for us.

The next morning after we woke up and got dressed we made our way down to the local Waffle House, making sure to snap a picture on our phones and send it to all of our boys back at home. When we walked in it wasn't anything special, in fact, I was surprised that the place was still operating, it seemed pretty ran down but that didn't stop us from getting waffles. When the waitress handed us our food it wasn't at all what we expected, I'm not very picky when it comes to food, but that breakfast just did not taste good. We decided that the next morning we would be eating the hotel's breakfast.

After we were done eating we paid the lady making sure to tell her to have a nice day. I knew that the atmosphere of the south wasn't the most exciting, but the people that surrounded the area made me feel the way I did when I was down there. Everyone was so friendly and polite, they would always use their manners, tell you good morning, hold doors open for you and most certainly always had a smile on their face, it was the type of place I wanted to raise my kids and live for the rest of my life. In Chicago if I told a stranger good morning with a smile on my face while I was at the grocery store, chances are they would look at me crazy and walk the other way. Not to mention the grouchy attitudes and the road rage in Illinois. I felt like people up north were always in a hurry to get somewhere and do something, they never know how to just slow down and enjoy life the way that it's meant to be.

We were running a little earlier than we planned, so before meeting Marcie at the building we drove around the local neighborhoods and scouted out houses that might be for sale or rent. We were already down there looking at a gym we figured we might as well kill two birds with one stone and check out houses while we were at it. We entered a neighborhood that you could tell was brand new, with only a few dozen houses that were complete, there were others in the process of being built. They were so beautiful, some of the most unique designs I had ever seen for a home. There were signs with balloons that read open house so we followed them and made our way to three model homes that we could view. When we pulled up to the driveway, we were very skeptical, it didn't seem like an open house, there wasn't anyone else around but we still managed to peek through the windows. While we were looking in a window of one of the houses an SUV with black tinted windows pulled in the driveway, we were unsure of what was going on until the driver rolled down his window and asked us "Do you like what you see?" Taken aback we answered that we loved the outside but we wish we were able to see the inside. The guy then told us that we were in luck and he was our guy, turns out he contracted and sold all of the homes in the neighborhood. He let us tour three incredible homes and told us that we could have the exact same ones duplicated if we had liked it. When Brittney was told this she asked how much the houses sold for. The man told her $180,000, she about had a heart attack, not because she thought it was too expensive but because of how cheap it was. Houses like these in Illinois sold for a lot higher and for the price he was giving us you could barely afford to live in a very small house in Chicago. He and Brittney exchanged business cards and then we made our way over to the gym to meet up with Marcie.

When we pulled up to the gym it wasn't what Brittney had expected. It was on a very rocky graveled road, with cats walking along the side of it and potholes almost every which way you turned. In

Mississippi on one side of the road you could have a million dollar mansion and on the other side you could have shacks with weeds and over grown grass. That's just how things were though. Families that have lived there for years upon years refused to sell their land thus the reason for such a difference. When we pulled up to the building Brittney had a disgusted look on her face, my mother and I were a little more creative though and we had smiles on ours because we saw the potential this huge building could have.

Once Marcie and her husband pulled up she jumped out of her black SUV with a huge smile on her face. When she introduced herself and shook my hand I got the feeling that she was a strong and genuine woman. She told us that she knew the building obviously needed to be cleaned up but that when it was up and running that it was a spectacular space to have.

When she opened the door we walked into what would be the front desk area and parent viewing area. It was a very nice space, large enough to have chairs and a computer and even a pro shop to buy apparel. When we walked into the gym it was a lot bigger than I had thought it would be. It was nowhere near the size of Famous but it was definitely a lot bigger than I had planned on starting with. While Brittney walked around and took pictures for Matteo, I sat there and tried to vision what the place would look like cleaned up and with equipment. I got a very clear and vivid image.

After Marcie was done showing us around we told her that we loved the gym and that we had to talk to the boys first but that we were more than interested and that we could hopefully work something out. We told her that we were also looking at a building the following day that was smaller and that we would keep her updated with how the meeting went. After we said goodbye and parted ways we went out to dinner at another one of my favorite restaurants, McAllister's, to discuss what we had thought. Brittney said that she liked the building, but that there was going to be a lot of startup cost to get it up and running. She said that the amount of space was perfect though. I agreed with her the space of the building was phenomenal but it did need a lot of work. Marcie was very flexible though and more than willing to work with us on anything that we needed. We drove back to the hotel for the night and while Brittney sent pictures to Matteo and discussed the building I fell asleep next to my mom it had been an exciting day and I couldn't wait to see the other building tomorrow.

The next morning, we woke up and got ready. We made sure to eat at the hotel this time instead of the Waffle house. While we sat at breakfast we discussed our plans for the day, we were to meet with the owner of the new building in about two hours. Unlike Marcie, he knew nothing about cheerleading and just had a warehouse that he was looking to rent out. From the pictures we saw online it looked as if this place was a lot nicer and in a better location but it was also about half the size of Marcie's gym. We decided to go in there with an open mind and make the best decision for the business.

When we arrived the owner introduced himself. He was a very young and polite gentleman. We asked him why he had a warehouse and he told us that he used to be a professional jet skier and would keep all of his jet ski's there. When we walked into the building I was astonished, the place was so up to date and brand new. As soon as you walked in the doors there was a counter to your left that would make a great front desk and behind it were shelves where we could keep merchandise. As we made your our way down the hallway and took a left, there was a kitchen with a fridge, a counter, microwave and sink, something that could be very useful for employees and athletes. There was another room to our left that would make a great parent waiting room. The best part of that room was that it was not connected to the potential gym area.

Being part of an all-star gym I knew how important it was not to just keep the parents happy but to keep them contained as well. I never liked the idea of parents being allowed in the gym unless asked by a coach. I definitely did not like the idea of having a window that looked into the gym for them to press their noses against while they watched their children and gossiped with other parents. In my opinion this was a recipe for disaster. Instead I wanted to have a parent room with their own bathroom, couches and a TV that would display what was going on in the gym with cameras, this way the parents wouldn't be a distraction to the kids while they were learning, but the parents could still observe.

After viewing the front area, the owner took us into the gym area where all the equipment would be. In my eyes it was perfect, just big enough to fit a cheer floor and in my opinion that's all we needed to open with. Brittney instantly had issues with the small space, she knew that there wasn't going to be enough room for the equipment her and Matteo would want. After we were done touring the building we grabbed the owner's business card and told him that we would let him know within the week what we planned on doing.

As soon as we walked out of the building Brittney said something that made me suddenly have a change of heart. She said "I can't wait to own a gym and eventually one day have people run it for me where I don't have to work at all. I just get to make all the money and I can't wait to dress up in cute outfits every day." Something about what she said made me cringe. I didn't want to open a gym to make money, and I most certainly would never NOT want to be in my gym while having other people running it for me. I came from a background of hard workers, it ran in my blood, I couldn't imagine a life where I didn't work and got paid to do nothing, I had a job ever since I was 16 and working brought me a sense of pride and well-being. It wasn't about the money for me, it was about the kids and giving them the place that I had when I needed when I was in high school, a place to come to vent, to be supported, to have fun and to learn hard work and respect. I kept my thoughts to myself about what Brittney had said until my mother and I were alone but I had a feeling that something just wasn't right about this situation.

As soon as we were finished looking at the new building we called up Marcie and told her how beautiful it was but that we might have some space issues and that after we were done talking to the boys we would let her know what we were going to do. I knew that in my heart the new building was exactly what I was looking for to open a gym. I wanted to start small and grow rather than start too big and take the risk of downsizing. Matteo and Brittney however thought that we "needed" Marcie's building. It had enough space to hold the equipment that they wanted to start with but I just didn't see the need for all the equipment that they needed, after all they had coached our team to Worlds with only a 7 ½ panel floor.

After our visit in Mississippi, my mother and I had a very serious conversation about what we thought would be best for our future keeping Cassady included in all our conversations and giving him the option to give us his input. We asked him to let us know if he had other aspirations and left the door completely open for him to give his opinion on anything. We wanted him to do what he wanted to do and not just follow us with what we wanted to do. He never told us he wasn't up for it in fact he and Trevor talked about getting jet skis when we moved, so we just assumed that he was on board for whatever we decided to do. After thinking and discussing everything my mother and I decided that Brittney and Matteo were wonderful people and knew that they were more than capable of running a cheer gym but in the end we had different opinions on how to open and run one. Their way was not wrong, it could be successful, but we did not want to start large, we wanted to start small. Once we made our final decision we sent them an email explaining that we believed we were going in two different directions with the business and ideas, we didn't want to end up in a bad situation down the road so we were going to discontinue working with them.

They didn't take this email lightly and we certainly don't blame them. We had gotten their hopes up and for that we truly did feel bad but we were purely trying to protect our future and we felt that it was in our best interest to part ways.

My mother and I decided that we still had a wonderful opportunity down in Mississippi and we asked Cassady and Trevor if they were on board to move down with us and help us open. They gave us the impression that they were so we continued to move along with our business plan.

Just as we thought things were falling into place we received a phone call from the owner of the smaller building that we had loved. He asked us if we were still working with Brittney because she had contacted him about the building and others in the area. When my mother and I heard this our hearts stopped. How dare they go behind our backs and try and open a gym in the place that we showed them? We knew that they knew we were sitting on an amazing opportunity and they wanted a piece of it. To deliberately go behind our backs without even asking though rattled our bones to the core. We sent them an email explaining to them that going behind our back was not only rude but unethical. They were trying to steal our opportunity right from underneath us.

After those emails were exchanged it was made very clear that we would no longer be speaking to each other. Matteo made sure to go out with a bang though and sent me a text that said, "You might want to ask Cassady about his real feelings on everything." When I received this message I was confused. I replied "What the hell is that supposed to mean?", but he never responded, and that was the last that I have heard from Brittney and Matteo.

I called Cassady after I had received the text from Matteo and told him that we needed to talk. He came home and of course Trevor was by his side. I told him that we needed to talk privately so we went into our bedroom. When he sat down on our bed he asked me what this was all about. I asked him why Matteo would send a text like this and I showed it to him. He panicked and spilled is feelings that he had obviously been holding back from me.

He went on a rant about how he thought the idea of moving to Mississippi to open a gym was insane and a horrible idea. He told me that I had never once asked him his opinion on anything and that I was just making these crazy plans up out of nowhere. He was acting like a wild person. I had never seen this side of him and couldn't understand where it was coming from. Shocked that he had the balls to say some of the things that were coming out of his mouth, I patiently waited for him to finish so that I could rip into him. I was taught growing up by my mother to only fight battles that you could win and to always admit when you were in the wrong,

Once he finished I started yelling at him about how ridiculous it sounded that I hadn't asked him his opinion because the truth of the matter was I did ask him his opinion on everything. I then asked him what was really going on and that for the past few months he's been acting strange and unhappy with our relationship. I couldn't possibly understand why he would not be happy. I thought I was a pretty cool girlfriend. I never nagged him about smoking weed, I never nagged him about helping with bills and I always let him hang out with his friends. I treated him like a God and everyone around us told him that he was so lucky to have a girl like me so I just couldn't understand why he would ever be unhappy with me. But it hit me, Trevor was a ladies man and because Cassady was always around him I think he secretly envied his lifestyle, which was funny because in my opinion I think that Trevor secretly envied his. The grass is always greener on the other side, right?

After the arguing settled and it got quiet in our room, I sat down next to Cassady and I asked him what he really wanted. He told me that he wanted to go to college to cheer. I told him to do that. He should do whatever he needs to do to be happy and if that meant going away to college to cheer then that's what he needed to do. I told him that I didn't do long distance relationships and that this was the end of the road for us. He said alright and walked out of our bedroom door to the living room where Trevor was waiting for him. As they walked out the door I obviously felt sadness but at the same time I felt a bit of relief. My mother had never liked Cassady and I've learned that mom is always right when she comes to her instincts, but timing is everything and everything happens for a reason.

26

ALTHOUGH MY WORLD was completely turned upside down I still had cheer practice the next day. Nothing was going to stop me from going to practice, in fact, being in the gym was what I needed the most and I couldn't wait to get there.

When I arrived at practice about 45 minutes early the girls were there lying on the couches in the lobby. I told them that I needed to talk to them in the coach's room about something. They got up and followed me into the room. We closed the door behind us, I didn't want anyone hearing what I was about to tell them. I didn't want any unnecessary distractions brought to practice, we had a World's bid we were after and that needed to be our primary focus. As I sat there and told them what had happened the night before, never shedding a tear, their jaws dropped. They couldn't believe what they were hearing. They explained to me that it seemed like Cassady and my relationship was flawless and that we looked so happy together. I told them that it was like that for a while until he started to hang out with Trevor then things started to change and it put a dent in our relationship. They were astounded that I had even showed up to practice that day and that I wasn't bawling my eyes out. They praised me for how strong I was and asked me how I did it. I told them that in life everything happens for a reason and that even when we are at our weakest moments we have to remember that there is a reason that things happen and it leads us to somewhere where we belong. I told them that

I wasn't sure what God's plan was for me but I knew he had one for me. My job was just to wait it out and be strong and patient until I found that reason out. They hugged me tight and told me that they were proud of me. Out of all the times to cry in the past two days this is when I chose to. Not tears of sadness but tears of joy. It was so nice to have real friends that I could be my real self. I was so thankful to have met them. After our talk I wiped my tears off my face and threw on my cheer shoes, it was time to get to work, we had a World's bid to obtain.

After Cassady and I broke up I found myself in the gym a lot to keep myself from being alone at the apartment. I focused on myself striving every day to work on new skills, I wanted more than anything to reach my full potential as a cheerleader and I knew that I was no-where near where I could be. I met a lot of new people in the gym and one of them was Nick Kiefer. He was at the gym one day stunting around with Steph and I wanted in on the action. I introduced myself and we began to stunt with each other. He was very built, had muscles like a mad man, long hair and tattoos and although he was newer to stunting I could tell that he had potential to become great at it. When I asked him where he cheered at he told me that he had only cheered on his high school team the previous year and now that he wasn't cheering any longer he came to open gyms to hang out with his friends and stunt.

We never talked much outside of the gym. The extent of our relationship was being Facebook friends and getting each other's numbers so that we could text each other if we were going to be at the gym. I think he just assumed that I had a boyfriend because I hadn't taken down that I was in a relationship yet on facebook, I wasn't ready for all the "I'm sorrys "from everyone.

Once I decided to put that I was single on Facebook, Nick texted me to make sure that I was okay. He had no intentions what so ever of hitting on me. I told him that he was very kind for asking and that Cassady and I had actually broken up a few weeks ago and that I've been doing great. He was glad to hear this I was okay and we continued to have casual conversation with each other. It was the first time in almost two years that I had talked to a guy for hours on end and I have to admit that it was nice, this guy seemed so genuine and real and the fact that he could hold a conversation with me was so nice.

After we talked for a while, I came to find out that he too had just gotten out of a long term relationship. It was nice that we had each other to lean on. I told him that he should come over to my apartment sometime soon so that we could talk in person instead of over the phone, he found this humorous and agreed to come over.

My mother instantly had a good instinct about Nick the moment after seeing a picture of him. She said there was something about this big guy with long hair and tattoos that made her feel comfortable. She knew that most of them were secretly big teddy bears, and she was right. The more I got to know Nick the more I started to realize how he had been stereotyped as this bad kid because of his image when in fact he didn't drink and he didn't do drugs. He actually got drafted by the Phillies for baseball but turned it down because his mother was ill and because the cost wouldn't have been worth the traveling that he would be doing with the team and he wasn't even guaranteed to play. He was working valet while he figured out what he wanted to do with his life.

I'll never forget the first time he came over to my apartment, it was the first time that we had both hung out with someone of the opposite sex other than our exes and you could tell that we both felt kind of uncomfortable at first. We put on a movie, The Notebook. Halfway through the movie we joked around with tears in our eyes about how dumb it was to watch a romance movie after we had both had just gotten out of a serious relationship. Laughter is the best medicine though and as we sat there and laughed, I couldn't help but feel happiness. As the movie went on I noticed that Nick had fallen asleep on the opposite couch. I couldn't help but stare at him, he seemed so peaceful and that's when I realized that this guy and I were going to grow into something special.

I crawled over next to him on the side of the couch while he slept and laid my head on his big arm, he woke up and was a little startled that I was there. I looked up at him with big tears in my eyes, probably the first time that I was admitting to myself that I was hurt and I told him "Nick, Cassady really hurt me" the next thing he did was put his hand on my head and say "I know" as if to say he understood and that he had been hurt too. It was reassuring to say it out loud. I know that I am a strong girl but I could only be strong for so long and sometimes I had to let my walls down and Nick was someone I could do that with.

After he went home that night I felt like I had finally exhaled. I was finally able to accept that Cassady was never the one for me and that we weren't compatible and had polar opposite personalities. I finally admitted to myself that I deserved someone that would treat me better. That was the day I decided that I would never settle for something less than the best and that whoever I decided to be in a relationship with next would have to treat me like a princess. I know it sounds selfish but I was sick and tired of helping and taking care of people and for once I wanted to be taken care of. I wasn't the girl that wanted to be showered with diamonds and fancy gifts, I am very independent but it would be nice to have a boyfriend that wanted to show me off, one that wasn't afraid to hold my hand in public or take pictures with me.

I texted Nick later that night and told him thank you for driving all the way out to visit me and that I had really appreciated it and I hope that I would see him again soon. He replied immediately with, "How about tomorrow night?" I told him that would be perfect.

27

THE NEXT NIGHT was a little different than the first, we were a lot more comfortable, not just with each other but with ourselves. We opened up a lot more and were laughing and having a great time. Out of nowhere there was a moment of silence and the whole world stopped. Our eyes locked and I found myself leaning in to kiss him. You know how people say that when you meet "the one" that you just know? Well, I never believed it until that kiss. As soon as our lips touched fireworks went off and my heart stopped and I knew that he was feeling the same.

After that kiss things changed between Nick and I. We instantly fell head over heels for each other. He walked around holding my hand, treated me like a lady and he respected me. He didn't drink, he didn't smoke, he loved cheerleading just as much as I did and all his friends were very nice. He took pictures with me and wasn't afraid to show that he was dating me. Actually, he loved showing me off. He was everything that I had ever dreamed of and more.

I practically lived at the gym. I was there during my free time and for practices. Practices started to increase since we were getting closer to our next competition and our next opportunity for a bid. We decided that we were going to try to obtain a bid at CSG Super Nationals. This was the same place that Famous had received their bid the previous year. Before we competed at Nationals we decided to sign up for a last minute competition the weekend before that was being hosted by the same vendor. We wanted to perform in front of their judges to get their comments and scores that way we could fix what we needed to in our routine to give us the best shot at a bid.

A week before our small competition something unexpected happened. I was sitting in the living room at my mom's house eating dinner and watching the news, when suddenly a news report on Jeff, part owner of our gym and one of our teammates on Power, came on the television. My mother and I stopped what we were doing and turned up the volume. A reporter standing in front of our gym went on to explain that Jeff, part owner of Cheer Illinois Athletics, and math teacher and cheerleading coach of a local high school was being charged for sexual assault against one of his high school athletes. My heart stopped as goose bumps on my arm rose, my mother immediately knew what I was thinking, "Here we go again." Tears started falling down my face and I started to freak out. Just as I was about to have a mental break down my coach called me and said that she was sure I had heard the news. I asked her what it meant and she told me that Jeff had resigned his position and would no longer be working or cheering at CIA. As much as I was concerned about what our team was going to do now with one person down, I was more concerned for Jeff. He was always such a sweet, happy and loving guy and I knew that there had to be more to the story. I knew that Jeff would never intentionally assault someone, especially one of his athletes. In my opinion, I felt that some girl probably took something he did or said the wrong way and decided to sue him. I texted him and told him that I would miss him and to keep me updated on what he was doing and that we all cared for him. We knew he would be able to pick himself up and be strong but his life was being turned upside down. He had to resign from a gym he loved and he was put on leave at the high school that he also loved. He appreciated the text and you could tell he was devastated from everything that was going on but it was nice to hear from him and that he was making it through this incident.

The gym owner and coaches made sure to call every single athlete in the gym that night and let them know that they were there for them and that if they had any questions or concerns to ask. Instead of shutting down like ICC had, this tragedy brought everyone closer together in the gym. Out of the entire gym only one athlete left because of the situation. I was told that they really didn't want to leave but because they were related to the girl that was pressing charges, they felt like they were obligated to stand by her side. It was so reassuring to be in a place where everyone leaned on each other for support instead of falling apart. We banded together and the bond that was already strong in the gym grew even stronger. We were unbreakable.

The practice we had after we found out about Jeff was a rough one filled with tears. Lucky for us one of the male coaches in the gym volunteered to step in for the weekend's competition so we didn't have to worry about withdrawing from it. Jeff was one of my coed partners that I stunted with in the routine. I felt a huge void but we knew Jeff would want us to do our best so we practiced like crazy to get the routine perfect.

The night before the competition I had all the girls sleep over at my house. I lived closest to Illinois State University where the competition was being held. I figured it would give us a little more time to sleep in before we had to leave and give us some bonding time. We cooked dinner and talked about how crazy things can completely change in the blink of an eye. We couldn't believe Jeff was gone. In cheerleading the bond that you have with your teammates is more than a brotherly sister love, we fight with each other, we motivate each other, we support each other and most importantly we always have each other's backs, so losing Jeff felt as if we had just had a death in the family.

The next morning when I woke up I didn't have that giddy excitement that I usually had. Not only was Jeff a part of the reason I felt that way but we were also the only other level five team there with no competition so it was more of an exhibition if anything. When we arrived I walked over to where we would be competing and I about had a heart attack. When I had heard we were competing at ISU I assumed we would be in a stadium or a basketball court or something like that but the competition area was so small. It was being held on the school's theatre stage. I had never seen anything like it. When my mom arrived I showed her where we were competing and she started laughing. It was hilarious.

Once warm-ups came around a staff member directed us to a ballroom area which was not your typical warm-up room. We just had to remember we were there strictly to get our scores and comments from the judges to prepare us for Nationals the following week. After warm-ups we waited for about an hour behind the stage in an 80 degree room with three other squads. A cheerleader from another team had gotten sick while competing and they had to change out the floors before we could compete again.

After they were finally done cleaning up and rearranging the competition floor it was our time to go on stage. Cisco gathered our team in and said "I know that we have been through a lot this past week, but let's take what happened and use it to our advantage, let's do this for Jeff okay?" After he said this we all put our hands in the middle of our huddle and broke on "POWER!" I couldn't help but start to tear up after Cisco had said that. I knew that he was just trying to be kind and positive but it had the opposite effect on me and instead flustered me and my emotions started to get the best of me. The announcer called our team's name and I had to suck it up and take my spot on the floor and put a smile on my face for the judges like nothing had happened the past week.

The routine went fairly well considering we hadn't competed in over a month. We had a few mistakes here and there but overall the judges really liked our routine. After we exited the stage a lot of younger children walking around from other gyms stared at us like we were celebrities. They had never really seen a level five team before and they were amazed by our talent, some even asked us for photos and autographs. For a second I felt like I was a cheerlebrity.

When our team met up after the competition was over our coach told us that Melvin, the coach that had stepped in for Jeff would not be competing with us at our bid competition next weekend so we would have to either re-work the routine, which we didn't have time to do or we were going to have to try and find someone to do the team for the rest of the season. I had just the person in mind.

It was late when the girls and I got back to my apartment. They decided to stay another night. On our way back I told them that Nick would be a perfect substitution for Jeff and that he and I partner stunted very well together. I told them that I was sure he would be able to learn the routine in a week. They were skeptical at first, he had only cheered high school for a year and all-star was a completely different beast. The fact that this first competition was a Nationals competition scared them but it was really our only option.

I called Nick up when I got back home and told him our situation. I begged him to do the team. He told me that he would be willing to give it a shot and help us out. I texted our coaches and told them he would be at this weeks practice and that he was willing to step in. They were relieved just as everyone else was on the team.

Later that night Katie and Steph decided they wanted to drink while Courtney and I supervised. We played a long game of HeadBandz, which requires you to where a head band with a picture attached to it that you can't see, you have to try and guess what the picture is by asking only yes or no questions. Steph started to get super rowdy and Courtney and I were extremely tired so we decided to go to bed. As we were lying in bed half asleep, Courtney and I woke up to a loud "BANG". We both jumped up immediately to see what the hell was going on, we realized that Katie and Steph were not in the bed sleeping next to us. We walked out to the living room and the scene we walked in on was like out of a movie. Steph was screaming and crying over her phone that she had obviously threw at my front door. She was devastated that it had broken. Katie was curled up on my bean bag crying with a bottle of alcohol in her hand. Courtney and I looked at each other half asleep as if to say "Should we just turn around and go back to sleep?" but we didn't. We asked them what was going on and they explained to us that Steph and her boyfriend had gotten into a huge fight over something silly and she ended up throwing her phone at the door and cracked the screen. We asked Katie why she was crying and she told us that she and Trevor were a mess and that she felt like nothing in her life was going right. She had worked her ass off all high school to get good grades because her parents told her that she could go to any college that she wanted but now that it was her senior year they were telling her that they were having financial issues and that she wouldn't be able to go anywhere when she graduated.

Courtney and I did our best to calm the two down and let them know that everything was going to get better. Once they composed themselves we convinced them to come to bed. Being a year older than them, Courtney and I knew how stressful your senior year can be and with all the added stress from cheerleading we understood why they would be having mental breakdowns but we reassured them that it would all work out.

28

THE LAST TWO practices were spent working Nick into the routine. Because Nick was replacing my coed stunt partner we got to work together, which was very nice. We were familiar with each other when it came to stunting so we had no doubt in our mind that we would hit our stunts this weekend. He was able to pick up the routine. It looked like we were going to catch a break.

Although we had Nick in the routine now we still needed to do really well at Nationals this weekend in order to get a bid. We really couldn't afford to go to another competition this season so this virtually was our last chance to receive one. It almost felt like last year all over again except for the fact that this team had been together a lot longer.

Power constantly struggled to have full-team practices. Like I had mentioned before, not only were international teams hard to come by they were also hard to keep together. With everyone's work schedules, school schedules, family events and college schedules we ended up only having one full-team practice before Nationals. It was a huge difference from when I was on Famous where everyone put their whole hearts into practices

Anyone that's ever been a cheerleader knows how hard it is to get things done as a team when even one person doesn't show up to practice. Cheerleading really is one of the biggest team sports. With one person gone this doesn't allow you to practice your routine full out and the only way to become better at performing your routine is to well…perform your routine. Power had some of the rawest talent I had ever seen and if we would have had full-team practices year round we would have been unstoppable, but we didn't which is why we had the pressure of this weekend on our shoulders.

The night before Nationals the girls and I slept over at Courtney's house. Before Katie and Steph had gotten there I sat with Courtney in her room and we talked. No one knew about Nick and me dating, I didn't want to take the teams focus off of Nationals. However, I told Courtney that evening, she and I had grown a close bond and we were basically the same person. I knew she wouldn't tell anyone until this weekend was over. I told her everything about Nick and me and about when we first hung out and when we first kissed and how I haven't been this happy with anyone ever in my life. Having the motherly instinct that she did, she told me to be careful and to make sure that I wasn't using Nick as a rebound. I told her that I understood but I knew that there was something special between him and me. She was happy for us.

As soon as we finished our conversation, Katie and Steph walked through the bedroom door boasting about how hungry they were. I told the girls earlier in the week that I would cook them my favorite dinner, steak onions and white rice. They teased me about how I didn't seem like the type to cook and I told them that in all honesty I really wasn't and this was basically the only thing I knew how to cook. They laughed and after I finished cooking we sat at the dining room table and ate. Courtney's mom joined us as well, she seemed like a hard-working woman, who had a lot on her plate, but she was very down to earth and joked around with us. After we finished eating we went to Courtney's room for the night and relaxed while watching a little TV. Somehow all four of us managed to fit on her bed and while everyone was snoozing my phone was blowing up with texts from Nick, supposedly he had gotten into a fight with his grandfather, who lived with him and his mother. Nick had left the house and I was worried about him but as soon as he told me that he had found a place to sleep, I felt better. I told him that he needed to go to bed as soon as possible because we had a big day ahead of us and we needed him.

The morning of the competition I woke up a little earlier than the girls to take a shower. I could hear the girls a few minutes later starting to crawl out of bed making their way to the kitchen to get something to eat. I got out of the shower and dried my hair I made my way to the living room where Courtney was curling everyone's hair. While I was waiting for my turn the girls explained to me that one of our teammates, Dono, was stuck at his house without a ride to the competition. Our group text for Power immediately started to blow up. Everyone was frustrated that he wouldn't have made plans to get to the convention center instead of waiting an hour before we had to be there. This wouldn't have been such a huge deal if he hadn't lived thirty minutes away and no one was near him to give him a ride. Luckily one of the girls on our team was done doing her hair and makeup and told everyone that she would go pick him up.

After hearing this I texted Nick to make sure that he had a ride since I hadn't asked him the night before and he told me that he was driving himself. Once the girls and I finished getting ready we put our shoes on and headed out the door. I stepped outside and took in a deep breath of the fresh crisp air, I had gotten the same feeling I had a year ago on my way to the competition. The sun was shining and there wasn't a cloud in the sky. I knew that it was going to be a good day. When we arrived to the competition center and walked through the front doors I saw someone in a Famous uniform. I was surprised that the gym was still up and running, I knew it would be soon though before it shut down. I had heard that the owner of the building hadn't gotten paid the last six months for rent and that he had locked the doors on the gym. Apparently Heather broke in and they continued to have practices. My only guess as to why it was still open was because the court was taking several months to process everything but as soon as they did I knew that their doors would be closed for good.

Right before our team got ready to walk down to warm-ups, Dono who didn't have a ride showed up running and throwing his bags down while saying "I'm sorry I'm late, I'm sorry, I'm sorry." Our coach then pulled us in a circle and told us the order that we would be throwing skills in warm-ups. She told us that she believed in us and that we needed to give 110% to get a bid. We didn't walk in a line on the way to warm-ups like we had with Famous, we walked every-where and scattered about. I didn't have the same sense of pride as I had the year before. I couldn't help but smile. This team was goofy, laid back and a little un-organized, but nonetheless we were deter-mined, in our own way to make it to Worlds.

When we arrived in warm-ups, I saw the last person I had ever ex-pected to see, Jorge. My jaw dropped. I walked up to him I asked him what he was doing here. He laughed and told me that he had moved to St. Louis and that he was cheering on a full ride scholarship at the local community college as well as cheering on an international team. I gave him a hug and told him that I was happy to hear he was doing well and before parting ways we wished each other luck.

Warm-ups went very smooth, the only issue we had was Courtney's stunt, for some reason her 1 ¼ up was not hitting and she was stressing out under the pressure. She asked our coach if they could go straight up and she told her no. Our coach knew she could hit the stunt and that it was just all in her head. Before we went on the floor I pulled her aside and with my hands on her shoulder I looked her in her eyes and told her to calm down that she was an amazing flyer and that she had no reason to be panicking. She wiped the tears from her eyes and shook her head up and down as if to say okay.

As I waited in line to go on the stage with my eyes closed, think-ing about my grandfathers, the music from last year's routine with Famous started to blare on the speakers. My heart skipped a beat and I opened my eyes to make sure that I wasn't dreaming. I peeked around the curtains to see who was performing and it was Famous Athletics special needs team. They were using our music from last year. Relieved that I wasn't dreaming, a smile came upon my face, as strange as it was to hear my old music playing, I felt that it was a sign that we were about to have a good routine.

When the music cut off and the special needs team walked off the stage it was our turn to perform. With our hearts pounding and adren-aline running through our veins we took the stage as the announcer introduced our team. We took our spots with our heads down, wait-ing for the music to start and as soon as it did we started our routine.

The routine started off great. Everyone landed their standing fulls and standing tumbling with ease. As we set for our stunt with our left foot in first our bases threw their flyers into the air releasing us at the top so that we could switch to our right foot, one of our best flyers, Annie, who hadn't fallen all year, was suddenly fighting to keep her stunt in the air. As her bases struggled to keep her over their heads she swerved and bobbed around doing everything she possibly could to keep from falling, but she fell. You could hear from the crowd's reaction that something had gone wrong but we continued on as if nothing had. The rest of the routine was nearly flawless. Our pyramid was a little sloppy and we had two tumbling deductions during running tumbling. It wasn't our best performance, but it certainly wasn't our worst, leaving us some hope that we were still going to place well.

Later that night the results came in that we were in first place and in the running for a bid. It was a huge relief. Also, we were surprisingly ahead by quite a few points, so although we had room for error tomorrow we still had to perform a pretty clean routine. The girls and I packed up our things and made our way to Courtney's house again for the night, and while the boys stayed out a little later we decided to go to bed early.

On the way to the convention center the next morning the girls and I blasted the stereo to "What doesn't kill you makes you stronger" By Kelly Clarkson, it got us pumped for the competition. When we pulled up to the convention center we jumped out of Steph's car and made our way inside to meet our team. The atmosphere was a little different with our team that day, a little bit more excitement and enthusiasm and it brought a smile to my face as I sat there and put my cheer shoes on.

My brother and my mom was there before our team made our way to warm-ups, giving me hugs and wishing me good luck. After we had said our good byes to our family and friends our team gathered in a circle and listened to our coach preach to us about how well we needed to do today. As our team stood there I held hands with Katie, our palms were sweaty from all our nerves. Once our coach finished speaking our team started whooping and hollering to get ourselves pumped up, we were soon on our way to warm-ups.

Warm-ups was a lot different that day, they flew by perfectly without a single person making a mistake. This got our team excited but in the back of my mind (and maybe it's just the inner cheerleader being superstitious in me) I started to worry, rarely ever did a team have a perfect warm-up and a perfect routine. I shook the thought out of my head and got myself back in the mode to kick some butt.

We were in the same performance order as yesterday, so like before, I waited in line to go on stage while listening to the music I had performed to last year with Famous. It brought a smile to my face, and like always the thought of my grandfathers passed through my mind.

When the announcer called our team's name we ran out onto the stage waving at the crowd. We took our starting positions with our heads down and as the room got silent our coach gave the DJ the thumbs up and our music began. The beginning of the routine was going more smoothly than day one. Everyone hit their stunts with no deductions. After we dismounted and moved to our jump spots, the crowd yelled with us as we jumped and connected our standing back tucks. We transitioned to coed pyramid and lined up side by side and all the guys grabbed onto their partners waists and threw them in the air, caught their feet and extended them. When nick grabbed my waist and threw me we traveled a little to our right and bumped into our two teammates next to us. We were able to stay in the air but they could not. "That is a deduction" I thought in my head, but continued on with the routine as if nothing happened. Next came running tumbling, something we struggled with yesterday, but pulled off today with no deductions...baskets were flawless...the only thing left to do was our "fearamid". Yes, we called it "fearamid"; we feared our pyramid simply because of the fact that the first time we ever hit it full out with no deductions was during yesterday's performance.

The beginning went smooth, the bases set their flyers foot and tossed them into the air and threw them as they flipped. When I jumped into my bases hands for my part of the pyramid, I did a 360 degree spin and landed in their hands but when they tried to push me up to an extension one of my bases hands slipped from underneath my foot and I came crashing down. I wasn't the only one, the girl to my right was also falling...great...that's two more deductions. I was so furious but I had no choice but to move to my dance spot and work it out with a smile on my face like I hadn't just fell.

When the routine ended, I was not smiling and there was no happy feeling, no tears of joy...just anger. I stormed off the stage into my mother's arms while she held me. I told her that there was no way we were going to get a bid from that performance. She told me that the other teams hadn't done that great either. I didn't care though I honestly thought that if we did by chance get a bid to Worlds then we didn't deserve it. Out of frustration I thought to myself how other team's probably worked their ass off to get a bid, and how we had all the talent in the world, but we didn't work hard. I didn't feel we deserved the bid over the other teams. The only thing left to do though was to wait for awards.

Our team made our way back up to the area where we had met in the morning, laying on our back packs while we listened to our IPods. My mother told me that she didn't want to wait around for the awards ceremony she disliked them just as much as I did. I gave her a hug and told her that I didn't blame her for leaving, that if I could I would have too. She told me to text her as soon as we found out the results and I told her that I would.

After about an hour our coach gathered us all up so that we could walk down to awards together. It was exactly the same as the year before, with music blaring, staff members throwing beads and beach balls out into the crowd while all the cheerleaders danced. Our team was a little too old for this and just not in the mood so we sat in the back of the crowd until they started announcing team placements. When they got to our division, our team huddled close, holding each other's hands, praying that we didn't hear our name called first. The announcer paused...and...in third place... with a score of 80.79... Layton Athletics! Whew... okay, that's a relief, now just one more announcement to go. We needed to get first in our division in order to even be eligible for a bid so the pressure was on. The announcer took a deep breath...and...in second place...with a score of 83.46... Platinum Athletics! We held in our cheers until they called first place and when they did we jumped all over each other, we couldn't believe it. Once the announcer finished reading off all of the team placements, they gathered all eight of the Worlds bids and set them out on stage preparing to announce the winners. Once they were all done laying all the banners and trophies out our team gathered around once more in hopes to hear our team name called. This time it didn't matter in which order we just wanted to hear our name. The announcer gathered himself and walked back and forth on the stage announcing that it was time to find out who made it to the 2012 Worlds Championship in Orlando, Florida, our hearts sank. The recipients of the first bid...with a score of 84.02...in the international open coed 5 division... Cheer Illinois Athletics' Power! Half of us sank to our feet while the other half jumped on the teammate nearest to them, we were going to Worlds!

After all the World's bid recipients were announced we joined together on stage to take a group picture with confetti falling everywhere. Once the photographer was done, being the little kids that we were, Katie and I took hand-fulls of the confetti and threw it everywhere jumping for joy. Once everyone exited the stage, Nick and I made sure to get a stunting picture together with me holding the trophy before we left. I thanked him for all of his help. Without him stepping in last minute we probably wouldn't have been where we were now.

The first thing I did after the ceremony was texted my mom "I'm going to Florida!!!" She was so excited for me she knew that after last year's World's performance that I needed to end my cheering career on a good note, and this was my opportunity to do that.

29

AFTER CSG IT was no secret to anyone on the team that Nick and I were dating and everyone was very happy for us. As I had mentioned earlier, we fell head over heels for each other. Neither of us had ever been in a relationship so pure and so simple where we could just be ourselves around each other. I started to notice that he was sleeping at my house about 5 out of the 7 nights during the week and although he never officially moved in he basically lived there. The more we got to know each other the more I fell in love with him.

I asked him about his high school experience and why he dropped out of baseball. He told me that in high school he got targeted a lot by the administration because of his tattoos and long hair and that they just assumed he was a trouble maker. One of his biggest bullies was actually his baseball coach. He told me that he was always discriminated by him and that he never let him play in games. He told me that the only reason he really ever went to high school was to play baseball and since his coach was bullying him and he didn't get much playing time and he was not doing that great in school he dropped. Another deciding factor that went into making the decision to drop out was that his mom was very ill. He explained to me that she had a pump in her that pushed morphine through her. When he told me this, I immediately asked him if she had cancer. He told me that she didn't that she just had a really bad back. This seemed extremely strange to me, usually when someone is on a morphine drip it's because they're on their death bed with cancer; it's certainly not a drug to be messed with.

He explained about how when he dropped out his senior year that he got his GED. He then went to a local community college to get his general education and play baseball. He was a left handed pitcher and right fielder. He had to have been pretty good because he showed me the letter he received when he got drafted in the 27th round by the Phillies. I asked him why he would turn down such a wonderful opportunity and he explained to me that it wasn't worth the time if he wasn't going to be playing and that he needed to take care of his mother, who only weighed 95 pounds and had trouble doing things around the house by herself.

When I met his mother he wasn't lying, she stood at about the same height as me, 5'2 and looked way too thin. She was as sweet as can be though and really laid back. I could tell that she and I were going to get along very well. She showed me the pump that was located near her stomach it looked like a hockey puck bulging under her skin. I asked her if it was painful and she told me that she didn't even notice it anymore, she had had it for nearly ten years. Holy crap, ten years on a morphine drip, what kind of doctor prescribes that?

Practices continued normally after CSG, and when I say normal I mean that we never really had any full team practices and once again we were thrown another curve ball with a teammate quitting the team. We were all stunned on why he would quit the team so late into the season with only a few weeks left, it boggled our minds. We later found out that he had checked himself into rehab for weed and pill addiction. I knew that he drank and smoked like most young adults but I never thought that it was that serious. I was happy that at least he was leaving the team for a legitimate reason, I couldn't be upset with him. As much as our team had bad luck we had just as much good luck. The gym owner's daughter was able to fill in. She was a high school cheerleader during the all-star cheer season but their season ended in February so she was able to join our team.

When she came to our first practice we needed to adjust some of the groups for stunting since we had just lost an athlete. She was a very strong base, she didn't have the strength of a guy by any means but she was damn near close. While the coaches sat there pondering where to put her since she'd be the only girl basing, they looked for the strongest flyer that would be able to handle the change and they chose me. They took Ray out of our group and moved him to a weaker flyer that needed two guys underneath her. I was devastated, my group had been together all season and I loved my guys more than anything but I was willing to do whatever worked best for the team. Surprisingly she and Cisco worked fairly well together and it only took us a couple of tries to master the stunt. I made sure to tell her how amazing she was doing. I knew she was nervous because she had never done two-man basing before but she really was doing a phenomenal job and I was so proud and thankful for her.

Our last practice before World's was upon us and I couldn't help but feel a little nostalgic. These people had become not just my family over the past few months but my best friends plus they gave me the opportunity to cheer again. As we broke for the last time, my mom was videotaping it in the back ground, we put our hands in and yelled "FUCK SHIT UP!" a line that described our team so very well. After we broke, laughing with tears in our eyes and excitement in our hearts for the trip to come, we took in the moment, not just because of all we had been through and how far we had come, but because for a lot of us… it was our last practice as an all-star cheerleader.

30

THE NIGHT BEFORE we left for Orlando, Dono and Nick slept over at my apartment. My team fundraised as much as possible for our trip to Florida, but with only two weeks to do so there was only so much we could do. My mom has a very nice job that she received bonuses at the end of the year and this helped us tremendously. She was able to pay for mine, Nick's and even Dono's way to World's.

The next morning the three of us woke up early and gathered our belongings before heading out the door to the airport. As we locked the doors we made sure that we had everything we needed. Like last year I had managed to stuff all my clothes into a carry-on bag as well as Dono and Nick, so we had the luxury of not waiting for our baggage. As we walked outside to my mother who was driving us to the airport, I prayed that the flight would go more smoothly than the previous year; although we had a layover in Atlanta, Georgia, we didn't anticipate on any delays. The weather was beautiful.

Once we arrived at the airport we all jumped out of the van and grabbed our bags making sure to hug my mother and tell her thank you. As she wrapped her arms around me I took a deep breath in and enjoyed the comfort of her love. As I said goodbye to her I felt anxious, excited and nervous all at the same time. Unlike the previous year when I competed in the small senior coed division, this year I was competing in the international division which most would debate as one of the hardest divisions for America.

Unlike the rest of the divisions, the international division had teams from all around the world competing and the top ten from each country made it to day two and from there the top three in every country made in to finals. This put our team, and any other American team, at a huge disadvantage, not just because the United States holds the most cheerleading teams but also because of the raw talent that we had. Teams from other countries were sometimes the only ones from their countries to make it to World's so they automatically qualified for finals, whereas America had 50 teams that qualified for Worlds so we had to compete against our nation first and beat 40 teams just to make it to day two.

Our team wasn't expecting to make day two but our coaches told us that if we hit a clean and flawless routine that there was definitely a possible chance and if you give us a small piece of hope we will take it and run with it.

When we walked down the escalators to security in Midway my jaw nearly dropped to the floor, in all the years I had been flying, I had never seen a line so long for security. It stretched almost out to the airport's parking garage. I panicked a little inside because we hadn't planned on the line being this long so while we waited and I watched the clock tick by I started to get really nervous.

We finally made it to the TSA agent who checked our boarding passes and ID's. I will never forget how rude the ladies were, they were in fact one of the reasons why the line was probably moving so slow. They were making sure to talk to each other in between checking people's ID's and boarding passes. They were discussing their personal lives and taking their sweet time to stamp our boarding pass. I glared at her as she stamped my pass. I knew that it might have been rude, but really? Your job is to make the line flow as smoothly, quickly and efficiently as possible, you could chit chat about your lives when you were on your break.

After I yanked my pass from the lady, to make sure that she knew I was upset, I followed Dono and Nick into the next security line where we put our carry-on bags through those big X-Ray machines. As I threw my bag on the belt, flopped off my sandals and took off my jewelry, I made sure to make a note in my head not to forget anything on the other end, I couldn't imagine arriving in Florida without my cheer shoes or uniform.

Once I stepped through security, bare footed, I grabbed my items and boarding pass, threw on my sandals, and jogged to our gate with the guys as fast as we could. I handed the lady my pass with a smile on my face and she told me to relax that I had made it in time to the gate and there was nothing to worry about

We took our seats on the plane, Nick and I were sitting next to each other and Dono behind us. I watched as the last few people boarded the plane. As I was watching everyone walk down the aisle my heart sank, Cassady and his family were walking towards us. He too was competing at worlds and his family had decided to come along this year to watch. As Cassady walked by I made no eye contact with him, his mom tried saying hello and I didn't acknowledge her either but when his little sister walked by and said hello I enthusiastically told her hello. She was too young and didn't understand the situation we were in and I genuinely loved her. The plane ride wasn't as awkward as I had anticipated it to be, they sat far away from us so it was like they were never really there in the first place.

I had never been to the Atlanta airport but I had been told by numerous people that it was miles long and always jammed packed with people. With only a fifteen minute layover we would have to jog to the opposite end of the airport to catch our second flight. As soon as our pilot gave us the okay to take off our seat belts we were the first people to grab our luggage and storm off the plane. When we got off the plane we scanned the airport for directions to our gate it led us down an escalator to an underground subway train. Thank goodness for that train or we wouldn't have made our second flight. When the subway stopped and the doors glided open we rushed out into a huge crowd of tourists, I knew I shouldn't have been surprised since it was spring time, and a lot of families were going on vacation, but I still couldn't help but think to myself how crazy it was that there were so many people in one place at one time.

We finally arrived at our gate and we didn't have time to linger around, a lady was already announcing our boarding group and we had no option but to jump in line and give her our passes. As we handed our tickets to her, with smiles on our faces, we couldn't help but get excited, we were so close to Orlando now as well as the rest of our teammates and we could not wait for the weekend.

Once the plane took off I thought to myself that napping would make the flight go by faster so I closed my eyes and dozed off. When we were about to start descending to the Orlando airport Nick tapped me on the shoulder gently to wake me up and tell me that we were almost there. I was happy my plan worked and time had flown by. I eagerly waited as the plane landed. As soon as we arrived at our gate I texted my mother that we had made it safely and that I would talk to her when I got to the hotel.

I stepped off the plane and took in a deep breath of air I couldn't help but reminisce about the first time I had stepped into this airport. The air had a comforting warmth to it that made you feel like you had just stepped into a tropical paradise. In away that feeling was true…it was a cheerleaders paradise.

After riding the magical express we arrived at the all-star resort. This year I was staying at "Sports Resort" it was the most popular of the three resorts and we were right by the football field where everyone practiced the night before competition. I could already tell that it was going to be an amazing and eventful weekend.

When I arrived to the hotel room I quickly threw my bags down, our team was meeting up near the football field to run through our routine before the sun went down and I needed to change into my practice clothes. I met the rest of my teammates outside and we made our way to a patch of grass that wasn't being used. If you've never been to World's or you're a small gym that isn't well known, practicing at the all-star resort can be extremely intimidating. Big named teams meet at the football field to practice and show off. With them are their families and fans which made for a large crowd of people. Our team is what you would call a little aloof, we could got easily distracted by all the teams that surrounded us, so our coaches made sure to find a place that was somewhat discrete. As we practiced and whether it was from being distracted, intimidated or falling over the patches of holes in the grass, we didn't have a very good run-through with our routine. It not only embarrassed us but frustrated us as well.

Our coaches pulled us aside and told us to stop worrying about the people that surrounded us and to start worrying about ourselves. We listened to her and focused solely on our team and our skills finally started to hit.

After we were finished we got together and took a team picture, then made our way back to our hotel rooms. Tomorrow was our first day of competition and we needed a good night's sleep. I laid there in bed that night and I prayed to my grandfathers and to God that we would have a good routine. I wouldn't be upset if we didn't make day two but I wanted to hit a clean and perfect routine...It wasn't about winning for me I just wanted to know that our team did the best that we could and left everything we had on the floor. To me, that was the definition of winning. Anything else would be icing on the cake.

The next morning when I got out of the shower, the girls that I was rooming with were up doing their hair. Unlike all of the other competitions, this time I decided that I wanted to curl my own hair. Courtney's curls were too short and tight and I wanted my curls to be big and long to show off my hair. After I finished getting ready I called my mother to tell her that I was about to leave to go to warm-ups and that I would talk to her right after we were done competing. She wished me luck and told me that she would be watching from home on her computer and that she loved me. After we hung up I met up with Nick and some of the girls outside the hotel room. While we waited for the rest of the team we took a few pictures with each other in our uniforms. I loved that Nick liked to take pictures with me it was so nice to have a boyfriend that finally showed affection towards me. Once our team was finished getting ready we gathered ourselves together and made our way down to the bus stop where a bunch of other teams were also waiting for their ride to the competition.

Once it was our turn our team stepped onto the coach bus. Katie and I made sure to sit next to each other so that we could take pictures on the way over to the competition. Once we arrived we had a few minutes to spare until warm-ups so our team decided to be a little risky and try and take a team stunting picture in front of the huge globe that was in front of the park. We weren't allowed to stunt anywhere but in warm-up. We set all of our bags by a palm tree and had a quick team huddle to devise a plan to get a picture without getting disciplined by the staff.

One of our coaches came up with the idea to pretend we were taking a normal team photo while lined up in our stunt groups and as she counted to three we would all go up into our stunts for a split second as she snapped the photo and if we got caught to just play dumb. As we posed for our "team photo" with the staff members staring us down like hawks, our coach counted to three and we all put our stunts up in the air as fast as possible and as soon as we did the staff members came sprinting over to us screaming "NO, NO, NO, NO, NO, there is NO stunting allowed on the concrete!!!" We did as we had planned and played dumb as if we hadn't known and apologized and told the staff we were sorry. When we walked over to our coaches they showed us that they had successfully gotten the picture. In one of the pictures though, the staff members were in front of the team with their arms up in the air screaming at us. This gave us a good laugh and eased our nerves a little as we made our way to warm-ups.

When we got to warm-ups, I felt amazing. I was more than ready to hit our routine and end my cheering career on a high. I wanted to get that addictive feeling one last time, that feeling that every cheerleader strives for, a perfect routine. As I sat there waiting for the clock to tick down for our turn on the warm-up floor, Steph was to my right with a strange look on her face. It was her first time at World's and something just didn't look right with her. I asked her what was wrong and with 30 seconds to go until we took the floor she looked at me with those big eyes that I will NEVER forget, and she told me: "I don't have a good feeling about this Morgan." Shocked at the words that had just come out of her mouth, I asked her what the hell was she talking about. She told me that she felt like she was about to get injured and then she wouldn't be able to try out for Kansas's cheerleading squad, the college that she was attending next fall. I looked at her and told her the only thing that I could tell her in five seconds, that she was insane for thinking such thoughts and that she was one of the most amazing athlete ever. The buzzer went off and it was our turn to take the floor, as we lined up in our stunt spots to go through our stunt sequence our coach started counting and our team performed the skill with ease although I do have to admit that I over spun my double twisting dismount and hit my ear on my bases shoulder and lost my hearing for a second. I shook it off and moved on to our next skill. When our team began to throw our pyramid, the beginning went smoothly and then half way through..... disaster struck.

31

I WAS IN the middle of the pyramid doing a 360 spin with my bases when all of a sudden I heard a loud thunk and a bloody scream. As my bases caught my feet our coaches yelled at us to stop the pyramid. My bases set me down gently. When we looked to our right we saw Steph and Cisco, my base from our stunt sequence, on the ground screaming in pain. Cisco managed to get up before the paramedics ran over but Steph on the other hand was in no condition to move. I am told that I while they were throwing her in the air and she was performing a back flip that on the way down the bases miscalculated the catch and she fell hitting her head with Cisco's head. The paramedics determined that Steph may have had a concussion and because of this they weren't going to release her to compete. The first thing that popped into my mind was that we were screwed. We could barely put a team together before Worlds, let alone have alternates, and Steph was a huge part of our routine, I couldn't see how we were going to fix this situation.

While the staff figured out what to do with us, we stepped outside in the 90 degree heat with our long sleeved uniforms and tried figuring out changes that we could make to our routine. Dying from the heat, our team slowly began to lose hope as we searched for solutions but couldn't find any. After thirty minutes had gone by the staff approached us and told us that they would be able to give us floor time in an air conditioned tent across the way to make any changes we needed to our routine. They told us that we wouldn't be able to get on the floor for another thirty minutes though so with that time we pondered what we could do to fix the situation.

While our coaches were talking, I suddenly realized that we were supposed to compete thirty minutes ago and that my mother was probably at home watching on the computer and us not having competed she was probably having a heart attack trying to figure out what happened. Little did I know that she had texted a friend that was at World's watching her daughter. She told my mother that a flyer had been injured on Power. My mom started freaking out knowing that I was one of the few flyers on the team. She started calling my coaches but never got through to anyone. She said it was the most hopeless feeling she ever had. I called her up as soon as I could. She was so relieved to hear from me. I told her everything that was going on and she couldn't believe what I was telling her. She asked what we were going to do and I told her that the staff got us about 15 minutes on a floor nearby so that we could try and re-work our routine. I told her that it was going to be difficult though and that our only real solution was having someone step in for Steph but there was no one that could do that. I told her that we were supposed to compete at 5:30 p.m. instead of our previous scheduled time at 2:00 p.m. She told me that she would be by the computer waiting and that she was so sorry for everything that was happening, I told her that it was okay and that I loved her and I would talk to her later that evening.

As we hung up I had realized that Steph was sitting next to me bawling her eyes out. She looked at me and told me that she was so sorry and that she felt like she had screwed this up for everyone. I told her not to worry about it that I knew that if the paramedics released her that she would have cheered. This all felt so surreal to me, I had to be dreaming, I just had to be, there was no way this was happening… but it was and I couldn't do anything about it.

Our coaches snapped me out of my day dreaming and told everyone to huddle together so that they could tell us what plan they had come up with. We knew they were about to say something crazy, they just had that look in their eye. Jacqueline took a deep breath and said: "I'm going to fill in for Steph" That's insane I thought in my head, she hadn't cheered in five years plus she was our coach, is that even legal? Regardless, she was the only other person here that knew our routine and she was a badass at tumbling. She could definitely throw all of Steph's tumbling but flying? She never really flew when she cheered. She was a stacked little base on the University of Louisville's all-girl team, the only time she had really flown was in baskets occasionally and pyramid sometimes.

She told us that she wasn't going to fly the stunt sequence for obvious reasons and that the bases needed to do their best job marking out the stunt. She told me that I was going to be flying Steph's basket now instead of back spotting it. Was she insane? I hadn't flown a basket in my life. She told me that it was just a toe touch and that I needed to just whip it out of my ass. I told her okay and did as I was instructed and whipped it out. It wasn't the prettiest basket but it would make do for the time being. Since she had flown pyramids some, she told us that she was going to have to try and fly Steph's part in the pyramid. She also told Nick that he and I were stunting in the opening of the routine now instead of Cisco and I since he wasn't feeling well from the accident.

This was Nick's and my opportunity to shine. We had wanted to stunt together in the opening and never got the chance. Now we were being handed the opportunity on a silver platter. We chose to stick with something simple and we didn't want to do anything too elite that would get us deductions in our routine, so we decided to do a toss stretch. We knew that the few changes that were made wasn't going to be a huge set back on our routine, but our coach flying in the pyramid was going to be difficult to pull off.

While we waited for the staff members to give us an okay to go on the floor to fix the changes we had made, Jeff was texting us from back home making sure that everything was okay, he too was watching from home along with everyone from our gym. We told him what was going on and he told us that had been Power's luck and that he believed in us and would be rooting for us from the computer. We thanked him and told him that we missed him and by that time the staff members were giving us the okay to have the floor for a few minutes before we had to go back into warm-ups.

To my surprise, all the changes that we had made hit with ease. I was impressed that our coach was able to fly the pyramid and jump back into a routine just like it was yesterday but she had been competed at one of the top colleges for cheerleading in the U.S.

When our time was up on the floor we were directed back to the warm-up mats once again but this time we were surrounded by some of the most talented teams around. Not only was this intimidating but now we knew for a fact that the whole cheer world was out in the crowd or sitting on their computers at home about to unknowingly watch our team perform.

Warm-ups went smooth and afterwards we were directed to wait behind the curtains along with five teams ahead of us. After the first two teams had performed we found ourselves sitting on the floor basically crawling our way to the stage. We were so exhausted from the heat, the disaster and the loss of hope, that by the time it was our time to go on stage we didn't even feel like competing. Before they called our teams name though I looked at Cisco who was still in a daze and told him that I was going to fly the best I had ever flown for him so that he didn't have to worry about me. He looked at me as if to say thank you and then the announcer called our team to the floor.

When I walked onto the stage waving into a crowd of hundreds and thousands of people, my heart began to sank and I could barely swallow from all the nerves running through my body. As I stood in my starting position with Nicks hands around my waist and my head down, I prayed to my grandfathers to help me through this routine, my worst fear at that second was being the flyer that fell at Worlds.

As our music kicked in and my head flipped up, I jumped and Nick threw me in the air as I kicked my heel stretch. I waited to feel the comfort of his hands beneath my foot and when I did an even bigger smile crept onto my face. When he popped me down I moved to my stunt spot where I set for my bases and told Cisco that I had this. When I jumped and they threw me I performed my 1 ¼ spin, I landed effortlessly into their hands and could hear the crowd screaming, we were actually hitting our routine. After our stunt we moved to jumps which were never an issue and then from there we moved to coed pyramid. As I backed in towards Nick and grabbed his wrists for the second time I yelled at him that he had this and when he threw me and caught my foot, I could see that to my right that someone had fallen. He popped me down and as I ran to my tumbling spot this is when the routine started to fall apart. For some reason our team had started to break down, people that normally threw level six skills were having a hard time throwing level four skills. I threw a round-off back handspring at World's, that's a level two skill! This is so bad that it's a deduction in level five. After I had thrown my embarrassing tumbling pass I ran to the back of the floor where for the third time Nick and I stunted together in the back with two other couples, we were supposed to perform paper dolls, a skill that requires the flyers to connect with each other at the top that resemble…well…paper dolls. And when we all got thrown in the air and tried connecting I saw that one of the flyers had fallen…this routine was a disaster. I tried shaking it off and putting on a smile. When it came time to fly baskets I didn't do too badly and everyone else flew theirs well too. The only thing left to do now was pyramid. As we set for pyramid I prayed that since we had already had so many errors to please let this at least hit. The beginning started out fantastic, giving me a little hope that we weren't going to completely bomb this routine, but then during the same exact stunt that Steph had gotten dropped our coach did as well and with it a majority of our pyramid came tumbling down.

I thought I was mad with our performance at Worlds last year, that didn't even come close to how angry I was with this performance. I stomped to my dance spot after the train wreck of a pyramid and pretended to dance as if I had just hit a perfect routine but inside I was about to break down. When the music ended tears immediately streamed down my face as awkward claps came from the crowd. I had never been more humiliated in my life.

32

BECAUSE OUR PERFORMANCE was out of order our routine was not shown live online so my mother never got to see me compete but she knew from the phone call following the performance that I was deeply heartbroken. With anger and sadness seeping into my mind, fighting back and forth to see which one overpowered me more, I struggled to make words come out of my mouth when I spoke to her. I kept repeating to her that the routine was a disaster, a disaster, a disaster…It seemed to be the only sentence that I could muster up. She asked me over and over what went wrong and I told her everything. She asked me if my stunt had hit and I said yes. She was excited about that, and of course so was I, but it didn't matter when you're team performs bad, you perform bad. Somewhere down the road we didn't work together enough or long enough or hard enough…as a team. We had failed as a team. She told me to look on the bright side, that like last year, I would have a couple days now to relax in Florida, I shrugged my shoulders and decided that she was right. There was nothing that I could do to fix what had happened so I might as well have fun for the rest of my stay.

Later that day after we had gotten word that we had placed second to last our team decided we would go to Magic Kingdom to take a team photo in front of the castle to blow off some steam. Unlike the previous year when I had gone by myself this year I was even more excited to get a picture with my team. Being together in a stress-free environment was exactly what our team had needed after that day's event. It allowed us to take our thoughts away from the catastrophe that had just happened.

It was a very hot that day, temperatures in the mid 90's so instead of wearing our long sleeved uniforms the girls wore our team sports bra and skirt while the boys wore their team tank top and shorts. When we had arrived to the park and walked through the gates we were instantly taunted by staff members who yelled at all the girls to put on a shirt and told us that this is was family environment. I couldn't help but question why in the world wearing a sports bra and a skirt wasn't "family appropriate" and they came back at us with a snooty remark that there was a rule in the hand book that states that no one is allowed to walk around with their stomach's showing. I snapped back at them that I would love to see that rule because it was almost a hundred degrees out and I could see other people walking around with their shirts pulled up and why weren't they harassing them about pulling their shirts down.

The staff wasn't having it, so instead of getting kicked out of the park before we could get our team photo we asked all the boys if they had any extra shirts and if we could wear them since obviously the staff thought we entered the park looking apparently like "skanks", we were on the staffs' radar. They knew that we were up to something like most cheerleaders were around this time of year, and they wanted any reason to throw us out.

Knowing that we weren't allowed to stunt in the park, we crept around the castle for a little while, acting like tourist. After a while they decided to stop watching us. As soon as they did we took the opportunity to stunt. Although we weren't right in front because of the large amount of people in the crowd, our team still managed to get a pretty good picture on the side of the castle. It didn't take long for the park rangers to move us away when they saw us stunting. We broke one rule and if we broke one more rule it was out on the curb for us, so we decided to act like good citizens and go on a few rides.

Before leaving the park, Nick and I made sure to get a stunting picture with just the two of us in front of the castle. It was a lot easier to get away with just the two of us stunting rather than the whole team, so the photo turned out very nice. I loved having a boyfriend that I could stunt with anywhere we went.

Later that evening a bunch of the guys from the team went to the liquor store and bought booze for everyone, we were more than ready to have a good time. When the guys returned, Ray walked into the girl's room which was attached to the boys with two gigantic bottles of Bacardi, one that was already almost half gone. He handed it to Katie and I and we took turns taking swigs until it was finished. Nick decided that he didn't want to drink liquor and instead chugged 10 beers within a matter of 20 minutes.

Around the resort you could tell which teams had and hadn't made it to day two simply because of the fact that half of them were out partying and half of them had been in bed hours ago to prepare for the day ahead of them. At one point in the night we were all poolside hanging out with our coaches and while we were all laughing and having a good time Dono interrupted and told me to look at the tikki-bar that was a few feet away from us. When I looked over my shoulder I saw the last people that I had expected to see, Brittney and Matteo. They were obviously in town supporting their little mini-me, Cassady, and I couldn't help but feel disgusted when I saw them sitting there. Dono asked if I had wanted him to go get a drink for me since he was of age and I told him that that would be nice so I gave him my debit card and turned around and acted as if I hadn't just saw them. I wasn't going to let them ruin my time and if anything I wanted to let them see how much better I was doing.

When Dono returned with my drink he handed me back my card and before walking away he told me that he had bought himself a drink and that he hoped that I didn't mind. I told him of course not until I looked at the receipt and it said twenty two dollars, my jaw dropped to the floor, I guess drinks were eleven bucks at the bar. I wanted to turn around and tell him that I did mind that he bought a drink off of my card without asking, after all, my mother did pay his way to be here, but instead I kept my mouth shut. It was stupid of me to ever hand ANYONE my debit card in the first place and I blamed myself. Katie looked at me kind of chuckling and when I asked her what was so funny she told me that he had literally just done the same thing to her too. I told her that I wouldn't have been so upset if he would have just asked first and to show some common courtesy but we shook it off as a learning experience and continued with the rest of the night.

The booze had definitely hit Nick by this time and somehow he found a wheel chair to transport himself in throughout the night. Apparently one of the guys had stolen it from somewhere. He definitely had me on the floor laughing when I saw him wheeling around like a master doing wheelies. I asked him how he got so good at it and he told me that he had broken his hip back in eighth grade and that he was stuck in a wheel chair for a few months.

The partying continued all night and once everyone started to tire out we decided to play catch phrase, something our team was well known for playing. For anyone who doesn't know what catch phrase is, it's a little hand held machine with a buzzer that starts off ticking slow and gets faster and faster. The object of the game is to not end up with the machine in your hand when the ticking stops and the buzzer goes off. Our version of the game required us to take a sip out of the big Bacardi bottle. When you're handed the device a word will appear on the screen and you have to describe it to the people around you the word. For example, if I had the word dog, I would say that this is a furry animal that barks and once someone guesses the word I would pass the machine to the person sitting next to me.

While I was playing this game Nick was in the other room nearly asleep from all the drinking. After a little while it got hard to keep my eyes open so I left the circle and joined him in his bed and snoozed off for the night. It was so comforting to be wrapped around in his big arms as I drifted to sleep. It had been an awful and long day but I wouldn't have wanted it to end any other way.

33

THE NEXT MORNING a few members from the team and I woke up early so that we could go to Animal Kingdom. It was one of the only parks other than the Magic Kingdom that I had really wanted to see. I loved animals and I had heard that the Animal Kingdom was a must see. Nick was very sick in the morning, not only was he dehydrated from the day before but he was also very nauseas from the beer. Although he felt like crap he still managed to get out of bed and come to the park with me. He knew that I was excited about it and didn't want to ruin my day so he put on a smile and threw on some clothes and joined us. I told him that he really didn't need to come and that if he really did feel super sick that he should rest but he insisted that he come with us and I wasn't going to argue with him.

When we arrived I got all giddy inside, just as a little kid probably does before entering the park. As we walked towards the gates, which were painted in a giraffe design, I couldn't help but screech like a little girl from all the excitement. When I walked in I was greeted by what virtually seemed like a real safari with vines hanging everywhere and the sound of wild animals in the distance. As I sprinted to the first little exhibit with little turtles some of the girls and Nick went to use the restroom. Nick told me that he felt like he was going to throw up so I told him that he should try to so the nausea might go away.

After waiting outside the bathroom for what seemed like forever, Nick finally emerged looking slightly pale and with circles under his eyes. I asked him if he had thrown up and he told me that he had but that he didn't feel any better. I grabbed his hand and we started walking to what most would consider the best part of Animal Kingdom, the safari ride. When we walked up to what was the end of the line for the safari we ran into our coach. She told us that she had just gotten off the ride and that it was a freaking blast. She said she only had to wait in line for ten minutes. She had arrived a lot earlier than us though and by looking at the line now I thought we would be in for a much longer wait. As we waited in line the humidity from the day started to get hotter and hotter; which made Nick feel sicker and sicker. He started sweating and became weak. I felt awful but I knew that he should have just stayed back at the hotel room; he was in no condition to be out in this Florida heat.

After about 45 minutes of waiting had past it was finally our turn to go on the safari ride. When the huge jeep pulled up in front of us we all jumped in and held on to the sides. We listened to the tour guide as she explained to us to keep our hands and feet inside the vehicle at all times. As we passed through the marshes, the grasslands and the swamps, I saw all sorts of wild animals and all close up! It was honestly the coolest thing that I had ever done in a very long time. I was literally feet away from giraffes, elephants, alligators and tigers. I made sure to capture everything on camera to show my mom. I knew though that photos and videos would never be able to capture the real moment that I was living in.

When the tour was finished Nick decided to go back to the hotel room. I was very appreciative of him coming and we had so much fun on the ride together. I was glad that he was going back to the room to rest, he looked awful and he needed to sleep. He wanted me to come with him but I told him that I really wanted to stay and see the rest of Animal Kingdom, that it was a once in a lifetime opportunity for me. He was very upset about this. He didn't understand why I wouldn't want to be with him and comforting him. I felt horrible but I stood my ground and stayed at the park.

Once we kissed and parted ways I continued with the rest of my teammates to Mt. Everest, one of the largest roller coasters in the park. While we were waiting in line Nick texted me that he really did not feel good and that he told his coaches that he really needed help. They suggested going to the hospital. I tried calming him down and told him that after the ride that I would come back to the room, but in the meantime to keep drinking water. It was clear to me from the symptoms that he was dehydrated. Our coaches were telling him to drink Gatorade and that upset me because in my opinion when you are dehydrated you should drink water, since that is what your body is lacking. Feeding his body sugar and sodium was the last thing that he needed. He needed to lie down in a cool bedroom and sip on water until I made it back to the room.

When we got off the roller coaster we all made our way back to the resort. When I stepped into the boy's room a cold cloud of air hit me in the face. Nick had obviously turned down the air to 60 degrees. It was very dark in the room and he was lying under the covers on a bed. When I walked over to him I wiped his hair out of his face to see how he was doing. He looked pale and had bags under his eyes. The rest of the team had decided to drink again that night but I decided to stay in with Nick and rest. I wanted to get some sleep for the block party tomorrow. After last year's block party, rumor had it that they weren't having one this year but that didn't seem to be true. They were still blocking off MGM studios for us and handing out wrist bands to the athletes. I had hoped that they would not be cancelling it because Nick had never been and we had never danced together. I thought it would be a great experience for the both of us. Although everyone stayed up partying and we could hear all the laughter and excitement in the room next to us, we still managed to drift to sleep. I had been in the sun all day and because Nick was exhausted from being ill.

I woke up early the next morning and tip toed across the bedroom floor to put on my bathing suit. I wanted to catch some rays before the party tonight and decided to lay by the pool all day. When I made my way downstairs I could see in the distance that one of my coaches and some of the younger girls from the team were in the pool performing what seemed to be synchronized swimming. I sat down next to them while I rubbed tanning oil all over and couldn't help but laugh at how silly they looked. They literally put together a whole routine and had everybody that was sitting pool side laughing.

One by one the girls slowly joined me in tanning, telling me everything that had happened the night before. A few minutes later the boys started waking up and joined us too, bringing along with them speakers so that we could listen to music. Some of our favorite songs came on, making it hard to resist starting a dance party. As we danced it out some other groups of cheerleaders that weren't competing that day joined in. It was fun being in a place surrounded by people that had so many similarities to you, we were all cheerleaders and we all had the same common understanding and respect for each other. We were all so laid back with one another it was like we had known each other for years, when in reality, we had never met a day in our lives.

The block party was to start around nine and we still had some time to kill before the sun went down. Nick and I and a few other people decided to go to Epcot Center for an hour or so to walk around. I have to admit that Epcot was my favorite park to be at. It had multiple pavilions set up to represent eleven different countries ranging anywhere from Germany to Japan. The best part was that at each of these set ups they had food from the country that you were visiting. I loved getting to taste food from all the different areas. It was so intriguing to me to learn about other cultures and get a little glimpse of what life is like in different countries.

While we were there we ran into a couple of cheerleaders from Chile, thankfully Cisco was with us. We wanted to ask them how they had done today at the competition but they spoke Spanish. Cisco translated for us and told us that they had done pretty well so we congratulated them. Although it was hard communicating to them they were some of the friendliest people we had met during our visit. They were so nice in fact, that they let us try on their uniforms. They were some of the sharpest looking uniforms I had ever seen. We talked to them for a little while asking them what it was like to cheer in Chile. They told us that there weren't too many teams so World's was fairly easy for them. They explained that they worked long hours and fundraised a lot of money to come. We made sure to get pictures with them and told them that it was such a pleasure meeting them and that hopefully we would see them either at the block party or if not then next year at competition. Once we parted ways we decided to head back to the hotel to get ready for the night, making sure to get a stunting picture in front of the huge globe before we left.

Nick still wasn't feeling well from the night before and told me that he didn't feel up for going to the block party. He asked if I would stay with him and not go to the block party, just as he did when we were at Animal Kingdom, but once again I told him that I really wanted to go. I felt bad for leaving him there but I told him that he needed to rest and that I would be back in a little while.

I put on a cropped top tangerine shirt and some white shorts, scrunched my hair really big and put some feather earrings on as an accessory. Katie and the girls told me that I looked like Pocahontas. I couldn't help but chuckle when they said that, I actually get told that a lot because of my long dark brown hair and brown eyes and with my dark red Cherokee skin. After I was finished getting ready I kissed Nick goodbye and told him not to worry me and that I would be careful. Little did I know what was about to go down that night.

34

BEFORE I LEFT I took a shot or two of rum with Katie and then we made our way down to the buses. We couldn't help but be excited for the night ahead. You could tell that the rest of the cheer community felt the same way. It was not just a long weekend of competing but the end of a long cheer season and the block party was the place for us to let out all our stress. When we pulled up to the line to get in was almost a quarter mile long. I guess they had caught on to people sneaking in and bringing alcohol so they really cracked down on security. They went through everyone's purses and bags and they told everyone to throw away all open water bottles that were filled with "water". When we finally got through the line the girls and I ran straight to where the DJ usually is set up. Expecting to see a crowd of people dancing we were greeted with an empty lot. Confused at why there wasn't anything going on we searched the park to make sure that they hadn't moved the party but they hadn't, it turned out that the rumors were true, they had cancelled the block party.

Picture this....thousands of stressed out non-chaperoned cheer-leaders waiting all year to let out their stress from their seasons, ready to dance and have a good time but only to be greeted by an empty lot with no music and certainly no party. We did not know this but it only took about thirty minutes for a mass media message to go through text, Facebook, and Twitter to let everyone know that they, the cheerleaders, were starting their own block party at the football field at the All-star Sports resort at 10 PM.

By this time Katie and I were by ourselves and sober, wondering around the MGM studios looking for something to do. While we were walking a group of cheerleaders ran by us screaming that the block party was back at the All-star Sports resort. Our ears perked up and we looked at each other as if to say "You down?" And then we sprinted after the cheerleaders to follow them to the party.

When we arrived, nearly the entire cheer world was on the tiny football field throwing a rave party. Katie and I naively joined in. One athlete held a huge boom box over his head that played music. Families that were staying at the resort started to file out of their rooms, watching the chaos unfold. They were recording videos on their IPhones and taking pictures. It was like a scene from Project X, helicopters started to fly in shining their lights down on us with kids looking up to them flicking them off, all too drunk for their own good. Katie and I decided it was probably a good idea to leave so we started to walk towards our room. It had gotten out that the police were on campus arresting kids and all hell broke loose and everyone started scurrying around frantically. Luckily our hotel room was only a few feet away and we didn't have that far to travel but just as we were about to turn towards our room my old teammate from ICC Destiny, Nathan, spotted me and started screaming my name. I whipped my head around and he came running towards me asking Katie and I for our help, one of the girls from ICE was in the hotel lobby's bathroom extremely sick.

I couldn't turn down helping an old friend so I told him okay and we followed him to the girls bathroom. When we walked into the bathroom, Katie and I asked the girl, who was with Nathan, where this sick girl was, she told us that she was locked in a bathroom stall and that she wasn't responding. Katie and I knocked on the stalls calling out her name trying to get a response from her, but there was none. We found it appropriate to climb on the toilet in the next stall and peek our heads over the ledge to see if she was okay. When we did, we could see that she was sitting there with her panties pulled down and her head lying limply on her chest. She appeared to be passed out. I asked Nathan and the girl that he was with, if she had been drinking tonight and they looked at me with big eyes and shook their heads up and down and said "A lot!" Katie and I determined that she was passed out so Katie crawled underneath the stall to unlock the door. While she was doing this I received a panicked phone call from my mother asking me what the hell was going on, that she had gotten a phone call from Nick saying that I wasn't responding to his text and the Steph, who had been back at the hotel room for a while, told him that she didn't know where Katie and I were and that we were off running around drunk together.

Infuriated that Steph would say such a thing to scare Nick and my mother, I told her that I had taken a shot earlier and that it had barely done anything to me and I was completely sober now. I told her that Nathan had found me and asked me to help with one of his friends who had passed out in a bathroom stall. She was relieved to hear this, thankful that nothing had happened to me and told me that she was sorry. She said Nick was panicking on the phone like something bad had happened and she instinctively freaked out as well. After I had calmed her down and told her that I was fine she told me that she would call Nick and to let him what was going on. I thanked her and told her that I would let her know as soon as I got back to the room and that I loved her.

Right as I got off the phone with my mom, Katie had managed to open the stall. Katie was repeating her name so to try and get her to respond. After a few shouts and taps on the shoulder she finally opened her eyes a little and swayed her head back and forth, you could tell that she was trying to focus on what we were saying but she was way too drunk to do so. We came to the conclusion that we just needed to get this girl back to her room and asked Nathan who she was staying with. He told us that he wasn't sure but he knew that Cassady would know. Great out of all the people it had to be him. Concerned about the girl though, I told Nathan to call him and tell him to come get her. As he talked on the phone Katie and I helped the girl off the toilet and watched as she tried pulling up her underwear. Once she had managed to do that we walked her out over our shoulders to the bus stop in front of the hotel where Nathan said Cassady and Trevor were coming to pick her up. It only took a couple of minutes for them to arrive and help out. They called her mother and told her that her daughter needed to be picked up. She showed up angry but nonetheless relieved that her daughter was okay. She helped the boys while they put her limp body in the back of the taxi. Before we left to go back to our hotel rooms, Cassady and Trevor thanked us for our generosity and said we didn't have to help her out. We replied that anyone with a heart would have helped her out. She was completely helpless and the people she was with had no idea what to do with her. We were just glad that she made it home okay.

After our crazy night I didn't want to do anything else but snuggle up next to Nick and fall asleep and that's exactly what I did. I apologized for scaring him and he told me that he was just glad that I was okay. That night as I lay there I thought to myself, with a little bit of guilt, this isn't who I am. I didn't like to drink and I didn't like to party and I was never the one to get in trouble or break the rules but for some reason when I was around these type of people I couldn't help myself. I thought to myself that I was a lot stronger and better than this. I was 19 years old and shouldn't be doing these types of things. From that moment on I decided to stand my ground and be my own person.

My mother always taught me that in life you have to make mistakes to learn and that if you never make mistakes then not only are you not living but you're not growing as well. This was one of those moments that that saying applied. I had made a mistake this weekend, I had alienated the one I loved, Nick, while he was sick and when I should have been home comforting him, I was selfishly out partying. This is not the type of person I am. Before I dozed off in Nick's arms, I thought to myself, it was time to start being me again. It had been the weekend from hell but I had learned a lot about myself and for that I was thankful.

The next morning Nick, Dono and I woke up early and gathered our belongings making sure not to forget our participant medals that we had received just for competing. When we were done packing we made our way to the bus stop and hopped on board the Magical Express bus that would take us to the airport. I was so ready to go home.

The plane ride home seemed as if it took forever. I was so anxious to get back home to my family and the comfort of my own bed that the flight dragged on. Once we finally arrived home and I saw my mother standing at the end of the walk way I ran up to her and gave her the biggest hug ever, I was so happy to be back.

Like always, I immediately told my mother everything that had happened over the weekend. She knew that I was more than relieved to be home, as was she, she hated seeing me stressed out and wanted to do anything she could to make me feel better. Once she dropped me off at my apartment I gave her a hug and kiss goodbye and told her that I loved her and that I would talk to her soon. When I stepped into my apartment the first thing I did was drop my bags and crawl into bed. I had never been happier to be in my home as I was then. With a smile on my face I snuggled into the blankets and thought to myself how this weekend couldn't be the last performance of my career. I needed to end on a good note so that I felt content about letting go of my biggest passion, competing, and I was determined to make sure I would go to World's again to make that happen.

35

AFTER OUR PERFORMANCE at Worlds, Nick and I were in the gym every day, stunting and tumbling, working our asses off to get better for next season. We decided we would stay at CIA and ask the gym owner if she would consider giving the two of us a job. Because Nick wasn't pursuing baseball anymore, he decided that he too wanted to make cheerleading into his career and we both decided it would be best if we started building our resume as soon as we could and as fast as we could.

The gym owner told me that she had already been planning on offering me a coaching position. She told me that she loved how I interacted with my teammates on Power and that I was one of the leaders on the team. She assigned me to a junior level three team with another female coach in the gym that seemed to be very nice. She told Nick that he could start working some stunting classes in the gym with the rest of the guys and that he could pick up privates as well. Although I was ecstatic about my first ever coaching job, Nick was a little upset that he wasn't offered as much but I told him that if he could keep the hard work up and hopefully bring in some private lessons, that in time he would have a coaching job.

I was taking the first steps to my dream of becoming a gym owner; being a coach meant so much more to me than anyone could imagine. All my life I've wanted to make a difference in children's lives, whether it be one or a million. I wanted to give them a role model that they could look up to, one that taught them how to respect others and themselves, how to be confident but not cocky, how to appreciate what they have and not focus on the things that they don't, how to be humble and kind and most importantly how hard work and honesty will get you the furthest you can be in life and ultimately lead you to what every human being strives for...happiness. I knew that this first step was one of many to come and I couldn't help but feel warmth in my heart. I had a smile on my face and I was so ready to take on whatever the world threw at me in order to reach my dreams. No one was going to stop me.

When tryouts came around Nick and I got more and more excited for Power to start up again, our stunting was becoming very elite and we wanted more than anything to get back on the floor and compete. International athletes didn't really have to tryout they just showed up to tryouts and hung around. We were the older team and all the coaches knew what skills we had and because of our ages the only team they could put us on was the international team since most of us were over 18.

A few days after "tryouts" the gym owner gathered most people from Power in her office and told us that they were making Power a senior coed five team. When we heard this we about fell out of our chairs, Power was the only team in the gym that consistently made it to worlds every year, so why would they take it away? It didn't just confuse us but broke our hearts. This threw me into another whirl wind of confusion. I had been working my ass off to get better and now I was being told that there was no longer going to be an international team.

The owner calmed us down and told us that they were still going to have an international team but that we would be level six. Level six? Are you kidding me? That's a collegiate level, which means that ALL the girls on the team had to fly and they all had to fly coed with only one guy underneath them. For one, we only had three flyers on the team that even knew somewhat how to fly coed and only a few of the guys did as well. The rest of the team seemed fired up about it and gave ourselves the new team name Magnum. I on the other hand had a million thoughts running through my head. None of these girls, including myself, have cheered level six, we've never done level six baskets or stunts and I didn't see what they were getting so excited about. There was no way that this plan was going to have a positive outcome.

Later that night I went home and told my mother about everything, and as surprised and as shocked as she was she told me to stick it out, that I had a job there now and I needed to be building my resume for when we open our gym. I agreed to give it a try, as well as Nick. We tried to stay positive and kept going to the gym every day to stunt and get better, but as the days went by there were no signs that "Magnum" was coming together. Other teams in the gym, including the one that I coached were about to have their first practice and there was no word that "Magnum" was happening. There was no information being given out on what was going on with the team and Nick and I started to have our doubts.

When my junior level three team's first practice started I was very excited and nervous at the same time. All of the coaches lined up in front of the cheerleading floor and introduced ourselves and our experience that we had with cheerleading. When it came to my turn I told them that this was my first ever year coaching and that I was more than thrilled for the opportunity. I also told them that I had cheered on two World's teams After everyone was done introducing each other I met my girls. They were between the ages of 8-14 and they were very shy and sweet and I could tell that I would instantly fall in love with them. Another female coach and I lead team stretches with all the athletes while the other coaches sat around and talked. They told us that in summer that all the teams were going to be practicing together and I had never heard of such a thing before but I later found out that the reasoning behind it was that some of the teams only had two girls on them and the owner wanted to hide that from the parents so that they wouldn't ask questions.

After stretching, the other coaches directed the kids outside to run laps around the building, so I followed everyone as we made our way out the back door of the gym. While I was standing there with some of the female coaches, while the athletes ran, I listened to the way that they talked about the athletes. One coach talked down about some of them, as if to almost make fun of them. Standing there made me feel so uncomfortable. I didn't believe that talking about anyone in a negative fashion, especially an athlete of yours, was right.

After the children were done running laps we directed them back into the gym for tumbling. When I asked the coaches what we were doing for tumbling they stood around for about fifteen minutes trying to figure out to do with all the kids. Finally they set up stations for them to rotate to with different tumbling and conditioning drills. I couldn't help but think in the back of my mind what a hot mess this was. If I were a parent right now and I had witnessed this first practice I most certainly would have been having doubts or even questioning the gyms organization.

After practice I called my mom and told her everything, but most importantly I told her that I just had a horrible gut feeling inside telling me that this wasn't the place I should be. Almost like magic she told me that Kyle, a former coach at Famous (which had now been closed down for a few months) messaged me asking me to work for his choreography and skills camp business. I was like a sponge at this point trying to absorb every ounce of experience I could get within the next two years and I told him that I would love to work for his business. I also explained to him my situation at CIA and how I was looking for another coaching position and that if he knew of one to let me know.

Once again, everything happens for a reason and every day I am proven this theory correct. God has a chess board for each one of our lives and sometimes when he's playing the game you may not understand the moves that he's making until one day it all make sense and you will have an aha moment, this was one of those days. Kyle told me that he actually knew someone that was looking for coaches and that he thought I would love the gym, so I got the owners information and contacted her immediately to set up a time to come visit the gym.

36

THIS GYM WAS a lot smaller and when you walked in the front door a sense of home came over you. The walls were painted pink with cozy black couches for the parents to sit on while they watched their children practice. My mom was with me, as well as Nick, and when we all walked in we all sort of looked at each other and smiled, you could tell that we were all feeling the same thing…that we were in love. After we walked in and took in our surrounding, we looked over to our left where the front desk was and right next to it was a tiny blonde lady with a huge smile on her face asking if we were Nick and Morgan, as soon as we told her yes she gave us a huge hug and welcomed us. We already knew that we would like this woman, she seemed like a complete sweetheart.

She had us fill out some waivers before we went into the gym and after we did we walked through the star painted door and stepped into a large room with one cheer floor and a few mats. To our left another tiny room connected with two trampolines and a smaller cheer floor. It was small, but it was so original and clean. The gym had only been open for a couple of years now so all the equipment was brand new. What I had loved most though was that there weren't that many people there. It seemed to be a very small and friendly gym and I immediately wanted to work there.

Angie, the gym owner of Five Star Cheer Academy, took Kyle's reference and hired us on the spot, no job application needed. She told me that I would be coaching a minis team, between ages 5-8, which was a huge relief for me because I had originally wanted to work with the younger kids as my first year coaching. For me little kids weren't intimidating they were just big goof balls that wanted to have fun and didn't even know if they really liked cheerleading or not.

Angie also offered me to teach hyper flex classes, a class designed to show and help athletes become more flexible, especially flyers. She told Nick that he could teach some stunting classes just as CIA had told him and he was okay with that. She also told us that they were going to have an international team and that most of the coaches in the gym and a few high school athletes wanted to be on it, an even bigger plus for us since we would be getting to cheer.

After visiting the gym I immediately sent an email to the owner of CIA, telling her that I had found a better job offer and that I was so sorry for any problems that this may cause, but to have a good season and best of luck. She was completely shocked by my email, but nonetheless she wished me the best and hoped that this new job would be what I was looking for. Relieved that I had found a new home to work at, somewhere I knew I would be more comfortable, I texted my mother and told her that I had resigned from CIA and that I was officially working at Five Star. While I was texting her, my phone blew up with hundreds of texts, word had obviously spread throughout CIA that Nick and I had left. All of the guys from Power sent me a nice text telling me that they would miss me and they hoped to stay in touch, however the girls were not happy. I started receiving texts from Courtney. She was acting all confrontational and playing the drama card. She asked me how I could make the decision to leave CIA without even consulting one of them first. I asked her since when do I have to ask other people whether or not I should take a job. I was a big girl and I could make my decisions on my own. She said that she understood but she didn't see how I could just not tell anyone that I was leaving. I understood where she was coming from, they had believed that I was really close to them and I was, but I never get too close to friends because I didn't trust anyone.

I have this ability to just pick up my life and some of the people in it and just move on without talking to them ever again. Although people get close to me, in my heart I would never get close to them. Maybe that was because of my past experiences with trusting people or just because I was raised always to be cautious, but whichever it was, I had no problem just picking up my life and changing things. I could understand why Courtney was so upset about me leaving, we had been good friends and she confided in me, she already had trust issues as it was, and this was not making them any better.

Courtney also accused me of leaving CIA to go work for their rival gym, Ultimate Athletics. She and the girls had heard me talk about how Ultimate was supposed to have a good international team this year. I snapped back at her and told her that she was wrong to assume that I would do such a thing and that she shouldn't accuse me of something she had no knowledge of what was happening. I told her I was working nowhere near CIA or even Ultimate for that matter and she immediately apologized and said that she was wrong. That was something I always loved about her, she was always the one to admit when she was incorrect or out of line. Her saying those words to me made it easier for me to leave them behind though, I knew that I was heading to somewhere better suited for me and I wasn't going to let her know where that was. I didn't believe she deserved to know.

While I was texting Courtney, I was also texting Katie, who was basically telling me the same thing but in a way more immature way. I responded to her a lot more shortly than I did with Courtney. I didn't want to deal with her childishness. Steph surprisingly was not texting me but I had just assumed that since she was attached to the other two by the hip that she would be upset with me as well. A lot of feelings were hurt that day and once again I had burned a lot of bridges with people but I was excited for my new journey with Nick at Five Star and more importantly I was excited to continue taking steps towards my dream. I knew that it was going to be a bumpy road but I was in it for the long haul and my heart was telling me that Five Star is where I needed to be.

PART IV
Five Star Cheer Academy

37

THINGS AT FIVE Star were going really well, just as I had expected them to. I was teaching my hyper flex classes as promised and Nick was teaching his coed stunt classes. Everyone was very friendly there and to my surprise, Nathan, my good friend from ICC Destiny, and also the person that asked Katie and I for help at World's with his sick friend, worked there. Something about him had changed though (or so I had thought). When I cheered with him on Destiny he was very snappy and emotional a lot of the time, now he seemed to light up the room when he walked into it with his bubbly personality. I believe it was because he finally came out that he was gay. I couldn't imagine the stress he had been dealing with and I'm sure he got teased for it a lot in school. You could tell that a weight was lifted off his shoulders and he was stronger for accepting and embracing who he was. I defiantly liked this Nathan a lot more, he wasn't going to take anyone's crap.

The day before I started coaching minis, Angie pulled me aside in the gym and wanted to talk to me privately. I jokingly asked if I was in trouble and she laughed, both of us knowing that I wasn't. I really liked Angie, she seemed to be the first gym owner that was genuinely truthful and family oriented and for that I looked up to her and how she ran her business. It was exactly the same way I wanted to run my gym, with a homey atmosphere, no lies, no scandal, no drama, just honesty and respect. When she pulled me aside she told me that she really liked me and that she wanted me to know two things. My heart sank a little, I couldn't tell if it was from nerves or from not knowing what she was about to say. She told me that there are two people in the gym that I needed to watch out for, Mrs. Nay, and Stacey. This kind of shocked and appalled me, since Stacey was a coach at the gym, and Mrs. Nay was a parent with two daughters in her program. I asked what she meant by that. She told me that these two people caused the most drama in the gym and to stay away from them and ignore them if they ever say anything or try to start anything with me. I nodded my head and trusted her, after all she was the gym owner and she was looking out for my best interest.

As the weeks went by my mother decided that I needed to kick my resume into full gear. She said that teaching one class and coaching minis wasn't enough. She told me that I needed to start giving privates so that I could start showing people my passion for helping athletes progress. She came up with an awesome idea to make a Facebook resume page for Nick and myself, not just to get our name out there, but to show people what we're all about and to show our hands-on work that we do with our athletes, posting pictures and videos of their progressions.

Along with the resume page, she came up with the idea to make flyers to post around the gym to advertise stunting privates with Nick and myself. We came up with the idea to teach these privates together so that the student gets advice from both the base and the flyer. We started off with a five privates for two hundred dollars. This may sound like a lot of money, but it's really not. Most stunting privates go for a minimum of fifty dollars per hour and we were only charging forty. This deal got our foot in the door and we started racking up privates, one of which was Kelly Nay, Mrs. Nay's daughter. She was a flyer for her junior high school and she wanted to take lessons to prepare her for high school cheerleading tryouts.

When you receive a private lesson at gyms, the parents will either pay the front desk lady or they will pay the instructor directly. At Five Star we got paid directly, so I got to meet Mrs. Nay for the first time and I could see what Angie was talking about. She came off kind of negative, almost as if she didn't like Five Star but she stuck it out for her kids. I did what Angie told me and just nodded my head to everything she said and did my best not to get too deep into conversation with her. I didn't want to be pulled into unnecessary drama like Angie had advised me.

Privates and the size of my hyper flex classes really started to grow. All of my mini's kids took tumbling privates with me to get skills they needed for their routine and flyers in the gym needed to get more flexible to perform better in the air. Nick was also starting to make some money with privates; he now had five regular girls every week paying him fifty dollars an hour to stunt and he had his classes on top of it.

We kept up our resume page, posting videos and pictures of our athlete's, and soon the page reached over 200 likes. It got to the point where I had students asking me to record them while they performed a skill, and if they did well I would put it on Facebook, this cracked me up, mostly because it was coming from a lot of my six year old athletes from minis.

As our resume grew bigger and bigger, Kyle contacted me and told me that he had a first ever skills camp for me to work. I was so excited to hear this news and responded immediately that I would love to join him. He sent me an email a week before the camp explaining the pay, the details, the location (which was in Madison, Wisconsin) and what to wear. He told me that because it was my first camp that he would be there to help so for me not to stress out about it too much. It was such a relief to hear that he would be there with me. I have to admit I was a little nervous, I had never taught a camp before but I trusted Kyle and I knew that he would take care of me.

The car ride to Wisconsin was a couple of hours giving us some bonding time to get to know each other. I learned a lot about him that day. He was a straight up business man, but not your typical black suit and tie business man, he was gay, loud, honest, fun, caring and he loved every job that he had (which was quite a few.) Not only did he run his own choreography and skills camp company, he also is a GK representative, one of the top uniform companies in our industry. He is also a coach at a gym. He definitely had a lot on his plate. He actually roomed with Brittney and Matteo for a little while and told me all about his experience there and how he moved out because they weren't the best people. I too, am not a fan of Brittney and Matteo's so we had that mutually in common. He was a very honest person and I respected that and I was so grateful that not only did he hire me to work for him, but he also recommended me for the job at Five Star.

When we arrived in Wisconsin, he stepped out of his car with a bottle of Listerine and took a swig and swished it around in his mouth and spit it out then he took a bottle of cologne and sprayed it on himself. Aware that I was watching, he laughed and said that it was always important to smell good in front of clients, that it would actually increase your cliental. I died laughing but he did have a point, everyone told him how good he smelled as soon as he walked in the doors.

He introduced me to the owner and coach, two very friendly people and they showed me around. Kyle had already done camps there before so he knew the place. It wasn't even a cheer gym it was actually a gymnastics facility. The cheer program was just renting out the space until they had enough money to open their own gym. I found it strange that they practiced on a gymnastics floor, not only was it a lot smaller, it was a lot harder too. I gave them props though, they made it work, and later on in the season they would produce some top teams that would win consistently at their competitions. Kyle had asked me earlier if I was good with little kids, and I told him of course. I loved them and coached a minis team at Five Star. He said that this was perfect because he preferred to work with the older kids. He told me he was going to start me out working with the gym's mini team, teaching the skills they could learn for their routine. I told him that this was perfect and my nerves were calmed. Not only were little kids not intimidating but I was also experienced working with them. While Kyle worked with some of the older kids between the ages 9-14, I worked with the little ones and had a great time teaching new skills and playing games with them.

Once lunch came around those two teams were done for the day and one last team was coming in after our break, a senior team between the ages 14-18. This was a little intimidating for me to hear, considering I was only 19, but Kyle would be with me and I knew that he would have my back plus I told myself that if I was confident that they would look at me as a lot older, and they did.

After eating Noodles for lunch, the senior team started to roll in and I couldn't help but feel extremely anxious. Once they all arrived we had them warm up and while they stretched we introduced ourselves. They were a smaller team and had very laid back respectful attitudes and a great sense of humor. After we were done stretching and warming up we had them line up in their stunt groups and began to teach them the new skills that they could use in their routine. I have to admit that while watching them get new skills and seeing the excitement on their faces I had the most rewarding feeling come over me. I had always known that I wanted to open my own gym for this exact reason but this made it even more concrete for me. I loved seeing athletes not only progress in skills, but as a person, nothing was more rewarding than to watch someone feel the emotion of achievement and success.

At the end of camp Kyle had the girls play his signature game "princess pony rider". When he told the girls we were playing this game they all looked at him like he was crazy. He told them to grab a partner and to keep in mind that there was going to be lifting involved. Once everyone found a partner he explained to them that he was going to call out a combination of words involving princess, pony and rider. When he called one of those words there was a certain move that you had to perform with your partner, and the last couple to perform that move was eliminated. When he called out the word pony you had to jump on top of your partner's back as if your partner was a horse on all fours. If he called out rider, you had to jump on your partners back like a piggy back ride. If he called out princess, you had to jump into your partners hands like a princess. I know this sounds easy but you and your partner are walking in opposite directions around a floor and when Kyle calls out a combination of words you have to sprint to you partner as fast as you can and perform those moves making sure not to be the last couple to do so. Once the girls started playing, the game got really intense; there were a lot of shoving and elbowing involved, but nonetheless it was all out of fun and games. They were all screaming and laughing from the fun they were having, I couldn't help but giggle to myself at how funny they looked.

Once camp was over we all said our good byes and I wished them good luck with their season, telling them that I'm sure I would see them at a competition. As soon as I left the building and got into Kyle's car he immediately handed me a check for the day. I was totally surprised and very impressed. He really knew how to run a business well and treated his employees better than most bosses do. I was exhausted on the car ride home and as I sat there and listened to Kyle talk on the phone to some of his clients from GK, I couldn't help but think to myself how he did camps back to back all summer long. They were extremely tiring and that this one was just a one-day camp! Most programs do a two or three day camp. I assumed that he had just gotten used to it over the years.

When he dropped me off at my apartment I thanked him for everything and told him to let me know if he needed me for any other camps. I also said that if he needed more male staff that my boyfriend Nick would be more than happy to help. He told me that he would keep that in mind and that I had done an amazing job today. As we parted ways I couldn't help but feel proud of myself, I had accomplished instructing my first camp.

38

AS THE SUMMER went on Kyle called me a few more times for skills camps in Indiana and some closer to home in Illinois, this time with other staff members, of which I all got along with fantastically. Kyle seemed to have a good eye for hiring employees, they all knew what they were talking about and they were all very friendly. Around the middle of July he contacted me and asked me if I wanted to work a skills camp in New Jersey with a few other staff members for two weeks. I told him that I would be honored to but I needed to talk to my mother and Angie first to work out my work schedule since I would be gone for so long. I talked to Angie and since there was another coach for minis, that as long as I got someone to cover my hyper flex classes (which Nathan would end up doing) then it would be fine. I also talked to my mother and she told me that it was such an amazing opportunity that I would be silly not to take it. I called Kyle back and gave him the okay. Nick wasn't too thrilled about me being gone for two weeks, we had just gotten a new puppy, who I had fell madly in love with, a rottie named Diesel. I prefer to call him Bubbas, and I knew that he would miss me too. Although Nick was bummed about me being gone for so long he was also very excited for me. He knew that this would help with my future and it was something that I needed to do and he supported me all the way.

As soon as I had made the decision to go to New Jersey, flyers all over the gym were being posted that Gabi Butler was coming to visit.

Anyone that's a cheerleader knows who Gabi Butler is. She's not just famous for her outstanding flexibility and flying skills, but she's also cheered on some of the most famous gyms in the United States. She was an inspiration to so many young athletes and one of the most known cheerlebrities. I told Nick that since she was going to be here while I was gone that he needed to get a stunting picture with her and that it would look great to put on our resume page. He told me not to worry that he would and he'd send the pictures to me right away and let me know how meeting her went.

When the day came to leave for New Jersey I packed up all my belongings, making sure not to forget my uniform and made my way out the back door making sure to give Nick the biggest kiss because I knew that I wouldn't be seeing him for two weeks. That killed me inside. I was going to miss him tremendously. I made sure to give Bubbas a big hug and kiss too and one last pet before I jumped into my mom's van. I waved good bye to my boys as we drove away. I prayed that this trip would go well. It was going to be the longest that I had ever been away from home. When I arrived at the airport I gave my momma a huge hug and told her that I loved her and that I would text her when I was on the plane. She hugged me goodbye and after saying I love you, we parted ways. When I walked down the escalators I saw that the line for security was extremely long. As I was waiting in line, time started to move faster and faster and I was still stuck in slow motion trying to get through security. I started to panic a little when I checked my phone and my flight was scheduled to take off in fifteen minutes. I heard someone's voice coming over the intercom looking for Morgan Fairley, I started to freak out even more. I was THAT person running through the airport holding my shoes and flailing my arms everywhere trying to make it to my gate in time. When I finally made it to my gate the lady took my boarding pass and asked me if I was Morgan, gasping for air I told her yes, and she replied that I had just made it to the gate.

As I sat in my seat trying to catch my breath I pulled out my phone to text my mom that I was on the plane. As I started typing I had this weird naked sensation come over me and my stomach fell to the floor. I had left my grandfather's ring at security. I texted my mom frantically praying that she would get my text before I lost service. I told her to call security immediately that I had forgotten my ring. Just as the text went through my phone lost service and all there was left for me to do was pray that she had gotten the message. The next few hours were the longest of my life, I couldn't help but think of what I would do if I had ever lost that ring, it meant more than anything to me and I would be devastated. This was not how I wanted this trip to begin.

As soon as the plane landed I turned on my cell phone and got bombarded by saved texts from my mother telling me that she had picked up the ring and to relax and enjoy the rest of my trip. It was a huge relief that she had gotten the ring, now I would be able to enjoy the rest of my trip without worrying. I told her thank you and that I would have no idea what I would ever do without her and she laughed and told me that she was happy that I had made it safely.

Once all the staff members had met up by baggage claim and gathered all of their things we made our way to the rental car place to get our two cars that we would be driving around for the duration of the trip. There were three boys and four girls. We had two separate rooms at a Super Eight not too far from the New Jersey shoreline. Once we all settled into our rooms we went over our agendas for the next two weeks, with only two days off, we'd mostly be working nine hour days on our feet and at some camps that would be outside in the heat. As I lay in bed that first night I felt a little bit of sadness and a little bit of excitement; I missed my family more than anything but I was more than ready to begin my adventure.

Our first camp was in a gymnasium at a local high school. I got to work with the little kids, which I loved. Working with the smaller kids you have to have a lot of patience and especially with recreational cheerleading. New Jersey was my first experience working with recreational cheerleading. Unlike all-star cheerleading, recreational is usually ran through the park district and they only compete once a year. It was more for fun. They also cheer for the park district football team. Although they both had the word cheerleading in their name, recreational and all-star cheer were two completely different sports. All-star had a much higher skill level and competitiveness to it, whereas recreational cheer is focused around football games and cheering.

Working with recreational teams was one of the greatest opportunities I was given, it not only showed me a whole different side of cheerleading but it taught me how to teach lower level skills which is surprisingly a lot harder than teaching higher leveled skills. It's like teaching someone the basics, just as an elementary school teacher teaches a child how to read, or a parent teaching a child how to talk. It taught me how to expand my mind and be more creative to make it easier to teach kids skills that they had never seen or done in their short lives.

Nick texted me a lot while I was gone. He told me that he was doing really well and that meeting Gabi was so much fun. She was an amazing flyer. He made sure to send me a picture of them, it seemed so surreal. I was happy to hear that Nick was doing well it was nice for him to be independent without me at the gym. It really allowed people to get to know him and it gave him more opportunities. On the evenings or mornings that I had off I found myself running 5K's just to pass the time so that I could get home sooner. I found myself starting to get really home sick and just as I was in my most depressed state, a knock came from our hotel door and when I answered it a mailman was there asking if I was Morgan. When I told him yes he handed me a teddy bear that held a vase of roses in it. It had a note that read "Only a few more days until I get to see you, love you and miss you so much! Xoxoxo Nick." My heart melted. This was exactly what I had needed to get me through the rest of the week. I texted Nick and told him that I loved him so much and thanked him a million times. I let him know that I would be snuggling with the teddy bear the remainder of the trip. He was glad to hear that it had made my day and told me to keep my head up, that I would be home soon.

I absolutely fell in love with the girls at my last camp, and vice versa. Not only were they respectful, cute and funny but they were great listeners. This made teaching them so much easier and it made the time fly by. I made sure to get a bunch of pictures with them and before we parted ways I told the coach to keep in touch with me and let me know how they do at competition; which she ended up doing,

I sent a video message to them the night before their competition wishing them good luck. She sent me a video of their performance, which I have to admit made me feel warm inside, I loved seeing them do so well.

The last night in Jersey, Kyle flew down to take all of us out to the Rain Forest Café as a thank you for being such wonderful staff members. He once again was showing his respect for his employees. We all dressed up nice and went to the board walk and got a table for eight. Kyle told us to get whatever we wanted on the menu. I ordered a delicious shrimp pasta and scarfed it down like a mad man. I had been living off of mac and cheese for two weeks so it was nice to have a good meal. After we finished off a huge volcano dessert we made sure to get a staff picture before we left.

As I laid in bed that night I couldn't have been more excited for the sun to rise and the time to come for me to be home but I was also thankful for this opportunity I was given. I met so many nice people, learned more than I ever thought I would and most importantly was taking steps towards my future. I wouldn't have had it any other way.

When I got back in town the first thing I did was give Nick and Bubbas a huge hug and kiss. I had never been more excited to see them. After saying hello I ran to our room and plopped down on my big comfy bed. As summer was nearing the end I couldn't help but think about what the future held for me and about where I was now and where I was a couple of months ago. I was amazed at how many things can change so fast..................

Kyle had taken my suggestion earlier on in the summer and hired Nick to work a skills camp with him, me and two other girls. Nick couldn't have been more excited, he had wanted more than anything to work for Kyle. Nick too was like a sponge wanting to absorb every ounce of experience he could get in this industry. He worked his first camp ironically at a high school right next to Five Star. He knew a bunch of the girls on the team so he wasn't nervous at all for his first camp. It was a great opportunity for him to show off to Kyle that he knew what he was talking about and could be a great instructor if given the opportunity.

By the end of the camp Kyle told Nick that he was VERY impressed at how well he worked with the athlete's and that he actually wanted him and I to drive down to a skills camp by ourselves in Carterville, Illinois. We were excited that he not only trusted us with this but thought highly enough of us to allow us to instruct a camp completely on our own. We told him that we would love to and to send us the information via email about the location, hotel, times…etc. and we would be there.

39

I WOULD HAVE never guessed that a trip out to Carterville, Illinois would have such a huge impact on my life, but it did. After the six hour drive to southern Illinois, Nick and I finally arrived in Carterville. After checking in at our Super 8 motel we decided that we would go to the Applebee's right across from the hotel. You could tell that town had just had a Friday night football game because as we were sitting eating our dinner, football players and coaches walked in and filled the restaurant. Maybe it was their southern accents or maybe it was the way they used their manners, but whatever it was, there was something about this small town that made Nick and I feel so at peace and so comfortable. After we finished our dinner we made our way back to the motel for the night. We had a nearly ten hour day ahead of us and we would need all the rest we could get. It would be our first time working alone together, and it would show us a lot about how we would run a gym with one another. I was eager to see how the day would play out.

The next morning I woke up with a horrible sore throat and could barely speak. I had caught a bad cold overnight. This was not a great way to start off a camp but I still had a smile on my face though and couldn't fight the excitement I was feeling. I told Nick that he would have to be doing a lot of the talking or at least help me out.

After we finished getting ready we made our way down to the tiny lobby where a waffle maker was. We made ourselves some warm waffles. For such a small motel the place was very well kept. It was almost like a nice little vacation for the two of us. Once we finished our waffles we gathered our back packs and headed out the door to go to the high school. We had made sure to take a trip there the night before just to make sure we knew where it was so we wouldn't get lost. When we walked into the school, Nick and I couldn't help but be impressed by how new everything was. Everything about the school was modern. We heard voices to our left and assumed that the cheerleaders were the only ones in the school since it was the weekend. We followed their voices to the gymnasium.

When we walked in the first thing we saw were two girls vacuuming a cheer floor. When the coach saw us walk in she stood up with a huge smile on her face and welcomed us. She told us that she was so excited for us to be here. Her name was Linda and I immediately fell in love with her. She pointed at the girls vacuuming and told me that they had been late to the football game last night and as their punishment they had to vacuum the whole floor. The girls laughed when the coach said this and I couldn't help but chuckle along and agree with her style of coaching, it was almost motherly.

Once everyone filed in I had them sit down and with my hoarse voice I introduced Nick and I. I cracked a joke that I sounded a little like Miley Cyrus which broke the ice. After we were done warming them up I had them line up in their stunt groups and we began teaching them new skills. Until this day I have never met a more respectful group of girls, maybe it was because they were in the south or because it was a small town but for whatever reason they used their manners, always saying yes mam and no sir. They were hands down the best listeners I had ever taught. I've always preached to my athletes to be quiet and listen to what your instructors are telling you to do because if you're talking over them then you are not doing nobody any good. Talking over me and not listening was just wasted time because I would have to repeat the whole instruction again. Because these girls never talked over me we accomplished way more than I ever could've imagined. We were flying through new skills left and right and all of these girls had determination and they weren't gunna stop.

Once the day was over I gathered all the girls around and told them how impressed I was and that I had never, in all the skills camps I worked with thus far, met a group of girls so hardworking, so determined and so respectful. You could tell that their faces, even though exhausted, lit up when I told them this. They thanked Nick and me and before parting ways we made sure to tell them to eat a good dinner and go to bed early because they had an even longer day ahead of them tomorrow. Before we left, the coach pulled us aside and asked what we thought of the girl's skill level. They had placed 11th at state last year and were dying to place top ten this year. We told her that in all honesty if they kept up the same work ethic that they were showing us today, that there were no doubts, in our mind, that they would place in the top ten. Some of the skills we were teaching them today were difficult for level five all-star cheerleaders to learn in one day. This made the coach's eyes light up and she was so thankful for all of our help. She told me to rest up because I wasn't looking so well, and I told her not to worry, that I would.

Later that night I was having a difficult time breathing and couldn't manage to stop coughing for more than two minutes. I decided that I needed some medicine to ease my symptoms so Nick and I jumped in the van and headed towards a Walgreens to get some medicine and some things for the hotel room. With a blanket wrapped around me, Nick told me to hang tight while he went into the store to get me medicine. It was 9:50 pm and they were closing in about ten minutes. When he came back with two bags filled with things he had a look of astonishment on his face. When I asked him what was wrong he told me that he had forgotten his wallet at the hotel room. I asked him how he got the groceries he had with him and he told me that an elderly woman had bought them for him. I couldn't believe how nice people were down here. When I asked him how much everything was he told me forty dollars. I couldn't help but feel awful inside. Nick replied "Yeah how do you think I felt?" He said he tried telling her that it was okay that he could go to the hotel and get his wallet and go to another store but she told him to buy someone else groceries if they ever needed them and to pay it forward. A warm sensation came over my heart, this is why I loved the south, people had this mentality of "paying it forward" If everyone could just show an act of random kindness once a day, that it would cause a ripple effect and spread cheer amongst the world. This feeling made me miss the south. I couldn't wait to get back to my roots someday, things were just so much more care-free and laid back in the south; people knew how to appreciate the little things in life.

Later that night things weren't getting any better, I was starting to feel worse so I decided to text my mom and Linda asking where an emergency medical clinic was so that maybe during tomorrow's lunch break I could go get some medicine. Linda told me of one that opened at three, but our lunch break was from one until two. She told me that it was completely okay to switch their lunch time if I need to. Once again, I couldn't believe how gracious and kind people were here. I told her that that wouldn't be necessary and that she was so kind to offer. I decided to go to the emergency room two miles down the road. My mom told me that it was a good idea, so I grabbed my blanket and headed out the door with Nick to the ER. When we arrived there wasn't any waiting, they got me in immediately. When I checked in at the front desk the attendants were so friendly, joking around about how busy they were. After they gave me a wrist band with my information on it they sent me straight back to a room and had me sit on the medical table. When the doctor came in he asked me what my symptoms were and determined that I had some kind of upper reparatory infection. He told me that he was going to give me a shot. Although I have five tattoos, when it comes to shots, I'm a complete baby. I must admit I have gotten better over the years and I can take shots in the arm fairly well but not the hip so much. When the nurse came in she told me that I'd have to pull down my pajama pants because I was going to have to take the shot in the butt. I asked her if I could get it in the arm. I told her that I couldn't stand getting pricked in the butt. She told me that maybe if I was 400 pounds she could give it to me in my arm but I had no fat on them, so the butt it was.

When I bent over she wiped a cold alcohol wipe on the injection site and told me that I'd feel a pinch. When she dug the needle into my butt I couldn't help but clench but the pain actually wasn't that bad and I joked around laughing and saying that it wasn't as bad as

I thought it'd be. The nurse chuckled then left the room and told me she'd be back in a few minutes. As soon as I started walking the worst pain came over the injection site and I started to scream, it felt like my butt muscles were cramping and twisting into a knot. I started screaming in pain and grabbed Nick's arm. You could tell by the look on his face that he was terrified. I told him that I was about to pass out that I couldn't see and I couldn't hear anything. He called for a nurse and she came running in and laid me down on the table and got a cool rag for my forehead. Once my hearing came back I asked what had happened, she told me that sometimes when people are in so much pain they're tense up so bad that they'll slow their heart rate down and cause themselves to faint. I felt like a big baby as I sat there and waited for the pain to subside, but it really was the most pain I had ever felt.

After the pain was tolerable and I could walk again the nurse released me, by this time it was about three in the morning and we were exhausted. When we got back to the hotel room we both set alarms for the morning and fell asleep as soon as our heads hit the pillow.

The next morning I woke up feeling like a new person, although my voice was still raspy, probably from trying to use it so much the day before, I felt amazing. We packed up our things, we wouldn't be staying in the hotel another night, although we debated the day before whether we should because after the camp we'd have a six hour drive home during the night and we weren't sure if we could handle that, but we decided that we could. When we arrived to camp on day two the girls looked a lot more fatigue but just as excited to learn as the day before. We had to put together a routine for the parents by the end of the camp and they were eager to show off the new skills they had just learned.

The morning was spent putting together a pyramid for the parent's performance and before we knew it time flew and it was lunch time. Before we left for lunch Nick and I stunted for a little bit to show the girls what we could do and Linda joked around that when we get married our wedding cake topper should be a girl and a guy stunting; this cracked us up, it was a pretty clever idea though.

When we got back from lunch a little early, Nick and I talked to Linda about how amazing these girls were and that we wish we could make them an all-star team and try to take them to a nationals, or even better World's, that they had the determination to do it. The girls overheard us and got extremely excited about this and I believe it opened their eyes to how good they really were. Nick and I certainly were not the ones to lie.

After lunch we finalized their performance and practiced it a couple of times before the parents started coming in. Once everyone was seated I made an announcement to all the parents about how they've raised amazing daughters and they should be very proud of how far they've come over the past few days. The parents were taken aback by our words and huge smiles crept up on each one of their faces, you could tell that they were honored by our words. The girls lined up and I started counting out loud for them, the parents couldn't help but laugh as my voice cracked like a little boy, Nick, also laughing, told me to stop and took over the counting, giving me a break to rest my voice. The girls had an amazing performance, hitting all the new skills they had learned over the past two days. The parents were so impressed, clapping after every skill. Once the performance ended we made sure to get a group picture and say our good byes. I told the girls that we would try to come to one of their competitions and that we would definitely try to be at state to cheer them on. As we walked out of Carterville High School a peaceful feeling came over me. I had learned so much over the weekend and I was so thankful for everything that had happened. I learned that there are towns where people respect each other; there is kindness in the world. There are good-hearted people that pay it forward. But most importantly I learned that there are some parts of cheerleading that are being ran correctly… and this not only inspired me, but gave me hope for the future.

PART V
Nova

40

WHEN WE GOT back from Carterville which was the last skills camp that Nick and I did for the summer, things began changing at Five Star. I had mentioned to Angie about my plans for opening my own gym one day and if there was anything I could do around her gym to help me gain some experience I would be more than happy to help her out. I wanted to gain as much knowledge and experience that came with running a cheer business. She told me that I could shadow her but she warned me that she wasn't going to be the person that she portrayed to outsiders looking in. She told me that I was going to see a side of her that most people don't. She said that she cries almost every night worrying about the stresses of owning her gym and that the money coming into the business was barely profitable and that she was paying out of her own pocket for bathroom supplies and hair ties for the athletes. She told me that the best advice she could give someone that wanted to open their own gym was to not do it. Just hearing these words come out of her mouth instinctively made me feel protective over my athletes for some reason. This wasn't the peppy Angie that I thought I knew, the one that acted as if she loved her job. At that moment I had a gut feeling that something wasn't right.

As soon as summer ended and the fall session began at Five Star, a whole new wave of people entered the gym and I soon began to see why Angie would say some of the things she said to me. The gym that seemed to be organized and well put together over the summer was now a tornado of chaos. I guess they failed to mention to me that summer was just their slow time. The lobby that I thought was set up perfectly for the amount of people I perceived to be in the gym, was now a boiling room for parents to sit on top of each other and either gossip or listen to gossip. I found myself at times sitting at the front desk during my free time observing everything that happened in the lobby. I listened to parents talk about how unorganized the gym was. I watched the parents with their noses pressed up against the glass windows staring at their children. This would put pressure on the kids to do well during their practices or classes. I watched the quieter parents observe others and keep their ears perked trying to catch every ounce of gossip that was being spoken. I soon realized, in my opinion, that these parents were the ones that really ran the gym whether Angie wanted to believe it or not. I was learning that I would make sure that when I opened my gym that I would not have any parent or family members of an athlete working at the gym. Why you might ask? Because while I observed Five Star and their procedures I realized parents would try and succeed to get away with using Angie. She was too soft on them and she, in my opinion, would allow them to do whatever they wanted. I watched as Angie would storm into her office and have mental break downs, screaming that she was done and that they were closing the gym and that she was sick of it all. I watched as Dawn, her partner, calmly tell her that closing the gym wasn't going to happen. She would tell Angie to take a deep breath. Dawn, also in my opinion, seemed to be the stronger of the two. I listened to both of the owners tell me how they didn't get to see their families much and that all their time was either spent on the phone with a parent upset about something or a parent asking questions about something. Although I witnessed the behind scenes of what was really happening, I still loved working at Five Star. I just kept my concerns in the back of my mind and continued to take advantage of Angie letting me make observations.

Although I was happy, it was now the beginning of fall and all the teams in the gym had their routines for competition season. The international team that Angie said was going to happen was nowhere to be seen. I kindly approached her one day to ask her if there was still going to be an international team and that Nick and I were actually being offered to be on another local team. I told her if there wasn't going to be one at Five Star then would she give her approval to us to allow us to cheer at another gym. She told us that she was sure there would be an international team at Five Star but if we wanted to go cheer for the other gym then it would be okay. Nick and I thought about it for a long time, it was already fall and most teams were about to compete in a month. Even though we wanted to compete, we came to the conclusion that we wouldn't want to see our athletes see us competing in a different uniform. Along with the cost of the other gym's team and the drive being long, we decided to stick it out at Five Star and hope and patiently wait for their international team to be organized.

A few weeks went by and there was still no sign of a team so I approached Angie again nicely, she told me that she was just too busy to start one and that if I wanted to take full reigns of starting a team than I could. I took full advantage of this opportunity and went straight to work recruiting people that I had previously cheered with or knew through Nick. Within two weeks I had found more than enough people to be on the team. To my surprise everyone had amazing skill and if we practiced our butts off hard enough we could easily make it to World's, which was my goal. Most of the potential athletes on the team had never been to Worlds and I wanted to give them that experience more than anything. I was determined to do anything I could to make it happen.

Because our team was older, I talked to Angie about making the prices for the team as low as she possibly could. She advised me that that was completely okay and gave me the lowest they could do for monthly fees. I got these fees down to $60 a month, which was nothing compared to most gyms who usually charged a minimum of $125. I also asked Angie if it was okay if I designed our own uniforms. The ones that she was ordering for the rest of her teams in the gym were way too expensive for the athletes on my team. She also told me that this was okay. I was able to find a customer friendly uniform company, Rebel Athletics, who was able to make cute uniforms for $150 instead of Five Star's approximately $300. On top of the savings cost, I was also able to get my mom's employer to sponsor our music. This was another $500 saved. We set up two really good fundraisers that were expected to bring in a lot of money. We named the team Nova.

Once our first practice came around I felt the biggest sense of accomplishment. I was standing in front of a great group of kids who were all determined to work their butts off and have a great season. Not only that, a few weeks ago a student in my hyper flex class told me a story of how she had to switch schools because she was being bullied, this touched my heart deeply since I had the worst senior year in high school due to bullying. I decided that instead of just cheering for our gym, our team should cheer for a cause and that cause would be anti-bullying. I told the athletes about my idea and they were all on board and more than excited to cheer for a cause, to a lot of them, it actually touched them personally. I had found out that a majority of the teammates had been bullied themselves throughout school and wanted to do whatever they could to prevent that from happening to another child.

Nathan was a huge help to Nova, he was a Junior Ambassador for a cheer organization. He was an advocate for anti-bullying because he knew firsthand what it was like to be bullied. Him, Nick and I sat down and came up with a uniform for the team. We decided to put an orange ribbon on our hips to support the cause. And not only that, we even took it as far as to put a voice over in our music that said "Our colors may be pink, but we wear the orange, this is for the kids, you all stay strong." which another teammate had come up with. I loved this team more than anything. I loved the fact that we were all in this together and listened to everyone's opinions. Being that Nick and I were the coaches and organizers for the team, we always wanted to make sure we spoke to and got everyone's opinions on uniforms, music...etc. We didn't want anyone to feel left out. It had only been four weeks and I was already sizing the athletes for our uniforms, gotten our music and put together two awesome fundraisers, one of which was already in full swing. My mom was driving to work one day, and at a red light she stopped next to a big truck that read on the side "Fill me up and you could make $1,500 for your organization" My mom took the website off the side of the truck and the first thing she did when she got to work was research the company. She found out that it was a clothing and textile recycling company that took used clothes, blankets, shoe….etc. and recycled whatever was too dirty to give to the needy and made wash clothes and wood chips for playgrounds out of the material. They paid by the pound of articles that they received. My mom and I did the math and if everyone brought in at least ten bags of used clothing everyone could have their uniform paid for. Everyone loved this idea because it wasn't your typical cookie dough fundraiser and more importantly it didn't require any money to start or to ask people for. We would make a 100% profit while at the same time helping a good cause. The bags of clothing started to flow in from everywhere, families, friends, churches and athletes… and soon we started filling rooms full of clothing. I had no doubt in my mind that we would easily be able to fundraise the money for our uniforms.

While this fundraiser was happening, my mom also found another one that we decided to kick off as well. Unlike the recycling company this one did involve selling to people, but it was almost too good to resist. It was unique and original and we had never seen it being used in our area before. My mother found a "Fun Pasta" organization which made little bags of pasta in all shapes, sizes and colors, anywhere from cat shapes to collegiate teams and even to cheerleading shapes. We advertised this everywhere to be a good stocking stuffer or a present for the holidays. There was something for everyone. The bags were reasonably priced so people bought them like crazy.

41

OUR TEAM WAS moving along perfectly and in a very short time. It was crazy how fast Nick, my mother and I had put everything together. Things were going so good. We were representing Five Star and Team Nova the best we could and doing a great job at it. However, I've learned in life that when things seem too good to be true, they usually are, and that's when my mother received a phone call from Kim, our agent at the textile company. She called us to ask if there were two fundraisers going on at Five Star, confused, my mother said no and that we were the only people in the gym doing it. Kim said "okay" she just wanted to make sure because someone else had called from Five Star wanting to set up the same fundraiser. My mom thanked her for calling and then called me right after extremely frustrated that someone else would try and do the same fundraiser in the same gym without even consulting us first.

My mother sent an email to Angie and Dawn letting them know how upset she was that someone else decided to do this at the same time as us. It almost caused us to lose our fundraiser and that she found it extremely disrespectful to me to not approach me first. We were under the impression that we were allowed to work separately from the booster club. Not only did they contact the textile company, but one of the parents, who is a part of the booster club, saw our pasta fundraiser on Facebook and commented on one of our post *"Who is doing this fundraiser, because the whole gym was planning to do this fundraiser in a few weeks."*

The booster club is in charge of all fundraising that goes on in the gym. There is a fee that we had to pay to be a part of it so to save money we decided to do everything on our own with the approval of Dawn. The booster club and the owners of the gym are legally not allowed to mingle finances with each other but that doesn't mean that they can't communicate to them what fundraisers they are setting up in the gym. Dawn told me that she had no idea that the booster club was setting up any kind of pasta fundraiser. It was clear to me then that this parent hadn't really set up any kind of pasta fundraiser, that she was just making it seem like she had come up with the idea first and we were the ones taking the idea from her. My mom even took it as far as to call the pasta company and ask if anyone else from Five Star had contacted them about doing a fundraiser, and they said no. We knew that we caught her in a blatant lie. This is when we found out that all of our ideas were being taken from us. We wouldn't have minded sharing our ideas because they were great ones, but the booster club did not have any respect for us to come ask us first.

Angie and Dawn told us that from now on I would have to go through the booster club first with any fundraising ideas so not to have any overlapping ideas. My mother and I immediately took offense to this because if we did that they would steal our ideas from us, just like they tried to do with the clothes and pasta. Angie and Dawn did circles avoiding the issue, telling me that they appreciated me and our hard work. My mom got extremely frustrated and told them that our concerns were not if they appreciated me or not, but that the booster club was in fact stealing our ideas and that we did not want to go through them first because who's to say they wouldn't say it was their idea and not ours and again emphasized that she felt as if they were being disrespectful towards me. We decided to move on from the issue though and focus on the team and making it successful until Angie sent an email back to my mother calling her disrespectful. She told my mom that she had spent hours texting her the night before while her children cried and begged her to spend time with them. She told my mom that all she wanted to do was to make sure that no one in the gym was hurt. I wasn't going to get involved with the dispute until Angie said my mother was being disrespectful. I was furious. I sent an email to her with months' worth of pent up anger and emotions towards her about my opinion of her gym and how it was being ran. That put a fire in their ass. Even though I mentioned throughout my email numerous times that I meant not to offend anyone, they got offended and I couldn't blame them. I was calling them out on all the flaws in their gym. I was running a more successful team in their gym than they were running themselves. The one team I was in charge of already had their music and was about to get their uniforms. The other teams in the gym were starting to question why this four week team was getting things done before them. Their teams had been together for months now and not to mention they were competing in a week and they didn't even have their uniforms. They also didn't have their music and didn't have parts of their routine finished. They would end up having to drop out of their first competition. Parents started to ask questions, as did I. Why didn't these athletes have their uniforms and music that they paid for? And now they were down one competition that they had paid for. I also started getting paid in cash instead of checks. It didn't seem right to me, but I put a fake smile on and continued coaching my teams as if nothing wrong.

Angie and Dawn called a meeting with me to discuss the email. Nothing got solved. In my opinion, they basically just wanted to put me in my place but there was nothing they could really say because everything in the email was true. I apologized for hurting their feelings, but told them that I had begun the email with a clear statement that said I meant to offend no one and ended with that same clear statement. Their only defense was that I should have talked to them sooner and so I nodded my head and apologized.

Ever since that email Angie acted different towards me, almost as if she didn't want me in her gym. She told my mother during a phone conversation that if it wasn't because everyone loved me in the gym that she would fire me because of what I said to her. This seemed outrageous to me. Why an owner would ever say that in the first place confused me. If she felt that way she should have just fired me, but in my opinion, she didn't want to taint her good image. She knew that if she fired me that there would be a lot of anger and a lot of questions from parents.

About a week went by and I started to come home from the gym every night crying. I couldn't stand being around Angie any longer. It is my guess that she was trying to make me quit so she wouldn't have to fire me. It got to the point where Nick and my mother told me that I should just leave. I couldn't bear the thought of not coaching my minis and international team. I had grown so attached to the children on minis that they were like my own children. Seeing their faces every week and watching them progress and grow up made me so proud and happy. I just couldn't see myself not being their coach and the same thing went for international. I was now running this team and had these kids' hopes up high that we were going to have a great season and possibly make it to World's. I honestly believed we could and I couldn't bear the thought of letting them all down.

I decided to try to stick it out but things didn't get better and I started to get depressed. Nick pulled me aside and told me: "Morgan, you have to stop thinking about others and think about yourself. If you can't be happy then you won't be able to make other people around you happy. If these people truly know who you are they will understand your reason for leaving. If you tell them the truth then they won't be mad at you and they will support you." He made a very valid point and after a few nights of thinking about it I decided that ultimately he was right. I decided to resign my position and sent an email to Angie, as well as posting it in a status on Facebook on my profile for all the parents and athletes to see. I didn't want anything to be misconstrued or misinterpreted and I wanted everyone to have the same explanation coming directly from me. Nick had been right about the out pouring of love and support by the parents and athletes. It was amazing. I didn't directly receive any negative comments, posts or messages from anyone but instead I received messages that they were saddened by the fact that I would no longer be coaching their sons and daughters. They wished me the best of luck with whatever future endeavors I encountered and that I would be missed tremendously. Although I was happy that no one was upset, at the same time it made it even harder to part ways with these people that I had grown so close to. I had to admit though it felt like a weight had been lifted off of my shoulders and every step I took felt a little lighter.

Later that evening I was lying on the couch trying to figure out what my next step would be since I was no longer coaching. Because I was no longer a part of Nova, my mother and I decided to continue our anti-bullying campaign along with another partner and decided to open a non-profit organization named Just Say No to Bullying. The cause was still dear to my heart and I still wanted to continue to raise awareness.

Right before I had resigned from Five Star, my mother had made bracelets for the team to sell that that read "Just say NO to BULLYING, Stay Strong" on them. With the money raised we were going to raise awareness for bullying by visiting schools and telling our own personal experiences and what to do and how to recognize bullying when kids see it happen, not only that, but to share acts of kindness with people every day because a kind gesture can go a long way.

I was no longer working at a gym so my new mission now was to get a job as soon as possible, it was so important for my future. As I was lying on the couch that night after I resigned, researching some local gyms that I could apply to, I stumbled upon a post that Nathan had made on Facebook and noticed that it had a bunch of comments on it, it read:

It really hurts me to see people sporting the words STAY STRONG and ANTIBULLYING without understanding the true meaning. Posting statuses about how pissed you are about something that happened and putting other people down IS bullying. And it is the worst form of it. So please keep your negative thoughts to yourself instead of spilling them publicly for younger influential kids to see that it's okay to see these things. It really makes me mad to see people getting involved in ANTIBULLYING and they can't even realize that they are the bullies themselves.

I knew instantly that the post was about my resignation email that I had written to Angie and posted on Facebook. When I saw the status my first instinct and what I wanted to do more than anything else was to post "Are you fucking kidding me? You're going to try to sit there and preach to me that I don't know what bullying is? I went through it my whole senior year and dozens of my athletes have confided in me their struggles with bullying every day. I know nothing about bullying? I didn't post a status about how pissed I was about something, I posted a status that was heart breaking for me to write and to let people know my reasoning behind my resignation. They deserved to know why I was leaving and I most certainly was not being a bad influence. If anything I was being a good influence by showing kids that you should always stand up for yourself. And really…you're going to try and call me a bully? I was the furthest from being a bully. I treated everyone equally and with respect. I couldn't help it if people didn't like to hear the cold honest truth. I sure as hell wasn't going to be the one to lie and put on a front. But… I didn't post it. I decided to be the bigger person and let him rant on about it and it didn't take long for other people to defend me. After Angie commented on his status saying "Well said, I love you!!!" with a smiley face, a few others joined in with her, praising his words.

Debbie, a close family friend of mine and who knew everything that had happened between the gym and I, replied to Nathan explaining to him that he was a bit confused on the definition of bullying. She explained to him that calling someone out who is stating the truth about a situation she was in isn't bullying. She said it was a nice concept, but not real. Nathan snapped back that he was an avid anti-bullying spokesperson and that he has gotten bullied 75% of his school years and that there is no worse feeling in the world. He said posting statuses about his gym and his boss, who he thought was in fact the sweetest thing on the planet, was extremely disrespectful. He went on to rant about how I was opening the non-profit for my own personal gain. When I saw this I couldn't help but comment, he needed to be put in his place.

I said to Nathan that I was glad that he thought I opened my non-profit for my own personal gain and that he, out of all people, should know I'm the most selfless person and have been bullied myself. I told him that there was a lot more going on than he or anyone else knew. He snapped back that he knew everything and that he had read the emails and seen the hurtful things I had said to Angie and that I out of all people should know not to bully and that I couldn't always get what I wanted. He said that I shouldn't have thrown a fit about it. He told me that being the coach of Nova didn't give me power to dictate everything that happened and that there are two owners of the gym that have complete control over the team. He told me that I should look in the mirror sometime and just say no to bullying. Some of my athletes began to defend me as I wrote out my lengthy come back to his immature and unknowledgeable comment. Once I was finished and sent the comment over I knew that there was no way he would be able to come back with something, I never picked fights I couldn't win because of one reason...I always admit if I am in the wrong and this time I most certainly was not in the wrong. I replied to his comment asking him if he knew that Five Star gave me complete control of Nova. I asked him if he was in all the meetings and if he had heard all the phone calls that happened between us. I asked him if he had saw the email that I had sent to Angie and did he see the part where I repeat over and over that I meant no disrespect and that I meant to upset no one and that it was strictly what I was observing. I asked him to please point out where I didn't say that in the email. I told him that ever since that email was sent out I was constantly targeted because some people just couldn't handle the truth. I told him that I felt sorry for how mislead and how immature he was acting and that I could promise him and his mother that they didn't know everything because they weren't there. I told him that my intentions were to make a successful team and get deserving kids to World's while supporting a great cause at the same time. I told him how hard it was to work in a gym that does not support or respect you and that I for one was the furthest thing from a bully. In a sarcastic manner, he thanked me for my opinions and told me that they were greatly appreciated and called me a bully for calling him immature and disrespectful. This was my favorite part of the argument. I responded quickly by saying that I never called him immature or disrespectful that I simply said he was acting like it. This is not a form of bullying and that this is a discussion or argument. Debbie topped my comment off with a cherry saying that his definition of a bully is broad and misleading and that when someone is acting immature and disrespectful that it is not bullying to tell them how they are acting. She told him that he should be able to handle some criticism without calling it bullying. All he could do after that was say that he was going to delete his post, not because he didn't want to stand up and plea his case but because he was ending the discussion. Right before he deleted his post I managed to get one last comment in that said he was deleting the post because I made him look bad. Before he deleted the post he continued with hurtful words and told me that I will always be a bully and that I think I'm some kind of saint and for me to look in the mirror. He then deleted the post. I wanted to say to his last comment that he was not using "bullying" in the correct definition.

After the post was deleted everything subsided and Nick and I began to look for new coaching jobs. It didn't take us long to get offers from a lot of places. Our resume page had helped us out a lot. One of the places that wanted to hire us the most was Five Star's rival gym, Ignite Cheerleading. I told Nick that we should go check it out and that it wouldn't hurt. When we met the owner she was young and actually looked a lot like me. She came off very nice and I loved her philosophy on running a gym. Instead of her asking the questions I actually asked most of them to her. I was basically interviewing her and not the other way around. I was so worried about being mislead with a gym again and my walls were up. I really liked the program and I could tell it was going to grow within the next few years. It bothered me that they were only five miles from Five Star. I was already picturing the drama that would come along with us working there. We told the owner that we would keep her offer in mind but that we wanted to keep our options open.

When we got into the car after talking to the owner, Nick immediately told me "no". When I asked him what he meant, he said that he didn't want to work there. I told him that there were pros and cons and that we'd actually be able to keep a lot of our privates since it was so close to Five Star. But, after further discussion and not wanting to deal with the drama that would come along with working there, Nick and I agreed that it wouldn't be worth it.

That night we were feeling really low, we hated not working in a gym and it had been almost a week now since we were teaching and coaching. Just as we were in our weakest state we received a phone call from my mom. She explained to us that one of her friends knew a gym owner about an hour from our house that needed a coach ASAP. She gave us the number to the owner and we called her immediately.

42

HER NAME WAS Rachel. She picked up the phone and immediately I knew she had a fun and bubbly personality. She explained to me that she was the owner of Lake Zurich Elite and that the local high school varsity cheer team that her daughter was on fell a part because their coach was no longer there. She explained to me that the team wanted to finish out their season competing with each other. They wanted to cheer for Lake Zurich Elite as a senior level four coed team. Rachel told them that she would be more than happy to let them cheer for her. The team had only been at her gym for three weeks and Rachel was coaching them but she is a nurse and told me that she was struggling doing both and that she was looking for coaches for the team. We told her that we were definitely interested and would stop by at their next practice to check it out. She told us that if we liked it that they were actually competing this weekend at Jamlive and that she could get us in as their coach. The next day, after driving a little over an hour north of our apartment, we arrived at the gym. When we walked in there was one red colored cheer floor and mirrors all over the wall. This was Nick's dream, to be coaching a team with me and the best part about it was that they were high school kids. Unlike me, Nick preferred coaching older kids.

We met all the athletes on the team and watched them do their routine. We were expecting to see a pretty sloppy team since they had just gotten their routine three weeks ago but they were actually pretty good and surprised the heck out of us. They had some really raw talent and I could tell that they all had an amazing bond with each other, which was a plus. I pulled Nick aside towards the end of visit and asked him about his thoughts on coaching. Before I could barely get the statement out of my mouth, he said "YES". He felt like this was a great opportunity for us to coach together and he loved that they were older, I nodded my head. Nick had always seemed to have really good instincts so we told Rachel at the end of practice that we'd love to coach the team. She was so excited. She gave us the information for the competition that was being held in two days and told us she would see us then. She thanked us and told us that she was so happy and thankful that we decided to coach Phoenix. The team also had a tumbling coach, Greg, who we got along with instantly. He was a shorter guy with bright red hair and a goofy personality; you couldn't help but love him. On our way home we stopped at my mother's house to let her know what had happened. She was so happy to see our faces lit up with excitement again. We told her that they were competing this weekend and she responded with a "holy crap, that soon huh?" and we laughed and said yes. She told me that she would be there supporting our team and that she couldn't wait for our first competition as coaches.

43

WHEN COMPETITION DAY came Nick and I dressed up in our flashy outfits, me wearing a black long sleeved fitted dress and some black boots while he sported dark jeans and a black button up shirt. It was our first time showing the world we were coaches and we wanted to make a good impression. To no surprise, Five Star dropped out of this competition as well. Word on the street was that they still weren't ready to compete and still had no uniforms. I was so happy that we were out of that gym.

When we arrived to the convention center, only a few minutes from our house, we couldn't help but feel strange walking in, it was our first time being at a competition and NOT competing. I couldn't tell if I felt proud or sad, I think a little bit of both. When we walked over to our team, Greg was standing there with a big smile on his face. He looked happy to have us there. The girls on the team were putting on their makeup and the guys were laying on their backpacks listening to music. Greg led us to the coaches stand to get our bracelets and when he told the lady that he needed two, she just handed them to him. We could have been anyone dressed up nice trying to get free admission. She just handed over the bracelets without checking names or ID's and I couldn't help but laugh. While the team sat in a circle getting ready I looked over my shoulder to my right and saw that the team I had done my first skills camp with Kyle in Wisconsin was sitting in a circle. I ran over to them and gave the owner a big hug and asked her if they had competed yet and she told me no, that they were actually about to go to warm ups. I wished the girls good luck and complimented them on their uniforms, they looked very classy. After parting ways I went over to our team and had them get in position for the beginning of their routine to mark it out. I could tell on their faces that they were nervous, for most of them it was their first all-star competition. After running through their routine a couple of times it was finally time to go to warm ups. Rachel made sure to explain to them how warm ups were ran and to not focus on other teams around them, that it was extremely distracting. When we walked into the room, Craig, from Ultimate was there. He is a local gym owner who had coached them last year and knew most of them. They were all really excited to see him and when he said hello to me he twirled me around and told me that I looked gorgeous in my dress. I thanked him and he wished us good luck and that he'd be cheering for us in the crowd. Warm ups went amazing, they hit everything perfectly and I was so proud of them. Once again, in the back of my head I thought that it wasn't a good sign, that perfect warm ups usually meant bad performances.

The looks on their faces were almost ghost like. I'm not sure if it was from all the nerves they had or from being intimidated by the teams warming up around them. I gathered them before they went on the stage and told them, "Any fear that you have, any doubts that are crossing through your mind, stops here. I know I've only known you guys for a couple of days but I can already tell that you guys are an amazing team and that this is going to be a good season. Go out there with a smile on your face and perform with confidence" and with that the announcer called their team name and they made their way on stage. As I followed behind, Rachel looked at me and told me that this was the hardest part about being a coach, not being able to be up there with them and letting them go, knowing all we could do now is hope and pray that they had a good routine.

When the music started two of the girls threw their standing tucks and they both touched down. It wasn't even five seconds into the routine and they already had two deductions. Half way through the routine a few stunts fell and after that it was over. The emotions on their faces were defeat and you could tell that they had given up. When their routine ended and they walked off the stage I walked up to one of the girls that touched down on her standing tuck, she was crying her eyes out, I asked her what she was thinking before she threw her tuck and she told me with red swollen eyes "That I wasn't going to land it." and I told her that's why she didn't land it. It had just dawned on me that this team had all the talent in the world but they lacked confidence and that was a lot harder to teach than skill. I knew Nick and I had a challenge in front of us, but we were ready to face anything.

PART VI
Lake Zurich Elite—Phoenix

44

COACHING PHOENIX WAS my first experience coaching not just an older team, but a higher leveled team. They tested Nick and me every day with their attitudes. They had been through nine coaches together in the past year and I believed they thought we were just another one passing along but we wanted to make sure they knew we weren't. At one of the practices one of the boy's back talked Nick. Nick is the last person to put up with that so he told the boy that if he was going to act that way for him to leave the gym. He also told him that if he didn't want to be a part of this team that the doors were over there. At one point we threatened to make the team a level three at Jamfest Super Nationals, the biggest competition of the season for them. A lot of the athletes were upset with that threat. We told them at the end of a practice that they weren't showing us that they were a level four team. No one was throwing their level four tumbling and that making them level three was the last thing we wanted to do but that we weren't going to set them up for failure. We told them straight up that if we were to compete at Nationals tomorrow that they would get stomped on by the other teams. Some of the athletes nodded in agreement that they understood. They were the leaders of the team. Some of the others athletes, to my surprise gave horrible attitudes from there on out. They were obviously mad at the fact that they might be competing as a level three team at Nationals. Instead of working harder they started to show acts of rebellion. We sat them down at the end of a practice and wanted to clear the air. We asked those who were upset to speak up and tell us their thoughts. The boy who back talked Nick told us that he thought it was dumb that we were making them level three. I told him that we weren't making them a level three that Nick and I were simply saying that they weren't showing us a level four team and we weren't going to set them up for failure. I told him that his bad attitude needed to change and that if he thought I wanted them to go level three then he was mistaken. I knew they were a level four team they just needed to prove it to me.

Later that night I received a text from that boy apologizing to Nick and me for the way he talked to us. He told us that he was just tired of losing and exhausted with what had happened to him over the past few years. He said that he was tired of going through coaches and most importantly that he was thankful that Nick and I were working our butts off to make this team happen. He said that he was going to start being more of a leader. I told him how good of a kid he was and that I completely understood where he was coming from. I told him that I knew the feeling all too well. I told him to keep his head up and keep working hard and that it would always pay off. He told me that he was ready to work his ass off. I told him that he may not realize it but the other athletes looked up to him and that his actions reflected how others would act. He was thankful for my words and promised me that things would change. With that conversation I fell a little bit more in love with this team. I knew they were all good kids and they had just been through a lot of crap. I wanted more than anything to give them a good remainder of their cheer season.

As the practices went by we prepared more and more for nationals. They were finally showing us that they were the team that we knew they could be. Nationals had a different score sheet than some of the other competitions we had been to. I had to re-work their routine and I spent seven hours doing it at home during my free time. I was so excited to show them the new routine and what I had in store for them. When I walked into practice that day ready to show them what I had worked on the last thing that I had expected to happen happened. A guy from the team, dressed in jeans and a sweatshirt and not in his practice wear, approached me needing to talk to me in private. I knew what he was about to tell me and it wasn't good by the look on his face. He told me that he had been offered to cheer for Craig, the gym owner who had twirled me around at Jamlive and told me how pretty I looked. My blood was boiling, because not only did Craig contact him, he contacted another one of our girls too who didn't even have the decency to show up and tell me in person. I asked him why he wouldn't just finish out the season with our team because the team that Craig wanted him to cheer on was a level five World's team and their season ran longer than ours. It didn't make sense to me why he wouldn't just wait it out and finish cheering with us and then go cheer for Craig. He told me that he had better opportunities over at Craig's gym. I was furious, I had spent seven hours of my own time working this routine for them to only show up with two people no longer on the team. I had been told by numerous people, athletes and coaches in the area that Craig was known for stealing athletes. I never made judgment about him because he never affected me personally but now if anyone asked me about Craig I would make sure to tell them my opinion on what kind of person I feel he is. I told the boy that was quitting to speak to Rachel or Rowe, the other gym owner. I told him that I didn't have time for this nonsense. I had a team to coach.

Nick saw that I was furious and tried calming me down. I just quietly whispered to him "what the hell are we supposed to do now?" Rowe also saw that I was upset and asked me what was going on. I told her everything that had just happened and she, just as I had, reacted like a firecracker and told me to continue to teach the new routine that she would find two athletes to replace the kids that were leaving if she couldn't convince them to stay. We continued practicing as if nothing had happened while both gym owners tried settling everything with the two athletes. I did as I was told and taught the new routine and everyone seemed to love it.

Later that night I received a text from Rachel telling me that we for sure lost the girl but that the boy decided to stay and finish the season with Phoenix. I was thankful for this news but at the same time frustrated that it had happened in the first place. I kept thinking in my head, that everything happens for a reason.

I loved being a part of Lake Zurich but because they were renting out part of a gymnastics gym I was not able to teach any privates or classes so I continued to look for another little side job at a gym and like fate one night when I was serving at Buffalo Wild Wings my old tumbling coach from years ago was sitting at one of my tables. I hadn't seen him in about eight years but he immediately recognized me and I asked him if he was still working at Elite, a gym that was only five minutes from my house. Elite is a gymnastics facility, not a cheer facility. He told me that he was still working there and I told him that I was involved in the cheer world now. He cringed and said that he had tried that once and couldn't stand it. I laughed and told him that I understood where he was coming from. There was a lot of drama that came along with the sport and unprofessionalism. He laughed at that statement and agreed. I told him that I would love to teach some tumbling classes at Elite and that if they ever needed extra help to give me a call and I'd be over there in a heartbeat. Seeing him that day, I knew that God had some plan for me, there was no way this guy just reappeared in my life for no reason and I couldn't wait to find out what that reason was.

45

IT WAS DECEMBER now and winter break was right around the corner. Phoenix was still looking for an extra athlete. Rachel told me not to worry that she would find someone before break ended and I trusted her.

For winter break, my brother, Nick and I decided we were going to Mississippi to visit my dad. The morning that we left a newspaper was in my mother driveway with a picture of me on the front page. Our non-profit was starting to grow and media outlets were starting to publish stories about me and the campaign that we had started. The article told my story of senior year. This was the first time I was telling the world and my town, my story. I was a little nervous. It was the first time telling anyone else besides my family and the few friends that I had what had happened. Even though it was common knowledge in my school I didn't broadcast it to everyone. I wasn't sure how people were going to respond but to my surprise I received an outpouring of messages from students, not just from my graduating class, but in other grades as well. They told me their stories of how they got or were getting bullied. I had no idea that it was such a huge issue in our town. Some of the people that I received messages from were the absolute last people I had ever expected to hear from. I just assumed because they made me laugh in some of my classes and were good looking and were athletes, that they never got bullied. Little did I know that some of my class mates would ditch lunch just so they didn't have to sit alone. Hearing these stories broke my heart and in a way reconnected me to some of the people I should have talked to since I was alone at school. I'm sure they assumed that I wasn't getting bullied either. I loved what I was doing and although I may not have been able to make everyone see the importance of kindness, I was doing something that touched home for some. It meant the world to me that they reached out and it gave me even more strength and encouragement to keep doing what I was doing with the anti-bullying non-profit.

On the way to Mississippi we hit a huge snow storm that lasted six hours. My brother decided that he wanted to drive the entire way and in between the slipping and the sliding there was no way Nick and I were going to get any rest. We were all on the edge of our seats the entire time looking at cars and semi's in the ditch.

Fourteen hours later, we had made it safely to our home town in Mississippi. We were excited, anxious and tired all at the same time. Nick was a little nervous that he was meeting my dad for the first time and wanted to make a good impression. I told him just being himself was enough and that I knew my dad would love him because he was the first guy that took care of me and respected me.

It was 5:00 in the evening when we got into town and my dad was still at work. We decided to stop by and say hello before we went to his house. When we stepped out of car on the gravel parking lot, my dad walked out of the shop with a huge smile on his face, I hadn't seen him in almost a year and he gave me a huge hug and then shook Nick's hand as they introduced themselves. We all walked into the shop and I introduced Nick to my younger half-brother, Mitch and my step mother, Suzy.

Later that evening I decided to take a nap by the warm fireplace in the living room. While I was asleep, Nick and my dad spent some time together talking while my dad grilled burgers. My dad asked Nick if he smoked weed and Nick laughed and told him no. Nick told him that he had tried it once and tripped out really bad and hated it and has never done it since. My dad liked that about Nick and continued to ask him a little bit more about him. Nick went on to tell him about his baseball career and if he ever wanted to get back into that he could but he loved cheerleading and was pursuing that with me.

For someone that doesn't understand cheerleading, especially my dad, it's hard for them to understand that it's a very profitable business. My dad was constantly telling me that I should go to college and become a physical therapist. I secretly think that he was worried that if I owned my own business, like he did, that I would always be stressed out. My business was going to be ran a lot different than his, he needed to see that. I wouldn't be stressed out like he was all the time because I had learn more over the past three years about how "not" to run a business and that I was more than ready to open a gym.

Talking to Nick, you could tell that my dad liked him. Nick was honest and respectful, and just an all-around good person. One of my favorite qualities about Nick is his ability to be so good around kids. He absolutely loves them. I watched him all week as he played with my little brother, throwing him on the couch and chasing him around the house, Mitch screaming from laughter. Mitch needed that more than anything. Mitch has very bad dyslexia and because of this he has a lot of trouble in school and never got to hang around many kids his age. He loved Nick and they became best friends within minutes of meeting.

There isn't a whole lot to do in Mississippi in the middle of winter so I called Marcie, the lady we were supposed to rent the gym from back when we almost opened up our gym. I asked her if Mississippi Cheer Academy was open, the gym that her two little daughters cheered at. She told me that Jake, her daughter's private instructor would be at the gym giving lessons and that we could stop by to stunt and tumble for a little bit. We were so happy, not just because it gave us something to do, but also because Nick and I hadn't stunted together in almost a month. It also gave me a chance to see Marcie again. I loved her and wanted to keep our relationship going.

When we arrived at the gym I introduced Marcie to Nick and she introduced both of us to Jake. He was our age who cheered at Mississippi State University. We instantly got along. He was just like us, very friendly and laid back. We were impressed with how nice the gym was, I hadn't ever been there and expected something a lot smaller. While stunting with Nick and Jake and Marcie's daughters, a sense of calmness came over me. Everyone in the gym was so well mannered and polite, it reminded me of Carterville and I had remembered why I had wanted to open a gym down here, people just seem to be much happier and less stressed. After being in that gym I wondered to myself if it was just Illinois that had such an issue with cheerleading, between the coaches sleeping and doing drugs with athletes, the gym hopping and the back stabbing and lying, I thought to myself that surely it had to be different in the south. I had hoped that it was because one day I'm going to open my gym here and get as far away from Illinois as I could get. The trip to Mississippi was well needed. It was a nice break from work up north and gave us some time to clear our minds. It also fueled and increased my desire to be motivated more than ever to build my resume and keep pursuing my dream.

46

THE DAY AFTER we got home from vacation I received a call from Jenny, the tumbling director over at Elite, asking me if I was available to come in and talk about an instructing position. I hadn't heard from her in years and she too was one of my coaches when I power tumbled at Elite. It was so good to hear her voice. I learned most of my tumbling at Elite and had some of my best memories competing on their tumbling team. We set up a date to meet the next morning and discuss what she was looking for in an instructor. This meeting easily turned into a catch up conversation on the past eight years. As we sat in her office, the first thing I noticed was her engagement ring. I was so excited for her, I had known her when she was just in high school and now she was in her mid-twenties and getting married, it is crazy how fast time flies by.

As we sat there I told her that after tumble team I actually joined all-star cheerleading, and that's what I've been involved with in the past few years. After I told her that she asked me if I had have ever heard of the name Craig. He was a guy that approached her about partnering up their two gyms. I told her "Oh yeah, don't even get me started on him." and she laughed. She told me that that was a common response that she got from people when she spoke his name. I explained to her what had happened with our athletes a couple of weeks ago involving him. She told me that her staff members told her it wasn't a good idea to partner up with him and that he would just steal all of her good athletes and put her out of business. She took their advice and turned down his proposal.

She went on to tell me that they'd only need me on Saturday mornings. I told her that this worked out perfectly with both my jobs at Lake Zurich and Buffalo Wild Wings. She also told me that next year they were looking at starting a cheerleading program and asked if I'd be interested in helping out. I told her that I and my boyfriend would be more than willing to help and she was excited to hear this. She gave me her number and told me to call her if I had any questions. She said that she would see me on Saturday when I started my new classes. I was so glad that I was finally getting back into teaching classes as well as coaching on the side. I was starting to become really busy now with my three jobs but I was okay with that. I was like a sponge soaking up all the experience and knowledge I could.

My first day working at Elite was everything I had expected and more. I worked mostly with younger kids, and they instantly became attached to me. I couldn't wait to watch them progress throughout the session. I had classes from nine in the morning until one thirty in the afternoon. After that I went home and took a quick nap before I started my shift at Buffalo Wild Wings. Saturday's were going to be a long for me especially since I closed the bar side of the restaurant until two in the morning.

That night my mom walked in around nine while the rush started to die down, she visited from time to time just to check on me and make my night. I loved seeing my family come into the restaurant. When she sat down at one of my tables she had a strange look on her face, like she had something bad to tell me. When I asked her what was wrong she told me that she didn't want to tell me while I was working. I told her to tell me anyway. She took a deep breath and told me that her house had been broken into and that someone had stolen my grandfathers' ring. I almost started crying but kept my composure so that none of my tables would see that I was upset. She told me that he was still looking down on us from heaven and that it must have happened for a reason. I didn't care though I wanted to hunt down whoever took it and get it back but I knew that there was nothing we could do. She stayed and talked with me for a little while and ordered some food to go. There was a Packer's playoff game going on that was almost over and the place was about to be empty. I was going to be left with a lot of cleaning to do so she kissed me good bye and told me to text her when I got off work.

As the night went on I felt like my feet were about to fall off, I was so tired and so sore from standing all day and so upset about my grandfathers' ring that I just wanted to go home and be with my doggie and boyfriend. After finally getting out of work I jumped in my car and headed home so eager to lie in my big comfy bed. When I walked into my apartment there was no doggie and no Nick to greet me. Confused, I called for my dog and when I heard jingle bells and paws running across the floor, I wondered what the heck was going on. I wondered if Nick had gotten Diesel a jingle bell collar or something. Diesel turned the corner of my living room and ran towards me, he had a heart shaped box around his neck with words that read "Be Mine" on it. I immediately started laughing and saying "awe" because of how cute he looked. Nick turned the corner as well with a big smile on his face. I opened the box while Nick sat on the couch with a panic look on his face. I saw that there were candy hearts in the box and I thanked him for his kind little gift and told him that I loved him. He told me that there was something else in the box and to dump it out, so I did. When I did a ring fell out with a note on it that said "Marry me?" I nearly fainted. I was looking for the right words to say, and the first thing that came out of my mouth was "did you talk to my mom about this?" and he said of course I did. Tears streamed down my face as I told him that I would marry him. After we kissed he asked me if I liked the ring. I told him that I did and that it was beautiful. I was still in complete shock that I was engaged, I hadn't felt this happy in so long. I love Nick more than anything and for the first time in my life, not only did I find someone to handle me and put me in my place when I needed to be, but he was the first person I couldn't imagine not having in my life forever, other than my family. I know it sounds cheesy, but when you know, you really do just know.

47

OUR ENGAGEMENT WAS a huge shock to everyone, mainly because we are so young but everyone was happy for us. With attention being drawn to us it caused a lot of people to start talking on social media, which lead us to a picture that Nathan posted on Instagram. Nathan had taken a snap shot of the front page of the paper I was on and posted it on his Instagram profile with the word "hypocrite" underneath it. People from Five Star started insulting me, calling me a bitch and a bully. His mom even joined in, saying "I hope she reads her bracelets a lot, maybe she will get the message eventually!" I couldn't believe what I was seeing. I had left Five Star three months earlier, and they were STILL posting things about me. They were calling me a bully! They were the ones STILL taunting and teasing me on a public social media forum. What made them think that this was okay completely boggled my mind and for a parent to be encouraging it blew my mind. I couldn't believe that a gym owner would allow their athletes and coaches to talk trash about another coach from another gym. My mother had had enough and the mamma lion was coming out. She took pictures of what Nathan was posting and sent it to the director of the program that Nathan was a part of as a Junior Ambassador. My mom sent him everything, showing how he was insulting another coach from another gym and how it completely goes against their code of conduct for a Junior Ambassador. He listened to my mom but kept dancing around the issue, saying that he would pray for Nathan.

My mom relentlessly kept bringing up the problem asking if he was going to do anything about it but the only response she could get from him was basically "It's just the cheer world." In other words, in her opinion, nothing was going to get done about the situation. He refused to believe the proof my mother sent to him. Frustrated, but not surprised by his not-taking action to fix anything, I decided to ignore Nathan and his little post and take the high road. I knew that karma would come around eventually, in whatever form it chose to.

Later on in the week I heard from one of the parents at Five Star, that the senior team that Nathan is on was addressed by Angie. She reportedly told them to delete me or any friends and family that were connected to me in anyway shape or form on any social media sites. Reportedly, she told them that I was starting drama and that I was going to report their gym for unsportsmanlike conduct. Personally, that's not how I would have handled the situation as a gym owner. The first thing I would have done was told Nathan to apologize for what he posted and then he would have been kicked out of my gym. In my gym there will be a handbook that will have a section that will state that any athletes or employees talking down about another athlete or coach from another gym on a social media site or in public in any way shape or form, will be immediately removed from the program. Not only when an athlete or coach or parent insults another gym or its members, does it make the individual look bad but it also makes your gym look bad too. I shook my head at what the parent had told me, but none the less I wasn't surprised. Once again another figure in the cheer industry wasn't being a good role model to children, which gave me all the more reason to open a gym in the future.

At Phoenix's last practice before Jamfest Super Nationals the team was finally starting to come together. We held a miniature pep rally for the teams in the gym to support each other before we got on the road to Indy. We sat in front of the practice floor and watched each team perform their routine full out one last time before competition, clapping and cheering each other on. After the lower leveled teams performed, it was Phoenix's turn and I pulled them aside in a huddle and told them that this was it; this was their last time throwing their routine before they competed. I told them that I knew the past couple weeks had been a struggle, with losing team members and attitude but that I was thankful and proud that they stuck with us through everything. I told them that they had more than the enough capability to hit a perfect routine. This got them pumped up and as they took their starting positions and waited for their music to come on, I waited with my fingers crossed as the room got silent. When I heard the two dings at the beginning of their music I started screaming my lungs out for them, cheering them on in hopes to see them hit a clean routine. The beginning went well, everyone landed their tumbling and stunts were solid; we had a few tumbling errors in the middle but they finished out strong with their pyramid, something we had been struggling with over the past few weeks. They danced their asses off to MC Hammer's "You can't touch this" at the end.

When their music cut off I started jumping up and down from joy, I hadn't seen them look this good all season; you could tell from the expressions on their face that they were thinking the same thing. After celebrating, Nick and I gathered the team in a circle one last time and told them to pack that routine in their suitcases and take it to Indy. We broke on "Phoenix" and on our way out a couple of the parent's stopped Nick and I and thanked us for how well we were doing with the team. They told us that they had looked great. It was so reassuring to hear those words come from someone new, it let Nick and I exhale and know that we were doing an alright job and that we weren't just going insane for no reason. Walking out of the gym that night I got a good vibe about this weekend, the kind you just can't fight. I knew that they were going to do well, I could just feel it.

48

IT WAS NICK'S first time to Indianapolis and I think I was more excited for him than he was. As we pulled up to the Westin trying to figure out how to get into the parking garage with all the confusing one way streets that Indy had, I couldn't help but jump up and down in my seat. Nick laughed and told me to calm down. I told him that I just couldn't help it, I loved Indy and I couldn't wait for him to experience it. Once we finally found parking we made our way into the lobby where Nick's facial expression reminded me of the first time I had walked into the Westin when I was cheering for ICC, his eyes lit up like a little kid and a smile crept up on the side of his face. The line for check in wasn't long at all but the lady that was checking us in had no idea what she was doing. It took her about twenty minutes and five different people to finally give us our room key. I felt bad, I knew what it was like working in an industry with computers and it could be confusing at times. Nick however was a little more impatient than I was and started to get antsy while waiting. Once she finally gave us our key we made our way to the elevators to the tenth floor and walked all the way down to the last door in the hallway. When we opened our room we had a spectacular view of Lucas Oil Stadium where the Indianapolis Colts play. We unpacked our things quickly, not only were we starving, we also needed to go to coach check in before our teams practice at seven that night. We threw on some coaches' shirts and Nike shoes and started speed walking to the food court in the mall where we ate Chick Fil-A. While we were eating I watched as Nick observed all the chaos around him. When there was a cheer competition in Indy, the mall connected to it, was filled to capacity with cheerleaders running around screaming, laughing and of course…cheering. I looked at him and told him that this was insane and he chuckled and agreed with me saying that this mall probably makes a shit ton of money on weekends like these. After we finished scarfing down our food we made our way to the convention center which was also connected to the mall. When we rode down the escalators to the hall where the coaches are, I noticed for the first time ever that Jamfest Super Nationals was not the only thing going on in the convention center there was also some sort of soccer convention. Sort of confused, since the soccer convention was in the place of where the cheer competition had been the previous years for cheer, I followed the signs to the new location. While I was holding on to Nick's hand I asked him what he had thought so far and he told me that it wasn't as big as he thought it would be. I told him that it actually was smaller than the previous years and that it was set up completely different but maybe it seemed smaller to him because I talked it up so much. When we found the coaches hall and tried checking in the lady told us that our gym owner had already done so. We thanked her and continued down the hallway to find our team; which should have been waiting by the practice halls since their practice time was in about twenty minutes. Scanning the chaotic crowd for our team we tried to focus on looking for black and red T-shirts. Once we located them we waved at the team and made our way to them. They all looked nice with their hair up in a high ponytail with their new practice bows. I asked them if they were excited, even though I already knew the answer, they replied yes with smiles and laughs. I knew that a lot of them were more excited for the Majors which was happening right after our short practice.

The Majors, in my opinion, is just a way for the vendor to make money. A board chooses approximately ten top teams in the U.S. They have them battle it out for a trip to Europe's Cheerleading World's. The team that won last year didn't end up even going. It was more for the bragging rights. I had been last year (the first year it happened) and thought it was just a waste of time and money, not only was the arena jam packed to the point where you couldn't even see the stage but I could have literally waited ten minutes after the performances and saw it on YouTube. But for the diehard cheer fans it was the place to see their favorite cheerlebrities perform. A few athletes from Phoenix, mostly the younger ones, showed me pictures that they had taken with the cheerlebrities earlier. I couldn't help but laugh. It was good that they had someone to look up to but most of these cheerlebrities, in my opinion, were not as good as athletes on some of the smaller gym teams. To me, cheerleading was a team sport and cheerlebrities take the team aspect away from it. Not just one person can determine the success of a team, no matter who they were.

I looked at my phone and it was five minutes until our practice so I gathered our team and headed to the practice hall, which was the same place that they would be warming up the next day for competition. The vendor gave us three strips of floor and a total of 24 minutes to practice whatever we needed before competition tomorrow.

The floors were on a rotation between all the teams so as the clock counted down with only a minute or so for our turn, Nick and I gathered Phoenix and told them what order they would be warming up their skills in. We told them that we had six minutes on the first floor where we would practice our coed stunts, our all-girl stunts, our basket tosses and our pyramid. They nodded their heads listening carefully. Then we told them that at the next floor that they had twelve minutes to themselves for whatever they felt like they needed the most work on, tumbling or jumps . On the final floor we would mark through the routine to our music, throwing which ever skills they felt they needed to throw, and pyramid, since that was my biggest concern.

As soon as I was done talking to them a staff member directed us onto the first floor where they began to stunt. As I counted out loud, with Nick cheering for them by my side, all of their stunts hit with ease; it was exactly what they needed, a big confidence boost. Excited from how well they did on the first floor they moved to the second floor and performed their tumbling with ease. After the twelve minutes wrapped up, we moved to the final floor and I told them exactly what I had told them at the pep rally that this was the last time going through the routine before competition and I needed to see cleanliness and perfection even though they were marking everything but pyramid. Once I turned on their music it was like most of them had forgotten how to count. A lot of skills were off timing and the pyramid looked horrendous. Once the music cut off that was all the time we got on the last floor so I pulled them aside, frustrated, and told them, " I hope you guys can learn how to count to eight by tomorrow, you sure as hell didn't look like you knew how to just then…" I paused and watched as disappointment creeped into their eyes… "How could you have a perfect warm-up and then as soon as I turn the music on you forget what you're supposed to be doing? You better go to your hotel room tonight and listen to the music over and over again and replay the routine in your head." While I was saying this the owner was talking to a staff member trying to get us more time so that we could mark threw the routine again with music. Just as I had finished talking to the kids she told us that she had gotten us more time. Relieved, because I didn't want to end the night on something negative, I told the team to stick around so that we could run through it again. This time they straightened up and took my advice; they counted out loud together and the routine looked 100% better. I told them that that's the team they needed to bring to warm-ups tomorrow and that's the team that I knew they could be on the competition floor. After talking to them about going to bed early and when to meet the next day and how to do their hair, we parted ways and I still had that same good feeling I had before leaving the gym after our last practice.

49

NICK AND I made our way back to the hotel so we could figure out what we wanted to do for dinner. It was late and the mall was closed so we couldn't go to the food court and we knew it would be hard to get into any kind of restaurant without reservations. As we walked into the hotel we saw that they had a steak house attached so we took a chance and asked them if they had a table for two and they told us that they did in the bar area, but not dining. We told them that as long as we could order food we didn't care where we sat. This made the hostess laugh and she led us to an open bar table where we sat and began to look at the menu. My eyes nearly popped out of my head when I opened the menu and saw the prices with the cheapest meal being thirty five dollars. Nick saw my expression and told me that it was okay that we never get to treat ourselves so we should order whatever we want and just enjoy it. Although it was hard for me to accept at first, he was right, we never treated ourselves and so I relaxed and enjoyed a nice dinner with my fiancé. After dinner we made our way back up to the hotel room and almost immediately fell asleep. I was surprised by how tired we actually were but were glad because we needed our rest for the hectic day ahead of us.

The next morning we woke up to a beautiful blue Indy sky which was hard not to smile about. I am sort of superstitious, so to me, it was a sign of good luck. After showering I threw on a pair of jeans, a red tank top and the coach's jacket I had received as a Christmas gift from the gym owners. I put my coach pass around my neck and with Nick by my side we made our way down to warm-ups. Although I wasn't competing, I was almost more nervous than if I were to be simply because I had no control of the outcome. All I could do was stand back and watch the team perform and I wanted more than anything for them to hit a clean, flawless routine, regardless of what place they take.

Once Nick and I arrived at the same meeting place as the day before only half our team was there the other half was out watching the younger groups from our gym perform. As I sat there and observed Phoenix, I was proud to see that they didn't seem to be nervous, just excited. For most, it was their first time in Indy and so I expected to see a lot more nerves.

Once the time came to make our way to warm-ups, I told them to line up in two single filed lines with all their jackets, sweatpants and jewelry left behind. As we checked in with a staff member I couldn't help but notice to my right, the director of the Junior Ambassador program that my mom talked to about Nathan's post. I couldn't help but feel bitterness but I saw that he was actually coaching a team that was competing in our division, and wiped the bitterness away. Just because I didn't like him as a person didn't mean I couldn't support his athletes, after all, they had nothing to do with his actions.

Right before our team took the first floor for warm-ups I pulled them into a huddle and laid down a couple of rules. I told them that my biggest pet peeve was bad sportsmanship and that there would be no such thing allowed. I told them they were to cheer for every team, clap for every team and absolutely no trash talking whatsoever; this made them giggle, as did I, because we knew they weren't that type of group to do that, but as a coach, I just wanted to make it clear. I told them that we were there for ourselves and no one else and that I wanted their attention to be on the team and not the other fifty teams surrounding them. I asked them if they remembered how we warmed up the previous night at practice and when they shook their heads yes, I told them good. I told them that that's the exact same way we're warming up now and they acknowledged that they understood. When the clock read that it was our time to take the first floor, they did, and they did exactly what I told them to do. They focused on themselves and hit all of their stunts with ease, which got all of them pumped up as we moved onto the second floor. Everyone threw their tumbling with ease accept one of the boys who was having trouble with a punch front (a front flip). I could see the nerves on his face and when I asked him what was wrong he told me that he didn't feel like he was going to land his punch front. I told him to take it out of the routine and that it was just there for show anyway, you could see the immediate relief on his face. They finished a little early on the second floor so I told them to take it easy and just wait for our turn on the third floor. They stood and watched the team ahead of them (which happened to be the team that was coached by the director of the Junior Ambassador program) once they finished marking their routine, our team clapped for them and wished them luck, as did I, and also complimented them on their flashy uniforms. When our team took the last floor I told them to throw any skills they felt they needed to, and to throw pyramid, most importantly I told them to count out loud together. As I pushed the play button for our music I prayed that this run through would go better than the first one the night before. They marked everything on time and a few people threw stunts that they felt they needed to one last time. Once pyramid came, Nick went beside them and started cheering them on. As I watched and counted along out loud, the pyramid flowed smoothly and hit perfectly. I was finally able to exhale, warm ups had went exactly how they needed to. After getting a quick drink we made our way behind stage where I gave the team our last goodbyes before we parted ways. This was one of the hardest things about being a coach. I gathered the team in a circle and told them that whatever happened in the routine to keep going and keep fighting. I told them that they should have no doubts and only belief that they were going to achieve a perfect routine. I told them that I was so proud of how far they had come and to leave it all on the floor. After saying a prayer I gave them hugs and took my spot in front of the stage watching the other teams in their division before their turn. All of the other teams had errors so far and although they had higher skill levels than us, I knew that if we hit a clean routine that we still had a chance to place well.

When the announcer called our teams name and I watched as they ran onto stage, I nearly fainted from all the nerves I had, I wanted so bad for them to just hit a perfect routine. When their music turned on, they performed their first tumbling skill all landing with ease, which gave them the fire they needed to keep going. Once stunts came I started screaming my head off. The first part hit and I held my breath as they began the second part. When the flyer gave their bases their left leg and switched up to the top with their right legs one of our best flyers' knee caved in and she came crashing down, it was the last thing I expected to go wrong, but I kept cheering for them hoping that the rest of the routine would flow smoothly. Tumbling went well, one girl accidently over rotated and tripped backwards to her butt which I knew would be another deduction, but nothing too serious. Once pyramid came around I crossed my fingers and prayed, I knew that this would be the make it or break it point in their routine; they needed to hit it. I listened to them as they all counted out loud, which helped, and watched as their pyramid flew smoothly just as it had in warm-ups. It was the best routine I had seen them perform all season. I was one proud coach. As they finished their routine dancing, I couldn't help but clap along with a huge smile on my face.

Once the music cut off I ran back stage to them, flailing my arms everywhere from excitement as they watched their instant replay. They too, were just as happy as I was. I told them that for the first time I saw a fight within them and that as a coach that's all I could ask for. I told them that during their first performance of the season that if one thing went wrong in the routine, they gave up; and now they were fighters, that when something went wrong, they fought back and ended the routine even stronger because of their mistake. I told them to enjoy the rest of their evening and that I would text them their standings once they were revealed.

For the first time at Jamfest, they had a scoring booth that you could go to immediately following your team's performance and see the deductions that the judges gave your routine. While I was checking our sheet with the staff lady I noticed that there was a legality deduction. It completely confused me. I asked what they had performed illegally in their routine and the lady told me that during the pyramid one of our flyers didn't stay connected long enough to the other flyer as she switched groups. I was very surprised about this, since we had competed this way twice already and no one had ever said anything about the skill being illegal. She told me that there was nothing she could do about it though and so I just thanked her and walked away. This legality hurt our score and put our team in fourth place out of six teams. When I told this to the team they took it well, still happy about their performance and ready to bring it even harder the next day.

After getting our score, Nick and I decided to head over to the coaches room and grab a bite to eat. On our way over we saw Craig and decided to stop him and ask him how his teams were doing. We had never really talked to him and wanted to see what he was really like. When he turned around he acted as if he really didn't know who we were, which was bullshit because he had taken an athlete from us and introduced himself to us at Jamlive a few months back. It was almost like his way of belittling us. We politely asked him how his teams were doing that day and he was short and snobby with his response. He didn't ask us how our teams were doing. We tried holding small talk with him asking him if he was still planning on starting the international team. He could barely look us in our eyes and acknowledge us. With that we said goodbye and turned around to look for a table to sit at. I really did want to give Craig the benefit of the doubt but after that conversation I had absolutely no respect for him and made my own decision that what everyone, that I had spoken to, said about him was true. That if you had something that he wanted he would treat you nicely and act like your best friend but if he wanted nothing to do with you, or he felt like you had nothing to offer to him, that he treated you like a piece of shit, and in my eyes, I had found this to be true.

While looking for a table, we tried to pick one with the least amount of people, not wanting to disturb anyone. We asked a small group of people with Green Bay Elite shirts on if they minded if we sat next to them and they were very polite and said of course not. Green Bay Elite was a larger gym in Wisconsin, a gym that I happen to look up to a lot, they were one of the few big gyms that didn't walk around cocky and they showed respect towards everyone else. I asked them how their teams were doing that day and told them how much I looked up to their program. They were some of the nicest people I had talked to since being there. They asked us where we were from and how our teams were doing. When we were finished eating I wished them good luck with their last performance of the day. It was one of their most well-known teams who had placed third at World's the previous year and I told them that I would be cheering for them. They thanked us and wished us luck going into day two and with that we parted ways.

Going into warm ups day two was just the same as day one. Phoenix had hit all their skills once again and I told them the few changes that they needed to do to raise their score. They all made sure to make a mental note. Behind the stage we all huddled together and I told them that I loved them and to go balls out; this was their last chance and no matter what I wanted to see no deductions. We prayed and broke on Phoenix and with that I took my spot in front of the stage with Nick. With my fingers crossed, I watched as our kids took the stage and waited for their music to come on. They had determination in their eyes today, I could see it. As their music started they nailed their standing tumbling and performed their stunts perfectly. I started to go crazy; they were performing a flawless routine! Once pyramid came around I yelled at the flyer to stay connected as long as she could so that we didn't get another legality deduction. They had hit a perfect routine…I started jumping up and down, clapping to their music as they finished their routine with dance and you could tell from the expression on their faces that they were the happiest they had ever been while competing. This brought a tear to my eye…I had finally found the one thing that was more addicting than hitting a perfect routine as an athlete, it was watching the team you coach hit a perfect routine.

Awards was only twenty minutes after their performance and as we waited I told them that no matter what place they got that I was proud of them for hitting a clean routine and that as their coach, I couldn't have asked for anything more.

When the announcer told them to take the stage they held hands in a circle with their heads down praying to not hear their names until top three; top three teams at Nationals got medals. We were hoping that after today's performance that they might bump up a spot. But when they heard their names called for fourth place and realized that they hadn't moved up, nor down, they still clapped and took their trophy with a good attitude. They were proud of what they had done even though they hadn't received medals. After awards, I told everyone to drive home safely and that I'd see them tomorrow night at the gym for practice and that they needed to be ready. They had one more competition left in the season the following weekend and I wanted to go out with a bang.

After we parted ways, Nick and I ran to our hotel room and packed as quickly as we could, check out was in thirty minutes and we hadn't packed a thing from the weekend. We finished just in the nick of time and as we threw our stuff in the van I asked Nick if he had had fun this weekend, he told me that it was an amazing experience but he couldn't wait to get home back to our doggie and our own bed, we were quite the homebodies. I was excited for practice the next day. Now that they had competed their routine full out in front of a crowd, I looked forward to being able to go to practice and not worry about changing anything around in the routine and just being able to practice it over and over again; I guess I shouldn't have jinxed myself though, cause there was always something with this team and I should have expected something to happen; I just didn't think it would be to this extreme.

50

ON OUR WAY to our first practice back from Indy I couldn't stop telling Nick how excited I was to see everyone; that it was going to be an awesome practice since we had just had an amazing weekend. That's when I received a text from one of the athletes…it was very short and with no explanation, it just read "Hi Morgan, I will not be at practice today, I'm sorry." Very confused, I texted her back "Why?" but there was no response. I called Rachel immediately and she told me that this was the athlete's third un-excused absence so I had the option to kick her off the team. I found it only fair to everyone else to follow the rules and decided that she would no longer be a part of the team but that I would talk to her after practice about the situation. I had too much to focus on now that I needed to change the routine once again.

Just as we were pulling up to the gym I received a text from her mother saying that her grades were not high enough and that they had made a deal with her that if they weren't better then she wouldn't be cheering. Although this made my decision of cutting her from the team a little easier, it made no sense to me why a mother would pull her daughter from a team the last week of the season, I mean what was a week of cheerleading really going to do? She told me that she had gotten into trouble at school and had a Saturday detention so she wouldn't be able to go to the competition regardless. This made more sense to me. I understood that school came first and that maybe there was more going on that I didn't know about so I decided to shake it off and try to stay positive at practice and make quick changes. The changes weren't hard for the kids to pick up, but whether it was because they were in a bad mood or because they were tired from the weekend, they didn't have much pep in their step as I thought they would. They weren't putting any effort into anything and they weren't listening to me. Nick noticed this and told everyone to come to the middle of the floor so that he could have a talk with them.

He asked them if they really wanted to be there because it didn't seem as if any of them did. They replied that they did and he told them that they needed to start acting like it. He told them that he knew that they were tired from this weekend but this was their last week of practice and they needed to step it up. This talk helped me out a lot they started listening to me, which made it a lot easier for me to make the changes that I needed to in the routine.

At the end of practice, since we hadn't done much that day besides fix the routine, we decided that we were going to condition a little and as soon as we said this most of the team immediately got snappy. They needed to understand that to become better you needed to push yourself beyond your comfort levels or you'd never see improvement. After fifteen minutes of conditioning Nick patted one of the girls on the back and told her "There you go, way to push yourself". He noticed tears in her eyes and he asked her what was wrong and she snapped back telling him to shut up and that he was so fucking annoying. My jaw dropped, as well as the rest of the teams, we couldn't believe what she had just said to him. Nick stayed calm and told her to leave, she tried talking back but he continued to tell her to leave and that she should never talk to a coach like that. Once she finally left the boy that had talked back to Nick earlier in the year tried defending the girl and told Nick that he shouldn't be yelling at her while she was crying. Nick told him to leave too and that he shouldn't talk back to a coach. He left also left the gym. Once they were gone Nick asked the team if anyone else had anything else smart to say and the team shook their heads no. With that, I told them to take it easy before their last practice in two days and that I would see them then and we broke on "Phoenix".

We went to my mom's after practice and told her everything that had happened. She was in just as much shock as we were. She then told me that she had some more news to drop on me. I told her to go for it that I had had so many surprises today what's another one going to do. She explained to me that one of our good friends, who happened to be a Junior Ambassador for the same program as Nathan, told her that over the weekend the director of the program approached her and told her to watch out for us. Being really good friends with us, she didn't ask for any explanation. She said that she just nodded her head to him. Supposedly he had told her that we were just out to start drama. In my opinion, Five Star had brain washed him and manipulated him into believing that we were out to do their gym wrong. How anyone could think that we were out to start drama when they were the ones publically insulting me? I didn't even make an ordeal out of the post. My mom just simply brought it to his attention as the director of his program that one of his Junior Ambassadors was breaking code of conduct and his decision to do nothing about it, reflects, to me on who he really is. We dropped it and moved on and that was that for us.

I started to realize that people were watching every move that my family and I did. People knew that we spoke the truth. These people tend to live in a "fake" world and would rather not deal with the truth. They didn't want their fantasy world interrupted with the truth. Even Cassady continued posting things on his twitter like "When your ex gets engaged, so glad I dodged that bullet." It was also clear that Five Star still kept their eyes on us as well. They were still trying to convince people that we are out to get them. They showed that by the meeting Angie had with her gym and requiring them to delete us as "friends" on the social media sites. The common denominator with all of these people and places is that I've left them. It seems as if they can't seem to believe the fact that I did leave. I go on with my daily life minding my own business simply because the past is the past and there are reasons that I left the things that I did. Some of these people still continue to talk and post things about me. Another interesting thing is that never once has anyone left me or I've been let go from a place. I have started to think that maybe people were not upset that I left but maybe they were upset with themselves. It is common knowledge that I leave something or someone because I either don't believe in their ethics or because I'm not being treated fairly. Maybe it is the feeling of guilt that they have, whatever it is it has become humorous to me now. Maybe the fact that I pay no attention to what they are doing with their lives is the reason they stalk my every move. It obviously means that either I am a big deal or a threat to them, otherwise why would they care. People know me for my honesty, they know that I am the first to call someone out on something if it is unethical, and to most, that is frightening. I continue my career and my future though, ignoring what people say and do because I know that I will make a change in this industry someday and nobody is going to stop me.

Last practice came around and unfortunately half the team was out with the flu. I told the few people that were there that we would do what we could and it would be more of a fun practice if anything and that we would get out early and eat cupcakes that the gym owner had brought for everyone. The practice went smoother than the one before, mostly because we couldn't do much of anything. At the end, before we handed out the cupcakes, I thanked the team for how much they've taught me as a coach and that they hold a special place in my heart. I told them that I will never forget them. This brought a few tears to some eyes. I truly did love these kids and through all of the struggle they went through they believed in Nick and me, and for that, I was more than thankful.

We put our hands in for the last time together at practice and yelled "Phoenix" at the top of our lungs; the next time I'd see them was at their last competition this weekend, it was a bittersweet moment.

51

WHEN NICK AND I arrived at the competition we knew it was going to be much smaller than Jamfest, but we had no idea that it would be this small. When we walked into the tiny convention center we were greeted by just one floor and ceilings that resembled triangles; starting at the highest point in the middle of the room and gradually winding its way down to the sides which were only about ten feet high. I was kind of shocked at the size because this was a World's bid competition and I expected the area to be a lot larger. ICE was at the competition, and they walked around like they owned the place because they were the biggest gym there. It made me gag. I thought to myself I would never let my athletes walk around the way they did. They were rude and obnoxious and disrespected the practice area acting like it was only theirs to practice on.

As we made our way over to a small area where our team met, I walked up to a sight that I did not want to see. Everyone looked pale and lethargic. I could tell that a lot of them weren't over the flu yet and seeing this worried me. I put on a smile and tried to get everyone excited, and a few of them did, but most looked exhausted. Once it was time for warm ups I lined them up and we made our way through a tight crowd to the warm up area which was directly behind the stage. When we checked in a staff member had the team line up from shortest to tallest and arranged them in a group to take a team photo. After this they were directed to the first floor. I gathered everyone in and told them that we were warming up exactly how we did in Indy. This competition was a lot smaller and when I mean smaller I mean that the floor we were on was under the lowest part of the ceiling so we had to throw baskets one at a time instead of two so no one hit the ceiling. The staff was very unorganized and they didn't have clocks set up anywhere to let us know how much longer we had on each floor. They were running around like chickens with their heads cut off which put stress on not just us as coaches but the athletes as well. They were very flustered from the chaos, but did their best to stay focused.

When we got onto the last warm up floor I told the team to mark their routine and throw pyramid. After they did, all the coaches looked at each other and said the same exact thing, they looked look zombies on the floor. We pulled them in and gave them a little pep talk while one of the athletes ran to the bathroom quickly to throw up. Her flu symptoms were uncontrollable and I told her not to worry and to just try and make it through the routine. We told the team that we knew they were sick, tired and injured but this was their last competition as a team and they needed to dig deep and find the strength to end the season on a good note. This woke them up a little more and gave them the motivation they needed to perform. Once we said our goodbyes I took my spot in front of the floor waving to my mom and brother in the crowd who were there supporting Nick, myself and the team. Seeing them reminded me of when I competed and I got that same feeling of comfort as I had when I was an athlete. When they announced our team's name and they took the floor, I held onto Nick's hand and prayed for a miracle. When the music turned on the first thing that went wrong was a tumbling fall. I wasn't too surprised though since it was the girl throwing up right before she had gone on stage. I started cheering for her as loud as I could, I knew that she was having a hard time and I wanted to give her as much strength and encouragement as I could. When she pushed through her standing tumbling pass and landed it I cheered for her as loud as I could as she moved to coed stunting where she flew with one of the boys. As everyone set in they all went up and hit perfectly. I threw my hands up into the air from happiness. When they moved to their stunt sequence I held my breath. They all hit and I again threw my hands into the air even more crazy than the last time. I was so proud of the fight they were putting into the routine. During running tumbling two of the athletes collided into each other but right away got up. I knew that that would hurt our score as well but I kept cheering them on as if nothing happened. When pyramid came I screamed for them at the top of my lungs and watched as everything flew by with ease. I clapped as they danced and when their music ended I followed them backstage and told them that the routine looked awesome for how sick they were. I always told them that I would never lie to them and I wasn't. It really did look awesome and I was so proud that they fought and pushed through everything. I told them to go home and rest and for each of them to drink a gallon of orange juice and wash their hands so not to get anyone else sick.

My family and I decided to stay and watch the level five teams compete and when we sat down we asked a group of ICE girls if the two chairs that were next to them were taken, they sort of glared at us. My mother asked if it was a "first come first serve" basis for seating and they told us "Not for ICE people." Nick laughed at their comment and found two other chairs. We couldn't believe what we had heard come from out of their mouth, and with their parents sitting next to them encouraging it. I watched as the girls made fun of other teams that competed and thought to myself if I was a gym owner and this was going on in my gym there would be some serious consequences for this behavior, like I've said before, bad sportsmanship and disrespect is my biggest pet peeve.

After most of the level five teams were done competing, the girls and their parents stood up and made their way out next to us but before leaving they made sure to make a snooty comment to Nick that he could have all the chairs he wanted. Being the outspoken person my mother is, she replied back to them "Way to have respect." All the girls and their mothers chuckled to themselves and replied sarcastically "Ohhh yeah, we don't have any respect?" I couldn't help but reply "Yeah, you're whole program doesn't." and with that they walked away and the vibe in the room got 100% better after they did.

Once level five was done competing we said goodbye to my mom and brother and thanked them for coming. We made our way back to our cars, making sure to grab our teams score sheets on the way out. My mother warned me that there would be a huge winter storm the next day, so to leave early and drive safe for tomorrow's competition.

On our way home I looked over the score sheets and saw that this competition counted deductions differently than the last. It is so frustrating, as a coach, to deal with different scoring systems at different competitions. When I looked over the judges' comments they told us that our team had good energy, which really surprised me because at Jamfest they told us that we needed more energy. In my eyes, they had much more energy in Indy and being sick at this competition they had less energy, but for what it's worth I took the compliment and continued to read through the score sheet. When I got to the last page where the standings were, I wasn't surprised to see that we were in third place (out of three teams) because of the deductions we had. I was surprised at how far away we were from second place, a whole ten points. I took a picture of the standings and sent it over to the owner, and she was just as surprised as I was, but there was nothing we could do about it. We let all the kids know where they stood going into day two and advised them to leave their houses a little earlier because of the storm. We wanted to be sure they all drove safe and took their time.

We woke up the next day to the storm my mom warned us about. It was an ice storm and it was supposed to gradually get worse as the day got longer. Thankfully Nick had put on winter tires for his car a couple of weeks earlier or else we would have been on the side of the road somewhere. Even with the tires, we still found ourselves sliding everywhere. We made sure to drive extremely slow and cautious so we could get to the competition in one piece.

When we arrived I was glad to see that everyone had made it safe and sound, and actually looked a lot peppier than day before. A lot of them had started feeling better. A couple of the girls gave me a coaches gift before we went into warm ups, thanking me for the season. I tried not to get too emotional, I didn't want to believe that this was the last day with them.

As they lined up for warm ups and pushed our way through the tight crowd once again, we waited for the signal to take the first floor. While we were waiting one of the younger girls came up to me and with a hopeful look on her face she asked if it was possible to get first place still. I looked at her with sympathy and I thought for a moment, keeping my promise of never lying to them, I told her "Of course there's a chance, there's always going to be a chance in cheerleading…but the other teams would really have to bomb." This made her giggle, which I was happy to see. I tried making her question into something funny. I didn't want to tell her there's no way we could get first place, because we did have a chance, it was a snowball's chance in hell, but the other teams would have had to have gotten at least ten to fifteen deductions today, which was a possibility, but highly unlikely. With that, we were directed to take our first warm up floor where they hit their stunts just as well as the day before, making sure not to hit the low ceilings with their basket tosses. As we moved to the second floor, the same girl from the beginning of the season that was having trouble landing her standing tuck, the girl who came off the stage crying from their first competition and I had asked why she was crying and she told me because she didn't land her standing tuck and I asked her what she was thinking before she threw it, she had told me that she was thinking that she wasn't going to land it, and I responded to her then that's why she didn't land it, again this competition she was having trouble landing her standing tuck in warm ups and started crying from frustration. Before she went onto the floor I told her to fake it, to play it safe in the routine so we didn't get any deductions. She looked at me and responded with no hesitation, "No, I CAN land it." She was a new person, someone that had suddenly started to believe in herself, someone I knew she was all along and I nodded my head and told her okay. When we huddled together for the last time I told them how proud of them I was this season and that they had nothing to lose today so to go out on stage and kill it but most importantly have fun. We prayed for the last time and broke for the last time. I knew that they were about to have a great performance. As I took my spot in front of the floor and watched them take their starting positions and listened as the music came on, I cheered for the girl who said she could land her standing tuck and watched as she nailed it perfectly. I thought in my mind, "That is exactly what makes a true athlete."

It was the best performance I had seen them do all season, they worked the routine like it was their job and sold their routine to the crowd. When their music cut off one of the boys through his fists into the floor and screamed out of happiness, they had just hit an awesome routine and you could tell that they were the most proud they had ever been all season.

Backstage, I congratulated them and told them to get ready for awards which were in fifteen minutes. While they were all waiting in a circle, knowing that they were going to get last place, they joked around about how if people asked, to tell them they got third out of eleven teams, not three team. It made me so happy to see that they weren't upset about their placement. They did end up getting last place but instead of being upset they were happy about the performance they had. They did end up winning a "Swag" award for the team that had the most swag. I'm guessing it was because the judges liked our dance to MC Hammer. After the award ceremony we took team pictures and said our good byes for the last time as a team, it was a bitter sweet moment for me. I was sad for the season to be over, but I was so thrilled that it ended on a good note. From experience I know it all comes down to your last performance. If you don't end on a good note you'll continue to have a feeling of emptiness, like something isn't finished. I did not want these kids to feel that feeling. Being a cheerleader is hard, you only have two and a half minutes to prove yourself and when you don't and you lose the opportunity to seize that one moment, it is the most heart wrenching feeling that only a cheerleader can truly understand.

The girl that swore at Nick ended up apologizing to him before she left the competition. She told him that sometimes she didn't realize the things that could come out of her mouth and that she should never talk to a coach like that. She thanked Nick and I for all the help we had given them. Although some of the kids on Phoenix talked back to us and gave us a hard time; they also taught us some of the most important lessons as a coach. We love every single one of those kids and to see them have such an amazing last performance like they just did, made us feel at peace and satisfied with what we did with this team. We knew that this is what we wanted to be doing for the rest of our lives. There is nothing more rewarding as a coach then to see your athletes grow and succeed.

52

NOW THAT OUR season is over, Nick and I need to sit down and decided what we want to do together. Elite is now contacting me about starting a cheer program and Lake Zurich offered us to continue to coach with them as well. My brother still has one more year of high school left and as soon as he graduates we plan on moving back to the south to open our gym. Until then we are still building our resume and soaking up as many experiences as we can.

Just when I think I've learned it all, and seen all there is to see, this industry still continues to amaze me with its ups and downs. The world of cheerleading continues to grow every single day at a rapid rate and I can now see why. Whether you are in it for the money, the passion or just simply because you want to help others succeed, it will easily become you're biggest struggle and you're strongest obsession.

Note from the Author

THIS MEMOIR IS strictly my experience that I've had with all-star cheerleading in the past few years. I'm not sure whether or not this applies to every area in the United States, but I do know that cheerleading has been the biggest struggle in my life, for reasons that I'm sure you can see.

I didn't write this book to get revenge, I didn't write this memoir to expose people, I wrote it because I genuinely feel that cheerleading, and maybe just where I'm from, struggles every day with issues that most businesses or sports don't have to deal with. Maybe there are "soccer worlds" and maybe there are "football worlds" maybe they have their own issues, but at least those sports aren't virtually owned by one brand and they have a universal scoring system. After all, that is what makes a sport a sport, right?

I feel like cheerleaders and coaches are constantly trying to prove to the world that cheer is a sport. I've tried almost every sport growing up and cheerleading is by far the toughest sport I've ever been a part of. But no one seems to be focusing on why it's not a sport. Maybe it's because we have no universal scoring system, maybe it's because society still views us as sideline cheerleaders cheering for a team, or maybe…it's because of all the scandal that these gyms and parents allow to happen. Whatever the reason, nothing is being done about it, and I'm tired of it. The evening that the two cheerleaders from Phoenix quit and joined another team, I broke down crying in my mother's arms. I told her that I was sick of this "world". I was sick of how it was being ran and that I was starting to lose my passion for it. I started to say things like I didn't want to own my own gym anymore. Hearing these words come out of my mouth, I knew that I needed to do something to help me get over this awful feeling that I had. I had grown a hatred towards cheerleading and that's not who I am. My mother always told me to write things down that I was upset about and that doing that it would make me feel better about everything. She was right. Now that I have all of this off my chest, I feel lighter and more at peace. I don't care what people say about going to college, there is no way that school could have taught me what I have learned over the past three years. Sure it might have taught me the technical stuff on how to run a business but college does not teach you how not to run a business and some of the real life situations you may encounter along with owning a business.

In the "cheer world" I've learned that you need to do back ground checks and drug test on employees. I want role models in my gym. I've learned to not let parents take control of your business or run any part of it. I've learned that you can't please everyone and you need to stick to your morals and ethics about your rules and that if you make just one exception then it leaves the door open for everyone else to follow. I've learned that honesty is the best policy and that is what creates good customer service. Most importantly I've learned that in order to get respect, you must give respect.

Until this day I am still learning how to run a cheer company and I am thankful for every step of the way. I am thankful for all the obstacles that God has thrown at me because it not only made me stronger it showed me how not to run a gym.

Cheerleading has become my biggest addiction, it's what I breathe, sleep and think about every day. Whether it's from the two and a half minute adrenaline rush that you get from hitting a perfect routine or whether it's from seeing your athlete's faces light up when they hit a perfect routine, I am not sure. But I do know that it is something that I will continue to love and hate every single day of my life. I will continue to learn and continue to grow and know that everything that happens along the way has a reason. I know that every person that I have met and will meet will have an impact in my life. I know that every obstacle I face is to make me stronger and that every happy moment is to remind me why I do the things I do. I know that ultimately everything that happens is leading me down the road to a bigger plan. I just have to sit back, hang tight and enjoy the ride.

Currently Nick and I are trying to build an international team at Lake Zurich. We hope to cheer at least one more time and hopefully make it to World's in Orlando. I am still teaching classes at Elite, while Nick continues to do private lessons. Elite is still planning on opening a cheer program. If they decide to this then Nick and I will pursue that together. We both continue to work for Kyle's skills and choreography camp which happens to be completely booked for this upcoming summer. We plan on being very busy with that.

As for our future, Nick, my family and his family will be moving back to Mississippi when my brother graduates in May of 2014 to open our gym. It has always been our plan to have a U-Haul outside his school on graduation. We plan on opening our gym in conjunction with our non-profit, which is doing phenomenal. We've actually started a new kindness campaign to try and promote not just anti-bullying but kindness as well. Unlike a lot of other anti-bullying organizations that blame the bullies and put them down it is our motto that "hurt people, hurt people" and that there are two sides to focus on when it comes to bullying. This is where our kindness campaign kicks in.

Nick and I still continue to teach respect, hard work, equality and kindness through coaching and plan on opening our gym with the same morals. We've started laying out the business plan, with my mother in charge of the business aspect, and Nick and me in charge of the cheer aspect. We are in the process of coming up with a plan to make cheerleading a better, all rounded atmosphere for children.

It's hard to call cheerleading a business because it has so many emotions involved. The business part is only half of what the owners deal with. In my opinion, the cheer business is more than just about the money, it's about being role models to young children. We want to give children a second home that they can come to, somewhere where they feel like they are not being judged for who they are or aren't, that teaches hard work and the values of family and respect.

We've even set up a program in our business plan that allows athletes to receive a discount on their monthly tuition fees in exchange for community service and volunteer hours. It's not about the money for us. We want to make a difference in people's lives, even if it's just one person. We want to show the world that through acts of kindness, honesty, respect and determination, that you can accomplish anything you set your mind to, no matter what people tell you.

CPSIA information can be obtained at www.ICGtesting.com
Printed in the USA
BVOW070605170413

318378BV00002B/424/P